# Accountability in Missions

# Accountability in Missions

*Korean and Western Case Studies*

EDITOR
JONATHAN J. BONK

ASSOCIATE EDITORS
GEOFFREY W. HAHN
SANG-CHEOL (STEVE) MOON
A. SCOTT MOREAU
YONG KYU PARK
NAM YONG SUNG

WIPF & STOCK · Eugene, Oregon

ACCOUNTABILITY IN MISSIONS
Korean and Western Case Studies

Wipf & Stock
An Imprint of Wipf and Stock Publishers
199 W. 8th Ave., Suite 3
Eugene, OR 97401
www.wipfandstock.com

ISBN 13: 978-1-61097-618-3

Manufactured in the U.S.A.

Biblical quotations are from:

New International Version, copyright © 1973, 1978, 1984, 2011, Biblica. Used by permission of Zondervan.

New Revised Standard Version, copyright © 1989, Division of Christian Education of the National Council of the Churches of Christ in the United States of America. Used by permission.

Today's New International Version, copyright © 2001, 2005, Biblica. Used by permission.

Manufactured in the U.S.A.

# Contents

# Foreword

I AM DEEPLY HONORED to be asked by Jonathan Bonk, executive director of the Overseas Ministries Study Center, to write the foreword for this publication, which is the product of the Korean Global Mission Leadership Forum held at OMSC, February 10–14, 2011. Forty-eight participants joined together to discuss the subject of missions and church accountability and to examine several case studies exploring strategic continuity issues.

We experienced spiritual unity through worship led by Jonathan Bonk and Bible exposition by Christopher J. H. Wright. Despite our various backgrounds, we all sensed our oneness in Christ for his mission through our genuine fellowship together.

The uniqueness of this forum was its focus on accountability in missions, from the perspectives of the local church, the mission agency, and the individual missionary, which represent what we could call the fundamental tri-unity of missions. In order to complete the Great Commission and reach the 639 yet unreached people groups of over 100,000 people, these three entities must be united in the Holy Spirit, but also in mind and strategy.

It was a humbling experience for me to hear from veterans of Western mission and their Korean counterparts who have decades of experience in the mission field. Their presentations critically examined past successes and failures in order to guide strategy for the future.

The contemporary church is in a spiritual battle for the souls of the unreached. I truly believe, however, that networks of local churches throughout the world do have the necessary resources to fulfill Christ's charge to make disciples of all nations. It is imperative that we be faithful stewards of these resources and talents, so that his name and renown may be proclaimed from every corner of the world.

I pray that this publication may challenge and motivate missionaries on the field, local churches that support them, and mission executives to work together as one body for the cause of Christ.

Won Sang Lee
Senior Pastor Emeritus
Korean Central Presbyterian Church
Centreville, Virginia

President, SEED International
Merrifield, Virginia

# Preface

THIS BOOK TRACES ITS genesis to a casual conversation with Sang-Cheol (Steve) Moon in the fall of 2007, when he visited the Overseas Ministries Study Center (OMSC) to attend a seminar being led by Andrew F. Walls. Moon, director of the Korea Research Institute for Missions and a professor at Hapdong Theological Seminary, Suwon City, Korea, suggested that OMSC organize and host a conference on accountability in mission, with a Korean emphasis. I was surprised, because it seemed then and still seems to me that there is little that we North Americans have to teach our Korean missiological confreres, and much that we have to learn from them!

Americans have the unenviable but sadly deserved reputation of being quick to teach others what they themselves have not yet learned. Furthermore, Western missionaries have all too often been implicated, however unwillingly, in European and American imperialism, wars of intervention and occupation, and general self-righteous meddling in the affairs of others. Even though Western missionaries (whose work, as a group, spans more than two centuries) should not be blamed for their nations' sins, they cannot escape stigma by association. Nor can they deny that they are material beneficiaries of their nations' morally dubious, self-serving behavior. However unwillingly, they serve abroad as symbols of their nations. Like nonsmokers in a room filled with smokers, they cannot escape the smell of smoke in their hair and on their clothes.

Korean missionaries, at least partly because they are not saddled with this dubious legacy, *can* and *do* serve more effectively in some of the world's most challenging sociopolitical environments. The last thing we as Westerners should do is taint them with our stale smoke! Such thoughts were in my mind as I reflected on the impertinence of spearheading such a forum.

Moon pointed out that, while there were indeed historical grounds for my discomfort, mutual discussions could enrich both Korean and non-Korean missionary communities, to the end of furthering God's mission in his world. He kindly noted that OMSC—being small, ecclesiastically neutral, largely non-Western, and reasonably well-known and trusted because of the *International Bulletin of Missionary Research* and OMSC's numerous international missiological forums—was uniquely placed to organize and host such an event. It would not necessarily be inferred that this event was simply another instance of "the West telling the rest." At last we agreed and got down to the hard work of conceptualizing and organizing a forum on mission accountability, which ultimately was held at OMSC in February 2011.

The phenomenal growth of the Korean Protestant (evangelical) church is well-known but is worth summarizing here. In 1900 the number of Christians in Korea was estimated to be just over 42,000—most of these Roman Catholic. By 1910 this figure had increased by an additional 9,000, mostly Protestant evangelical. By 1950 the number of believers was 1.6 million, by 1970 it was just under 6 million, and by 2000 it had risen dramatically to 19.5 million. Current figures place the number of Korean Christians at just over 20 million.[1] In his book *Born Again: Evangelicalism in Korea* (2010), Timothy S. Lee cites evidence from national surveys suggesting that, in the early 1980s, well over 90 percent of all Korean Protestants were solidly evangelical,[2] a figure that had declined to 75 percent by the late 1990s and is presumably even lower today.[3]

---

1. This information is from the World Christian Database (Brill), accessed January 22, 2010. The 1910 data is from Todd M. Johnson and Kenneth R. Ross, eds., *Atlas of Global Christianity* (Edinburgh: Univ. of Edinburgh Press, 2009). The most impressive English-language assessment of evangelicalism in Korea is Timothy S. Lee's *Born Again: Evangelicalism in Korea* (Honolulu: Univ. of Hawai'i Press, 2010). His epilogue, "The Beleaguered Success of Korean Evangelicalism in the 1990s" (pp. 139–51), is particularly insightful. I hope that Korean evangelical leaders read it.

2. In his classic study *Evangelicalism in Modern Britain: A History from the 1730s to the 1980s* (London: Unwin Hyman, 1989), pp. 2–3, D. W. Bebbington identified four markers of "evangelicalism"—what has become known as the Bebbington quadrilateral: *biblicism*, a particular regard for the Bible (namely, that all spiritual truth is to be found in its pages); *crucicentrism*, a focus on the atoning work of Christ on the cross; *conversionism*, the belief that human beings need to be converted; and *activism*, the belief that the Gospel needs to be expressed in both word and deed.

3. Lee, *Born Again*, p. 141.

More exponential yet has been the increase in the number of Korean missionaries over the past thirty years. In 1979 Korean churches sent out 93 missionaries. By 2000 this number had jumped to 8,103.[4] Ten years later, the number of missionaries had more than doubled—to over 20,500, according to Korean World Mission Association figures. The extraordinary growth of the Korean Protestant missionary force continues, with 2011 estimates placing the number at 22,500, which is more than 13 percent of the global Protestant missionary force. If current projections prove correct, by 2030 this number will increase to 20 percent. In other words, in twenty years, one out of every five Protestant missionaries worldwide will be Korean.

Not surprisingly, administrative and fiscal accountability processes and procedures within this dynamic and rapidly growing mission community are evolving. The explosive growth and dynamic energy of Korean mission endeavor on the frontiers of some of the world's most challenging mission fields has often far outpaced established policies and guidelines, which could not have anticipated these kinds of challenges. Veteran Korean missionaries, to mention actual examples, have purchased properties, built institutions, and established organizations in various countries that are registered in the names of the missionaries themselves, rather than in the names of their churches, denominations, or sending agencies. Not surprisingly, complex problems have emerged when the inevitable time for succession has arrived. Are there precedents for this in non-Korean missions? How have such issues been addressed by agencies and denominations? Can tried and proven accountability systems already in place elsewhere be adapted and applied to the Korean situation without stifling Korean missionary initiative, momentum, and creativity?

Western denominations and mission agencies, with their longer history, have confronted a wide range of accountability challenges, many of these ongoing. It is possible, we thought, that Korean churches, agencies, and missionaries might learn from this history, and likewise that the Western missionary movement could benefit from closer attention to Korean experience, insight, and policies. The forum would be an opportunity for genuine conversation. Half of the participants

4. These figures are taken from Steve Sang-Cheol Moon, "The Protestant Missionary Movement in Korea: Current Growth and Development," *International Bulletin of Missionary Research* 32 (April 2008): 59–64.

would be Korean; half would be non-Korean (as it turned out, they were American, Australian, British, Canadian, Indian, and Singaporean). All participants would be in responsible positions of leadership in the most significant evangelical churches and mission agencies at work in the world today. What would they need to learn or implement in order to achieve and sustain God-honoring systems of accountability? And where would missionary training—both pre-field and on-field—fit into all of this?

On March 1, 2010, a group of key Korean mission leaders met with me at the Seoul Club, in Korea, for an extended working luncheon, generously arranged by Mr. Young Hyun Jung and Mrs. Sook Hee Kim, staunch supporters of missions and of OMSC. We discussed questions such as those mentioned above with a view to shaping a possible forum on accountability. Present were Keungchul (Matthew) Jeong, Hyun Mo (Tim) Lee, Shin Chul Lee, Wonjae Lee, Sang-Cheol (Steve) Moon, Nam Yong Sung, Yong Joong Cho, Shinjong (Daniel) Baeq, Kwang Soon Lee, and Seung Sam Kang. They agreed that a forum on accountability should be convened at OMSC, and they assured me of their willingness to cooperate.

With the able assistance of my colleague Jin Bong Kim, serious planning for the forum got under way, and the event, which took place at OMSC in New Haven, Connecticut, from February 10 to 14, 2011, served all of us beyond our expectations. Some forty-eight invited leaders—a list of whom is included in the appendixes—took part. As agreed at the March planning meeting in Seoul, half of the case studies were Korean, the other half non-Korean. Koreans responded to non-Korean case studies, and non-Koreans responded to Koreans. The results appear in this book, published in both Korean and English editions. As is customary, the opinions of the individual writers are their own and are not necessarily those of the editorial committee.

It is appropriate in this introduction to acknowledge with gratitude not only the participants but also the cosponsors of the forum and the book. Generous financial support was provided by First Korean Presbyterian Church, Hartford, Connecticut; SaRang Community Church, Seoul; Rexahn Pharmaceuticals, Baltimore, Maryland; Institute for the Study of American Evangelicalism, Wheaton, Illinois; and New Haven Korean Church, Hamden, Connecticut. Other churches, giving practical and financial encouragement according to their means, included Korean Central Presbyterian Church, Centreville, Virginia; Council of Korean Churches in Connecticut; SamKwang Presbyterian Church, Seoul; and United Church, Westville, Connecticut. Word of Life Press, Seoul, Korea, underwrote the concurrent publication of the Korean language edition of this volume. Since each of the participants paid his or her own way, it must be acknowledged that every mission agency or church represented at the forum contributed substantially to its success. Without this generous spirit of cooperation, the forum could not have occurred, and this book would not have been possible.

To God be the glory!

Jonathan J. Bonk
Executive Director
Overseas Ministries Study Center
New Haven, Connecticut

# 1

# Historical Overview of Korean Missions

## Yong Kyu Park

B Y THE TIME OF the 1910 Edinburgh World Missionary Conference, the Korean mission field had gathered recognition throughout the world, even though missions activity in Korea had begun only a quarter of a century earlier.[1] The Korean mission had commenced with the arrival of Horace N. Allen on September 20, 1884, and had grown remarkably in this short period.

The Korean mission developed quickly after Horace G. Underwood and Henry G. Appenzeller, representatives of two American mission boards—the Presbyterian Board of Missions to Korea and the Methodist Episcopal Mission—arrived in Korea on April 5, 1885. The Presbyterian Mission of Victoria, Australia, began with the arrival in Korea in 1889 of Henry Davis and his younger sister Mary Davis. It was followed by the Presbyterian Mission, South, in 1892 by William D. Reynolds, Cameron Johnson, L. B. Tate, and W. M. Junkin; the Methodist Episcopal Mission,

1. In preparing this chapter, I relied on articles dealing with the mission history of the Korean church, especially Seung-sam Kang, "The Korean Presbyterian Church and Overseas Mission," in *Chonghoe Baegnyeonsa* (One hundred years of the General Assembly of the Korean Presbyterian Church), 2 vols., ed. Yong Kyu Park (Seoul: General Assembly of the Presbyterian Church, 2006), 1:403–52; Seung-sam Kang, "The Foreign Mission of the Korean Presbyterian Church, 1965–1990," in *Chonghoe Baegnyeonsa*, 2:327–53; In-ho Kim, "Hanguggyohoe Haeoe Seongyo-ui Yeogsa-wa Jeonmang" (The history and prospect for foreign missions of the Korean church) (paper, Mission Korea Conference, Seoul, 2001); and Steve Sang-cheol Moon, "Gwangbok 60nyeon-gwa Seongyo Hanguk" (Sixty years of liberation and mission Korea), *Mokhoe-wa Sinhak* (Ministry and theology), August 2005, pp. 68–73.

South, by Clarence F. Reid in 1896; and the Canadian Mission, a Presbyterian group, in 1898. These four Presbyterian and two Methodist missions, which led the Protestant efforts in Korea, thus began their work within fourteen years after Allen's arrival in Korea. Meanwhile, the Baptists and the Church of England began their Korean mission work in 1889 and 1890, respectively, as did various other missionary societies, such as the Oriental Mission, the forerunner of the Holiness Church, in 1907, and the Salvation Army in 1908. Of all these groups, the Presbyterians and the Methodists played the leading role in Korean missions.

As Arthur J. Brown pointed out, a considerable number of outstanding missionaries arrived in Korea very early.[2] These missionaries were committed to the authority of Scripture and historic Christianity; most of all, they possessed a burning passion for saving souls. Most of the missionaries who came to Korea in the initial period were greatly influenced by the worldwide evangelical revivals of the late nineteenth and early twentieth centuries, including the D. L. Moody revivals and the Student Volunteer Movement. Naturally, they were directly and indirectly influenced by the evangelical foreign missionary movement led by Moody, Arthur Pierson, Robert Speer, John Mott, A. J. Gordon, and A. B. Simpson.

Missionaries arriving in Korea spared no effort in promoting the foreign mission movement through their partnership with North American leaders who were having great impact interdenominationally, while closely associating with their own foreign mission boards. As a result, Korea soon became a focus of attention for mission workers worldwide. The passion for saving souls, the progressive mission policy and ministry, evangelical theology itself, and the faithful personal lives of the early missionaries all played essential roles in shaping Korean Protestantism as a solid, missionary-sending church.

In this historical introduction I divide the history of the foreign mission work of the Korean church into four periods: preparation, pioneering, new awakening, and amazing accomplishment. I conclude with final reflections and challenges regarding the next stages of Korea's missionary work.

---

2. Arthur J. Brown, *Mastery of the Far East: The Story of Korea's Transformation and Japan's Rise to Supremacy in the Orient* (New York: Charles Scribners, 1919), p. 540.

## THE PREPARATORY PERIOD, 1884–1907

The preparation period for Korean foreign missions lasted from the arrival of Horace N. Allen in 1884 until 1907, when the Korean church was officially organized after the Pyongyang Revival. What was the driving force in developing Korea as a singularly fruitful mission field after just twenty-five years of mission work? We should most deeply give thanks to the grace of God; historically speaking, we may credit the early Western missionaries to Korea for their clear sense of priorities, both personally and in their mission work. The early missionaries were outstanding figures, not only in their academic preparation and personal character, but also in their sound theology. George L. Paik described the evangelism of the early missionaries as "preaching by their deeds,"[3] highlighting their godly personal model. The mission approach they adopted also played a pivotal role, embracing medicine and education, literature and Bible translation, working cooperatively, a system of mission comity, and what has been called the Nevius Method.

Of all their activities, the Bible translation accomplished by the early missionaries was truly an outstanding achievement. It is not an exaggeration to say that the Korea mission began with Bible translation. Yesu-sungkyo-chunseo (the first Korean translation of the New Testament) started being printed from 1882. The Gospel of Mark, translated by Soo-jung Lee, was published in Yokohama, Japan, in February 1885, and the complete New Testament was published by John Ross in 1887; these two became an invaluable foundation for the Korea mission. Koreans participating in Bible translation (outside Korea) brought the gospels they had produced to their hometowns, which became the Gospel seed for the beginning of the churches in Jipanhyun Lee Yang-ja, Uiju, Sorae, and Saemoonan. As such, Koreans themselves were the active preachers, right from the beginning.

With the first translations by John Ross and Soo-jung Lee meeting the Koreans' early thirst for the Gospel, the early missionaries went on to translate and publish a joint revised version of the New Testament in 1906 and of the Old Testament in 1911. The fact that the New Testament was available in 1906, before the outbreak of the remarkable 1907 Pyongyang Revival, was surely a special gift of God. Very many believers with a thirst for the Gospel, after reading the Scripture, experienced

3. George Lak Paik, *The History of Protestant Missions in Korea, 1832–1910* (Seoul: Yonsei Univ. Press, 1970), pp. 243–45.

the remarkable power of the Holy Spirit working through and with the Word of God. In this regard, the Pyongyang Revival, occurring in close connection with an emphasis on Bible study and practice, was a special providence of God for the Korea mission.

The Protestant mission in Korea began just at the time when many Koreans had a burning desire to devote themselves to a new religion. It was Christianity that suddenly appeared like a comet in the sky, catching the attention of people who found themselves wearied with traditional Buddhism and Confucianism and estranged from Korean shamanism. The qualities, activities, and mission methods adopted by the early missionaries were unusually well suited to the Korean context, all of which helped to maximize the fruit harvested. These early Protestant missionaries carried on their mission work with a wonderful balance between direct and indirect mission methods.[4] They built numerous hospitals and schools, sensing from the outset the importance of medical and educational efforts. Besides the Bible, they translated foreign religious works, including John Bunyan's *Pilgrim's Progress*. They also translated the most significant Korean literature into English, thus introducing it to the Western world.

The missionaries acted wisely in regarding the whole Korean peninsula as a single mission territory, ranging from Hamkyeong Province in the northeast to the island-province of Qualpart (Cheju) in the south, divided only in terms of mission comity. No parts of Korea were left out. The practice of comity eliminated wasteful overlap of effort and, from the beginning, allowed the missionaries to keep denominational walls from blocking their view of the common goal. And we must not forget that the Nevius Method they adopted played a central role in maximizing the fruit of the Korea mission.[5]

The early missionaries to Korea were young, most of them in their twenties: James S. Gale was only twenty-five, Horace Underwood twenty-six, Henry twenty-seven, and William B. Scranton, the oldest, was only twenty-nine when he arrived. They were young and full of ambition, but they lacked mission experience. Thus they prayed for an

---

4. In contrast, the Roman Catholic mission to Korea focused more on direct evangelism, with less attention to efforts to meet a broad range of human needs. Young Kyu Park, *Hanguk Gidokgyohoesa* (History of the Korean church), vol. 1, *1784–1910* (Seoul: Word of Life Press, 2005), pp. 531–638.

5. Charles Allen Clark, *The Nevius Plan for Mission Work, Illustrated in Korea* (Seoul: Christian Literature Society, 1937), pp. 255–74.

experienced missionary to come help them. This prayer was answered in the person of John Livingston Nevius, an American Presbyterian missionary to China who visited Korea for two weeks in 1890, sharing his long mission experience with these young missionaries and imparting his vast knowledge to his attentive audience. These young missionaries listened eagerly to his experiences and methods as if they were their own fathers' last words. Out of this providential connection arose the Nevius Method, which became the basis of Protestant mission policy. Underwood and many other missionaries testified to the value of these interactions: "We believe the progress of the Korean mission is thanks to the blessing of God; that is, the Nevius Mission Method we adopted."[6]

As Charles A. Clark pointed out, the Nevius Method is sometimes known as primarily advocating self-support, self-government, and self-propagation. Its core, however, lies in its emphasis on Bible classes. The missionaries to Korea in fact enabled the Korean churches to become self-supporting, self-governing, and self-propagating, but they saw this as a result of their diligent Bible teaching, which touched individuals as well as church life. The Korea Presbyterian mission adopted the Nevius Method in 1890 and put it into practice throughout its mission field, from Sunday schools to Bible classes, Bible schools, and seminary. Overall, the results were marvelous. Another aspect of the method was its emphasis on every believer being a Christian witness in his or her neighborhood and occupation; each one must fulfill this task. Through their outstanding teaching and faithful lives, the early Western missionaries imbued the hearts of Korean Christians with the consciousness of being debtors to the Gospel.

A handful of Korean believers served in other countries, though not always with the title "missionary." Korean immigration to Hawaii began in 1902, and Sung-ha Hong was sent that same year to serve the Korean church there. In 1909 Hwa-jung Bang was sent to Mexico for the same reason. When the Chinese church experienced terrible oppression in 1900 because of the Boxer Rebellion, the Suncheon Church, from Korea's North Pyengan (now spelled Pyongan) Province, sent N. C. Whittemore and Seung-won Ahn to support the South Manchuria mission. The Presbyterian church sent Sang-do Joo in 1901, Sang-nyun Kim in 1903, Kyung-hee Han in 1909, and Jin-kuen Kim and Woon-

6. Horace G. Underwood, "Principles of Self-Support in Korea," *Korea Mission Field* 4, no. 6 (June 1908): 92.

ki Hwang in 1910 after taking over churches in South Manchuria from John Ross and John MacIntyre. Similarly, for mission work in Kando (East Manchuria), adjoining North Hamkyong, the Southern Methodist Mission in 1902 sent Canadian missionary R. G. Grierson and Bible teachers Soon-gook Hong and Soon-young Ahn, who had been living in Chongjin, North Hamkyong Province. The roots of the later blossoming of Korea missions can be traced to the mission work of these early missionaries. Without such preparation, it is difficult to imagine that the Korean churches could ever have begun their foreign mission work.

## THE PIONEER PERIOD, 1907–45

The Korean church started with a sense of urgency for mission from its very beginning. In the autumn of 1907, when the Pyongyang Revival swept across the Korean peninsula and was being called one of the most powerful revivals since the Acts of the Apostles, four Presbyterian missions organized the presbytery. It had been two hundred years since the first presbytery was organized in the United States (1706), and then only twenty-three years since the Korea mission began (1884). It certainly was very meaningful that one Presbyterian Church was established by the coalition of four Presbyterian missions, instead of each one creating its own denomination. At this first presbytery, the Korean church ordained seven graduates of Pyongyang Presbyterian Theological Seminary and appointed them as pastors. It was even more surprising that, among the first seven ordained pastors, they decided to send out Ki-poong Lee to Qualpart and to pay his salary from the mission board,[7] celebrating in this way the organization of the presbytery. The Evangelism Committee changed its name to the Foreign Mission Board on September 18, 1907, and one day later, it appointed twelve board members and adopted a resolution stating that, if the church ever ceased doing missions, it could no longer be considered the Presbyterian Church. They inculcated the attitude that all Presbyterian churches were missions of which all Presbyterians were life members.

The Korean Presbyterian Church sent missionaries to Japan, Russia, and Manchuria, China. In 1908 the presbytery decided to send Suk-jin Han, one of the first seven ordained pastors, as a missionary to Tokyo

---

7. Presbyterian Church of Korea, *Presbytery Records* (Seoul: Christian Literature Society, 1907), p. 18.

for Korean students. The Japan mission was conducted in partnership with the Presbyterian and Methodist churches. Despite many difficulties, the Japan mission grew steadily, reaching about fifty churches and three thousand members; in Japan, six missionaries, thirteen Korean pastors, twenty Bible women, and several lay ministers carried out mission work. In 1909 the presbytery sent Kwan-heul Choi to Vladivostok, the key port city in southeastern Siberia, Russia, to begin a ministry for immigrants. In 1913 three people were sent to Shandong, China: Tae-ro Park, Young-hoon Kim, and Byung-soon Sa. Since these three already knew the Chinese characters, they were quickly able to adapt to the Chinese language and culture.

Passion for foreign missions did not diminish thereafter. The church sent missionaries to Mexico and Hawaii to conduct ministry for Korean workers there. After Japan annexed Korea in 1910, Koreans began to endure great privation. Korean churches, however, never stopped their foreign missions, even under their extremely impoverished conditions. The missionaries that had already been sent continued to carry out their calling as debtors of the Gospel, despite the sorrow of losing their own country to the Japanese. And the Korea Presbyterian General Assembly continued to send missionaries overseas despite financial difficulties, such as Ji-il Bang to Shandong Province in 1937 and Hyung-joo Choi to Manchuria.[8] Though it was an especially difficult time for the impoverished Korean church to persevere in sowing the seeds of mission, it continued to do so. Eventually it saw the promise of Psalm 126:5 fulfilled: "Those who sow in tears will reap with songs of joy" (NIV).

## THE PERIOD OF NEW AWAKENING, 1945–80

From 1945 to 1980 was a period of new awakening for foreign missions within the Korean church. This awakening came as a special gift of God after the severe trials of the previous decades. After the Presbyterian General Assembly sent Ji-il Bang and Hyung-joo Choi to Shandong, China, and Manchuria as missionaries in 1937, the next missionary was not sent out until 1955.[9] The colonial usurpation by Japan, especially

8. Park, *Chonghoe Baegnyeonsa*, 2:654.

9. Despite an effort from 1957 to 1963 to revive missions, the actual numbers of missionaries sent out showed minimal increase. Kang refers to the period from 1938 to 1963 as "the mission of the recession" ("The Foreign Mission of the Korean Presbyterian Church," p. 329).

the forced shrine worship, became difficult in the extreme. Then World War II and mobilization under the terrifying colonial ambitions of Japan were further tunnels of darkness through which the Korean church and the Korean people had to pass. Though liberation was achieved in 1945, it was but a temporary lull, as the Korean War (1950–53) followed soon thereafter, the most fearsome and damaging invasion in Korea's history. The horrifying war between the South and the North severely threatened the Korean church and the very survival of the people. The Russian mission had to be stopped because of the outbreak of the Russian Communist revolution, and even the China mission, into which the Korean church had put its heart and soul, had to be suspended because of World War II and then Chinese Communism. "Pioneer missionary Hyo-won Bang retired in 1936, and his oldest son, Ji-il Bang, took over his ministry in 1937; but because of the Greater East Asia War, missionary teams faced times of tribulation. Missionary Soon-ho Kim had to relocate to a mission field in Manchuria in 1938, and missionaries Sang-soon Park, Dae-young Lee, and Ji-il Bang faced extreme difficulties in their work. Sang-soon Park returned to Korea in 1940, Dae-young Lee in 1948, and Ji-il Bang in September 1957, which brought a temporary end to the China mission."[10]

Although the China mission had to be suspended temporarily, the Korean church again launched foreign missions, even while suffering from the unhealed scars of the Korean War. Missionary awakening in this period occurred in four areas.

### Korean Denominations

The first area of awakening for foreign missions was the various denominations. The Korean Presbyterian General Assembly sent Chan-young Choi and Soon-il Kim to Thailand in 1956 as missionaries, and Hwa-sam Kae to Taiwan in 1957. Choi and Kim, both trilingual in English, Chinese, and Japanese, adjusted well to the mission field, mastering their new language and culture in a short period of time. Choi served successfully for fifteen years, until 1970, and Kim became highly trusted and respected in Thailand for his pioneering and itinerant ministry. The work in Taiwan of Kae, who had been raised and educated in theology

10. Kang, "The Korean Presbyterian Church," p. 449.

in Manchuria, laid important groundwork for the future missions to China.

On the occasion of the one hundredth anniversary of the martyrdom of Robert J. Thomas (the first Protestant martyr in Korea), on September 26, 1966, the Korean Presbyterian Church held a memorial service and decided then to send Eun-soo Chae to Taiwan. In 1967 the General Assembly declared that "the mission board will focus only on foreign missions, that is, only on indigenous people, not on evangelism for Koreans living abroad."[11]

The Presbyterian Church in Korea (Hapdong) was the leading body for foreign missions of this time. In 1969 the church sent Seung-man Yang to Brazil and Nam-jin Cha to the United States; in 1971, Man-soo Suh to Indonesia and Heung-sik Sin to Thailand; in 1972, Hwan Cho and Hyung-tak Kim to Japan; in 1974, Byung-soo Baik and Jung-sook Kang to Japan; and in 1976, Jong-man Hong to Hong Kong, Ho-gi Yuk to Germany, and Yeon-ho Lee and Sin-sook Kim to Egypt. Other missionaries were sent to the Philippines, Germany, and Argentina.

### Ewha Womans University

A second push for foreign missions during this period came from Ewha Womans University, in Seoul. In 1959 President Hwal-lan Kim participated in the International Missionary Council, where she saw the possibility of a Pakistan mission. Upon her return to Korea, she was instrumental in making this a reality. In 1961 the Mission Board of Ewha Womans University, the first interdenominational mission association

---

11. *Je 53hoe Chonghoerok* (The fifty-third General Assembly records, the Korean Presbyterian Church) (Seoul: Presbyterian Church of Korea, 1968), p. 118. In the following year the General Assembly made several critical decisions for foreign missions. It affirmed its intention to expand mission sites to all over the world; to give responsibility to the main office for selecting missionaries and mission sites, subject to the approval of the General Assembly; to have churches, organizations, or individuals pay the living costs of missionaries; and to have the Mission Department pay the costs of sending out missionaries plus operational costs. Furthermore, in cases where a missionary is not suitable in a given field or is causing trouble in certain mission projects, then that missionary would be warned or the Mission Department would send out one of its members to investigate personally or would ask that missionary to return home. The General Assembly also decided to open a seminary-level course in missions in its seminaries, it appointed an "honorary secretary" of missions, and it prepared detailed guidelines for stimulating foreign missions, such as the "Council Mission for Mission Projects."

in Korea, sent three of its graduates to the St. Teresa Girls' High School in Quetta, Pakistan: Sung-ja Cho, from the Education Department, and Jae-ok Jeon and In-ja Kim, from the English Department.

### Korea International Mission

The third contributor to Korean foreign missions was the Korea International Mission (KIM). Pastor Dong-jin Cho, who was in charge of the Hooam Church after graduating from Chongshin Seminary and taking further studies in missiology at Asbury Theological Seminary, in Wilmore, Kentucky, established the Institute of East-West Mission and KIM. This mission sent many missionaries overseas and became a leading promoter of passion for foreign missions in the Korean church. As collaboration with many international mission organizations became difficult, the All-Asia Mission Consultation, or "Seoul '73," was convened in August 1973. It was the first world mission strategy conference led by the non-Western world. As a result of the conference, the Asia Missions Association (AMA) was established in 1975.

Christian leaders in the non-Western world sharply criticized the indifference of Western church mission leaders and declared a new mission era focused on the non-Western world. The Summer Institute of World Mission, in Seoul, was opened in 1973 and trained dozens of young Asian mission volunteers, including Koreans, for two to three weeks every year. Those who were sent to overseas mission fields from the mid-1970s to the 1980s went through this school; with its global perspective, it was influential in inspiring young mission volunteers, as well as the missions of Korean churches, which were still immature. In 1971 KIM sent Hong-sik Sin to Thailand, and in 1976, Jung-woong Kim to Thailand and Eun-moo Lee to Indonesia. The latter two began active mission work appropriate to the two countries, and they played a role in introducing international mission organizations such as Overseas Missionary Fellowship and Wycliffe Bible Translators to Korea.[12]

### Mass Evangelism and the Worldwide Evangelical Movement

The final push for Korean foreign missions during this period came from mass evangelism, interdenominational mission organizations, and the international evangelical movement, which directly and indirectly

12. Kim, "The History and Prospect."

influenced the foreign missions of Korea. The mass evangelism represented by the 1973 Billy Graham Seoul Crusade, Explo '74, the National Evangelization Crusade in 1977, and the World Evangelization Crusade in 1980 accelerated the growth of the Korean church and brought in more financial resources, which allowed for more effective missions. The brisk activities of interdenominational mission organizations at the time provided a new engine for the growth of Korean mission. Activities of numerous interdenominational mission organizations, including Campus Crusade for Christ (CCC), InterVarsity Fellowship (IVF), Navigators, JOY Mission, Youth for Christ (YFC), and the University Bible Fellowship (UBF) imbued young people with an interest in missions and offered human resources for the foreign mission movement that quickly grew in Korean churches. Of all of them, UBF, launched in 1961 by Samuel Lee and Sarah Barry, was especially strong in its foreign mission emphasis, envisioning foreign missions under the slogan "Bible Korea, World Mission." After In-kyung Suh, Dong-ran Sul, and Hwa-ja Lee were sent to Germany in the early 1970s as missionary-nurses, 205 more missionaries were sent overseas by 1975. By the end of 2000, there were 1,500 UBF missionaries serving in eighty-three countries. These missionaries, all self-supported or on study-abroad programs, focused especially on lay ministry, college ministry, and native missions.

The international evangelical movement, operating under the Lausanne Covenant, was another key factor in accelerating the Korean mission movement. As an outflow of Lausanne, the Korea Evangelical Theological Society (KETS) was organized, as well as the Korea Evangelical Fellowship (KEF), and the Asia Center for Theological Studies (ACTS). Formation of these groups led to a new level of cooperation and exchange with evangelical leaders from other countries, including countries in Asia, Britain, and the United States, which further promoted foreign missions.

Meanwhile, the missionary ship *Logos* of Operation Mobilisation (OM) visited Korea three times—in 1975, 1978, and 1980—inspiring missionary interest among college students and Korean churches. The last two visits in particular were warmly received by the Korean government and by the churches, as the OM workers visited major churches in Korea and challenged people regarding foreign missions. Promising young Koreans who participated in a three-week evangelism campaign had their own passion and missionary vision refreshed through an

Operation World Conference that drew witnessing laymen in their early twenties from various countries to Korea. This conference "clearly demonstrated the importance of world mission, and the 210 participants played a significant role in preparing the Korean church for deeper foreign mission involvement."[13]

During roughly the same period, the Student Mission Fellowship was launched within the Presbyterian General Assembly Theological Seminary, often called Chongshin Seminary. Seminary graduates Yu-sik Kim, Hwal-young Kim, Hee-won Yun, and Seung-sam Kang were sent as foreign missionaries. There was a strong missionary awakening at the denominational level, and additional seminarians became involved. At this time the Korea Presbyterian Church (Hapdong) was the denomination sending out the most missionaries.

The Billy Graham Seoul Crusade in 1973 and Campus Crusade's Explo '74 were turning points for the many young people who opened their heart to the Gospel. During the time of the crusade, 23,000 young people made a commitment to world mission. Despite the politically unstable situation in 1979, when former president Chung-hee Park was assassinated, the Korean church never flagged in its interest in foreign missions. According to Martin L. Nelson, in 1979 the Korean church had a total of 93 missionaries serving abroad.[14]

## THE AMAZING PERIOD, 1980–2010

The passion for foreign missions among evangelical churches in the Second and Third Worlds has deepened remarkably, including in Korea, since 1980, when a World Evangelization Crusade was held in Seoul. From only 3,400 Third World missionaries in 1972, the number increased rapidly to 13,000 in 1980, and then to 42,000 in 1992. During this period Korea showed especially strong growth. In 1979 it had 93 missionaries serving in other countries, a number that by 1996 had risen to 4,402—a nearly fifty-fold increase. Then by June 1998 the number was at 5,948 missionaries serving abroad.

Several international gatherings involving Korea reflect the coming of age of Korean missions. In 1988 there was a Korean World Mission

13. Ibid.

14. Martin L. Nelson, *Directory of Korean Missionaries and Mission Societies* (Seoul: ACTS, 1979), pp. 44–45.

Conference (KWMC), held as always in Wheaton, Illinois; in 1990, the first Asian Mission Congress, held in Seoul, with 1,300 participants; in 1992, the next KWMC, held at the Billy Graham Center, in Wheaton; and in May 1995, the Global Consultation on World Evangelism (GCOWE), held in Seoul, with 4,500 leaders from 216 countries around the world participating. Throughout, the remarkable passion for foreign mission among Korean young people continued. Over 1,000 Korean young people participated in the 1996 Urbana Mission Conference, held in Urbana, Illinois.

The remarkable growth of Korean missions was indebted to the work of interdenominational mission organizations such as CCC, IVF, JOY, and UBF, as well as the mission promotion of Korean churches, the "Mission Korea" movement, the mission movement among Korean-Americans, flexibility in mission strategies, awakening for foreign mission through evangelical missionary conferences at home and abroad, and cooperation between mission organizations, such as OMF International (originally the Overseas Ministry Fellowship), OM, and SIM (originally the Sudan Interior Mission, later, Serving in Mission).

A relaxation in the foreign travel policy of the Korean government beginning with the Seoul Olympics in 1988 greatly assisted the missionary revolution. Before then, on January 1, 1983, the government began issuing tourism passports to all citizens aged fifty or over, for at that time experts saw a stabilization in Korea's international trade balance. Then on January 1, 1989, as South Korea's economy grew rapidly, the overall standard of living improved, and the country realized a budgetary surplus, the government fully liberalized overseas travel. Instead of the previous difficulties in traveling abroad, now there was a liberal passport policy, many people were able to leave the country for short-term mission, and missionaries went to other countries without specific restrictions. In this sense, freedom to travel provided new momentum to Korean mission. As a result, from 511 missionaries in 1986, the number grew rapidly to 1,178 (1989), 4,402 (1996), then 8,200 (2000). We need to acknowledge, however, that a large number of those being sent out during this period did not receive adequate training for their missionary work.

The "Mission Korea" conference, which was held every two years beginning in 1988, was an opportunity for impacting numerous youngsters with the missionary challenge and for imparting a strong missionary vision to all participants. The founding of the Korea World Missions

Association (KWMA) in 1990 was an important turning point in giving new direction to the foreign mission development of the Korean church. Beginning in 1994, KWMA has held a National Consultation on World Evangelization (NCOWE) every four years to discuss the policy and strategy of Korean foreign missions. At the fourth NCOWE, in 2006, all denominations and mission organizations of Korea gave their support to the Target 2030 Mission Movement, which hopes to send out 100,000 missionaries by 2030.

International mission organizations such as OMF International, Global Bible Translators (GBT), SIM, AIM (originally Africa Inland Mission), WEC International (earlier Worldwide Evangelization for Christ), Interserve, OM, Youth with a Mission (YWAM), Red Sea Mission Team, and New Tribes Mission (NTM) have recognized the mission potential of the Korean church and have begun establishing local branches in Korea or at least looking for collaborative relationships with Korean churches. Through this process, the Korean church has been able to learn many things from its Western counterparts. The church, through such collaboration, has gradually been able to build a foundation of mission specialization upon which to implement strategic missions, versus simply trying to send out more and more missionaries, armed only with their personal zeal and passion. Mission strategies and goals have changed significantly over the years. Korean churches have transitioned from missions for Koreans living overseas to intercultural foreign missions, from country-centered to ethnic-group-centered missions, from individual missions to an era of cooperative missions, from pastor-oriented missions to multiple missions including lay missionaries, and from deficient mission training to substantial mission training. Changes are still ongoing; in fact, it has become clearly evident that changes will always be necessary.

Korean missions have realized great strides through these various events and influences. One important factor has been the foreign missions of the respective denominations. After 1980 each Korean denomination influenced by evangelicalism has sent many overseas missionaries—almost as if the groups were in competition with each other. As Ho-jin Jeon pointed out in his article "The Status and Direction of the Missions of Korean Churches," denominational missions in Korea have sent out many more missionaries than have U.S. denominational missions.[15]

Until the 1970s, Korea had only one or two mission training centers. By the 1980s, however, their number had increased to more than ten. The mission training program now handled by the Global Mission Society of the Presbyterian Church (Hapdong); ACTS, established in 1974 for evangelization of Asia; a training center operated by the Presbyterian Theological College and Seminary (Tonghap); the Missionary Training Center, Hapdong Seminary; and missionary training programs by Baptist College and Seminary, Korean OM Mission, Korea Harbor Evangelism, Global Missionary Training Center, and Korea Overseas Mission—all are vital mission training centers. Of the 4,402 missionaries sent overseas in 1996, almost 60 percent—2,618—received training from one of these centers.

In the 1980s Korea experienced unprecedented waves of change. In the social sector, there was the 1980 Gwangju Democratization Movement, the 1988 Seoul Olympics, campus democratization, and overseas travel freedom. In the religious sector, activities of evangelical leaders were noticeable, leaders such as Joon-gon Kim, Sang-bok Kim, Jung-gil Hong, Han-heum Ok, Dong-won Lee, Yong-jo Ha, Myung-hyuk Kim, Tae-woong Lee, Bong-rin Ro, and Ho-jin Jeon. Furthermore, the foreign mission movement within the Korean church realized unprecedented growth, including the establishment of Korean Students Abroad (KOSTA), Mission Korea, and Yanbian University of Science and Technology, a base in China for work with, and through, Koreans. We see the effects of all such movements in the numbers of missionaries sent out from Korea: only 93 in 1979, but over 10,000 in 2001.

The twenty-first-century church of Korea, which only 120 years ago was referred to as a hermit nation, has developed seemingly limitless mission leaders, well equipped with human resources and a strong spiritual dynamic, elements seen in the latter part of the nineteenth century only in the British and American churches. Already in 1992 Yong-hyun Hwang could write, "It is evident that God has given responsibilities to the Korean church as a leading mission power in the center of world churches at the end of this century; consider its economic growth,

15. Ho-jin Jeon, "Hanguk Gyohoe Hyeon Hwang-gwa Banghyang" (The status and direction of the missions of Korean churches), *Seonggyeong-gwa Sinhak* (Bible and theology) 16 (1994): 68–72.

theological richness, ecclesiastical zeal and determination, educational advancements, the social recognition of Christianity, abundant human resources, and its evangelical spirit."[16]

Thomas Wang, chairman of the 1995 GCOWE, Seoul, wrote, "God indicated that Korea was a country to lead world missions in the twentieth century," citing the church's enthusiastic prayer movement, the trend of its theology (which is based on biblical faith), and its sacrificial support for foreign mission. It was not an exaggeration to forecast, as many mission leaders did at the time, that Korea would become "a country with a strong influence for world mission in a couple of years."[17]

## REFLECTIONS AND CHALLENGES

The quantitative growth of Korean mission has continued. In this new century, about 1,000 missionaries have been sent overseas every year, and the total number of missionaries now on the field exceeds 20,000. This amazing growth in foreign missionaries witnessed after 1980 has made Korea the second largest missionary-sending country, after the United States. And as Steve Sang-chul Moon has pointed out, the foreign mission training of the Korean church has reached world standard. It is very inspiring to note that the passion for foreign missions has shown no signs of abating, especially considering the period of stagnation and even decline in numbers that the Korean church has had to face since 1992.

We must admit, however, that the quality of Korean missions has not kept pace with its quantity. Many problems in this amazing foreign mission movement have started to surface within the Korean church and its overseas mission fields. This has forced us to look more closely at the mission agenda and at matters of maturity. Despite the continuing interest Korean mission leaders have in organizing small- and large-scale mission conferences, the Korean church, in its concentration on mission mobilization and stimulation of zeal for mission, has failed to pay attention to such areas as self-reflection and mission reform.

In 2001, noticing a series of problems that occurred among Korean missionaries, one mission mobilizer raised the question whether the

16. Yong-hyun Hwang, "Segye Bogeumhwa-leul wihan Umjigimdeul" (The movements for world evangelization), *Bit-gwa Sogeum* (Light and salt), September 1992, p. 57.

17. "5 wol 17 il Gidoggyo Yeongjeog Olympic Yeollinda" (On May 17th, open the spiritual Olympics of Christianity), *Bit-gwa Sogeum* (Light and salt), April 1995, pp. 21, 19.

Korean church mission was going in the right direction. There was criticism that a significant number of missionaries seemed more interested in furthering the renown of Korean church growth than in proclaiming the Gospel of the cross and the resurrection of Christ in the mission fields. They had a strong tendency to be more focused on quantitative missions than on proclaiming the Gospel itself; despite holding large mission conferences, thoughtful objectives and strategies of missions seemed to be missing. Setting the direction of the mission movement in the twenty-first century is definitely the most critical task for Korean mission.

The Korean mission has many issues to solve now. Most of all, mission resources have been running low. Management of the sending out of mission volunteers has been deficient, although resources for mission have been discovered through the Mission Korea movement. Seminarians are as important as young laymen, but the Korean church has failed to discover and mobilize mission resources among them. Korea needs a movement like the American Inter-Seminary Missionary Alliance, which, along with the Student Volunteer Movement for Foreign Missions, awakened God's call to mission in Horace Underwood and Henry Appenzeller in a previous century.

The qualitative improvement of missionaries is another task for the Korean mission to seriously consider. Sending out more highly qualified missionaries could well lead to a new period of fruitful and amazing missions, for we recall the results achieved when the early Western missions in Korea sent out singularly qualified missionaries.

There should be high-level discussions on member care, including issues of financial support, child education, the sabbatical (or furlough) year, provision for missionary retraining and retirement, leadership, mutual respect, keeping the "unity of the Spirit" by refraining from excessive rivalry, and, overall, upgrading of the missions. Korean missions, which have experienced hectic times in their abrupt quantitative growth, should now seriously consider how to sustain a growing world mission through greater self-reflection and reform. Though KWMA is leading in establishing a movement toward united effort and collaboration that transcends strictly denominational interests, there should be greater in-depth cooperation with denominations, as well as domestic and overseas mission organizations, in order to carry out effective world mission in the twenty-first century.

The failure to preserve historical records is another serious problem area. Letters and mission reports sent to mission boards and organizations by Korean missionaries are not being properly preserved, which will cause difficulties when it comes time to prepare the histories of the various missions. Korean mission still has a long way to go before it can match the practice and diligence of American mission boards in systematically organizing and preserving mission history through the letters and reports of the missionaries they send out. It is very encouraging that a Korean missionary handbook has been published that reports the mission status of each denomination and mission organization after 1979, thanks to the efforts of Martin Nelson and Sang-chul (Steve) Moon.

To properly evaluate Korean mission through its past mission history and to seek a better direction in the future is itself an important and historic task. In this regard, the 2005 Mission Forum in Bangkok that dealt with accountability in mission[18] and the 2011 Korean Global Mission Leadership Forum (KGMLF) held at the Overseas Ministries Study Center (OMSC) are very meaningful in terms of Korean mission history. In particular, the KGMLF should be highly appreciated for its in-depth discussions with domestic and overseas mission leaders on the topic of mission accountability. The future of mission by the Korean church will be brighter to the extent that the parties involved continue to conduct in-depth discussions and share concerns for their mutual growth in maturity.

18. The papers presented at the 2005 Mission Forum in Bangkok were compiled and published as *Hanguk Seongyo-wa Chaengmu* (Korean mission and accountability: The second Bangkok mission forum), ed. Bangkok Mission Forum Committee (Seoul: Hyebon Publishing, 2006).

# 2

## Samuel, an Old Testament Model of Accountability and Integrity

### *Christopher J. H. Wright*

THE ISSUE ADDRESSED BY this book and the consultation that lies behind it is timely and urgent. Mission leaders are increasingly aware that, in our passion to "do mission," we cannot ignore what is going on in the church itself. The credibility of our message depends on the integrity of those who live it and proclaim it. At the Third Lausanne Congress on World Evangelization, in Cape Town in October 2010, I was asked to present a plenary address on the topic "Calling the Church of Christ Back to Humility, Integrity, and Simplicity." I contrasted these great Christian virtues, which are taught and modeled by Jesus himself, with three forms of idolatry that are condemned in the Bible but sadly still rampant among God's people today (including mission leaders): the idolatries of power, success, and greed. Integrity and accountability ought to be fundamental to the character of those who are entrusted with Christian leadership. And yet, sadly, leaders themselves often display neither of them, partly because, before becoming leaders, they were never deeply discipled in what it means to be a follower of Jesus.

The Cape Town Commitment has a whole section (II.D.3) on Christ-centered leadership. It is worth quoting here because the section addresses a broad area that includes the challenge of integrity and accountability.

### CHRIST-CENTRED LEADERS

The rapid growth of the Church in so many places remains shallow and vulnerable, partly because of the lack of discipled leaders, and partly because so many use their positions for worldly power, arrogant status or personal enrichment. As a result, God's people suffer, Christ is dishonoured, and gospel mission is undermined. 'Leadership training' is the commonly-proposed priority solution. Indeed, leadership training programmes of all kinds have multiplied, but the problem remains, for two probable reasons.

*First*, training leaders to be godly and Christlike is the wrong way round. Biblically, only those whose lives already display basic qualities of mature discipleship should be appointed to leadership in the first place [1 Tim. 3:1–13; Titus 1:6–9; 1 Peter 5:1–3]. If, today, we are faced with many people in leadership who have scarcely been discipled, then there is no option but to include such basic discipling in their leadership development. Arguably the scale of un-Christlike and worldly leadership in the global Church today is glaring evidence of generations of reductionist evangelism, neglected discipling and shallow growth. The answer to leadership failure is not just more *leadership* training but better *discipleship* training. Leaders must first be disciples of Christ himself.

*Second*, some leadership training programmes focus on packaged knowledge, techniques and skills to the neglect of godly character. By contrast, authentic Christian leaders must be like Christ in having a servant heart, humility, integrity, purity, lack of greed, prayerfulness, dependence on God's Spirit, and a deep love for people. Furthermore, some leadership training programmes lack specific training in the one key skill that Paul includes in his list of qualifications—ability to teach God's Word to God's people. Yet Bible teaching is the paramount means of disciple-making and the most serious deficiency in contemporary Church leaders.

A) We long to see greatly intensified efforts in disciple-making, through the long-term work of teaching and nurturing new believers, so that those whom God calls and gives to the Church as leaders are qualified according to biblical criteria of maturity and servanthood.

B) We renew our commitment to pray for our leaders. We long that God would multiply, protect and encourage leaders who are biblically faithful and obedient. We pray that God would rebuke, remove, or bring to repentance leaders who dishonour his name and discredit the gospel. And we pray that God would raise up a new generation of discipled servant-leaders whose passion is above all else to know Christ and be like him.

C) Those of us who are in Christian leadership need to recognize our vulnerability and accept the gift of accountability within the body of Christ. We commend the practice of submitting to an accountability group.

A ringing call for "a cleansing wave of honesty" in mission leadership appears later in the Cape Town Commitment (sec. II.E.4):

WALK IN INTEGRITY, REJECTING THE IDOLATRY
OF SUCCESS [EPH. 5:8–9]

We cannot build the kingdom of the God of truth on foundations of dishonesty. Yet in our craving for 'success' and 'results' we are tempted to sacrifice our integrity, with distorted or exaggerated claims that amount to lies. Walking in the light, however, 'consists in . . . righteousness and truth' [Eph. 5:10].

A) We call on all church and mission leaders to resist the temptation to be less than totally truthful in presenting our work. We are dishonest when we exaggerate our reports with unsubstantiated statistics, or twist the truth for the sake of gain. We pray for a cleansing wave of honesty and the end of such distortion, manipulation and exaggeration. We call on all who fund spiritual work not to make unrealistic demands for measurable and visible results, beyond the need for proper accountability. Let us strive for a culture of full integrity and transparency. We will choose to walk in the light and truth of God, for the Lord tests the heart and is pleased with integrity [1 Chron. 29:17].

I would love to hope and believe that the Korean mission movement can have the openness, courage, trust in itself, and maturity to ask, "Can we look at ourselves honestly and face up to some of these issues?" And then to ask for God's forgiveness where necessary and God's help in other areas. Confidence that this is what the Korean mission movement wants gives me great hope. It seems to me that we are touching here on a nerve, something that the Holy Spirit wants to see happening. Trusting one another in this process is very important if there is to be a cleansing wave of honesty in the church that can lead to a far higher level of integrity and accountability.

In the Old Testament, resource materials on this issue are rich, but I decided to choose just one example, Samuel, as a model. First of all, let's look at what Samuel himself said and did in relation to his moral integrity, as recorded in his closing speech in 1 Samuel 12. Second, we will look back behind Samuel to ask where he would have gotten the resources, ethos, and understanding that he shows in his speech. Then, third, we will look beyond Samuel to the rest of the Old Testament and ask, What was the sequel? What do we find in the rest of the narratives, the Psalms, and the prophets of the Old Testament that reflects and reinforces Samuel's emphasis on integrity?

## THE SUBSTANCE OF SAMUEL'S CLAIM

At a critical juncture in Israel's history, the prophet Samuel spoke to the assembled people, directly addressing the issues before us.

> Samuel said to all Israel, "I have listened to you in all that you have said to me, and have set a king over you. See, it is the king who leads you now; I am old and gray, but my sons are with you. I have led you from my youth until this day. Here I am; testify against me before the Lord and before his anointed. Whose ox have I taken? Or whose donkey have I taken? Or whom have I defrauded? Whom have I oppressed? Or from whose hand have I taken a bribe to blind my eyes with it? Testify against me and I will restore it to you." They said, "You have not defrauded us or oppressed us or taken anything from the hand of anyone." He said to them, "The Lord is witness against you, and his anointed is witness this day, that you have not found anything in my hand." And they said, "He is witness." (1 Sam. 12:1–5 NRSV)

This is a significant moment for Samuel. It is a significant moment in the history of Israel because it is a transition of leadership. We all know how difficult leadership transitions can be. One of the biggest problems faced by churches, as also by mission organizations, is what happens when a good and godly leader who has been in place for a long time has to leave or is so old that a change has to be made.

Samuel tells the Israelites that he is old and that he has his own sons, but he is faced with the common problem that the second generation is not always of the quality of the previous one. Samuel has gone through the pain of hearing reports that his own sons were dealing illegally and taking unjust gain. His sons were not like him. There is a particular irony in that knowledge, for Samuel began his own ministry by having to point out exactly the same thing to Eli (1 Sam. 2–3). Eli's sons had been misbehaving, and Samuel had to bring God's words to Eli about their misbehavior. Now the same thing is happening to Samuel himself. It was a tragedy then, and it is a tragedy still.

As we introduced ourselves to one another at the start of our consultation, it was lovely to hear testimonies of those of us who are blessed to have sons and daughters who are following the Lord into various forms of Christian ministry or missionary service, and we all rejoice in that. Some of us, though, may feel our hearts drop when we hear this kind of report because we have sons or daughters who are not doing that, and it is grievous to us. And there may be no reason, no logic about why that happens. In the Bible we find some sons and daughters who follow their parents' examples and others who do not.

This difficult situation now faces Samuel. There has to be a transition of leadership; the time has come for him to lay down his office and step aside. In doing so, Samuel stands before the Israelites to open up the books of his public office and to hold himself accountable before God and the people for the role that he has occupied all his life. He says, "I have been your leader from my youth up," and indeed that was true; from his very earliest days he had been used by God as a prophet (bringing God's word to the people and exercising spiritual leadership). Also he was a judge. Rather like a "circuit judge," he had had an itinerary around the country year by year in which he dealt with judicial affairs and resolved disputes and conflicts. Because of his duties, he was involved in the everyday life of the people. On one or two occasions he was even a military leader. So Samuel had had a very significant combination of public offices that he had discharged throughout his long life.

In verse 3 Samuel makes two distinct claims. The first is that *he had taken no personal profit from public office.* "Whose ox have I taken? Or whose donkey have I taken?" He is saying that he has not stolen anything under the protection of his power or in any way legitimized by his office. He had not behaved as if to say: "I'm the judge, I can take what I like and get off with it." People in high office sometimes think they can behave with impunity; the ordinary rules don't apply to them. Sadly, even Christian leaders bend the rules in that way. But Samuel says, "I did not do that. I have not expropriated funds. I have not taken anything that belonged to somebody else for myself." He had not taken advantage of the access to resources that such power gives to those who wield it. He says, "If I did that, tell me. Whose ox did I take?" And they all replied,

"Nobody's. You have been clean. You have been honest. You have not stolen anything simply because you had the power to do so."

Samuel's second claim is not only that he had taken no personal profit from his public office but, further, that *he had allowed no corruption of the office itself.* He asks, "From whose hand have I accepted a bribe to make me shut my eyes?" Bribery and corruption are blinding. They make leaders overlook bad things that are happening and turn a blind eye to the real needs of the innocent. He says, "I have not accepted anything in order to twist the law or to show any kind of favoritism to somebody because they made my life easier with a tempting bribe." Of course, bribery is just one form of corruption. There are many others that are perhaps less obvious, many of them practiced within the Christian community. There are forms of nepotism, where we give jobs and privileges to people in our own family. Or we may show favoritism to people from our particular tribe or caste. Or we may allow close friends to have unfair personal influence, or we overlook their failings and cover up for wrongs they have done— just because they belong to our circle of family or friends. In such ways, our ministry becomes twisted, corrupted, and darkened. If so, we have become blinded by corruption. Samuel says, "I allowed none of that! My eyes were not blinded by any bribery or corruption."

This, then, is Samuel's claim. He claims to have resisted both personal profit *from* his public office and corruption *of* that office. This occasion, in 1 Samuel 12, is one of transparent public accountability. Notice how both God and the people are involved. Samuel calls God to witness, and he calls the people to witness. This is the nature of biblical accountability. Samuel did not merely go to God in his prayers at night and say, "Lord, you know that I am clean, aren't I?" and then have some nice dream and feel content before God. It is not just that he kept his life open before the Lord, but he is also courageous enough to stand before the people and say, "*You* be my judge; *you* are my witnesses. If there is anything you can point out that I have done that is wrong, then I will put it right. Let's make this an open, transparent public act of accountability before all those I have served in this ministry." This is the substance of Samuel's integrity.

## THE SOURCE OF SAMUEL'S INTEGRITY: COVENANTAL LAW

Where did Samuel get this sense of obligation? What was the source of such commitment to integrity, to a form of public accountability which was both horizontal and vertical—to the people and to God? I would suggest that he got it, on the one hand, from the rich tradition of Old Testament Torah, in whatever form the writings were known to him in the Scriptures of his day. On the other hand, it came from the narratives and stories that he would have known from the previous generations of the history of Israel—indeed, I would suggest, even from his own mother (not a bad place to learn accountability and integrity!). Samuel undoubtedly owes something to Hannah as the story is recorded in the opening chapters of the book by his name.

In this section we will look at examples of the resources Samuel found available in the Torah. The Old Testament possesses a very deep-rooted awareness of the covenant relationship between God and Israel, which had exactly this double dimension of the vertical and the horizontal that we see at work in Samuel. On the one hand, Yahweh, the living God of Israel, was the divine Lord of the covenant; he was the divine Auditor. He could see all and hear all and know all, and therefore the whole of life was lived *coram Deo*, in the presence of God, the great covenant Lord. The vertical obligation to love God, to obey God, to walk in God's ways stands out. Every Israelite, and especially every leader, was accountable to the God who sees and knows all.

On the other hand, the covenantal relationship is also horizontal; if you are bound to God in that way, then you are also bound to all the others who are within the covenant community, who are your brothers and sisters within the covenant. There is a very strong sense of obligation to others within the community, the obligation of truth, trust, love, and justice; this is what we owe to one another. We owe it to one another—as a covenant obligation—to tell the truth, to trust one another and to be trustworthy, to love one another, and to do justice. So the horizontal and the vertical are the double dimensions of covenant obligation that Samuel is here exercising.

### The Decalogue

We can see both these dimensions—vertical and horizontal—in the Ten Commandments in Exodus 20, as they summarize the people's obligation to God and to one another. Horizontal integrity is particularly clear in the eighth, ninth, and tenth commandments. In the eighth, "You shall not steal," is sounded forth the integrity of what belongs to others, which Samuel had obeyed. The Old Testament then builds on that commandment many other laws in relation to restitution, compensation, accidental loss, and the importance of treating other people's property with respect.

The ninth commandment is not merely the general command "Don't tell lies," but specifically, "You shall not bear false testimony." It is talking about the integrity of the law court, of the importance of witness and testimony. There will always be wrongdoing in society, but if the courts themselves become corrupt, then society quickly goes completely rotten. God places a very high priority on the need for integrity in situations where truth-telling (or its opposite) has very serious results for people at risk.

The tenth commandment is the root of all the others: "You shall not covet." Covetous greed, as Paul said twice, is idolatry. Break the tenth commandment, and basically you break the first commandment as well. Greed and covetousness lie behind so much wrongdoing and can so quickly destroy people's integrity—even within the church and among leaders of churches and mission agencies.

In addition to the foundational Ten Commandments, two other passages are instructive about integrity.

### Exodus 23:1–9

The verses of Exodus 23:1–9 contain a short series of laws about how court cases were to be conducted. They deal with issues of integrity and accountability within the legal system. Verses 1–3 are for *witnesses* in a case. "Do not spread false reports. Do not help a wicked man by being a malicious witness. Do not follow the crowd in doing wrong. When you give testimony in a lawsuit, do not pervert justice by siding with the crowd, and do not show favoritism to a poor man in his lawsuit" (NIV). So if there is testimony to be given, if you are called upon to bear witness in some case, then make sure that you do it with integrity. Do not just say what everybody else says if you did not personally witness the event. And do not allow your sympathy for the accused to distort your testimony. It is not a matter of whether you feel sorry for him or not; the question is what actually happened. So these verses speak about the integrity of the witnesses.

Verses 4–5 deal with the integrity of *relationships between the contenders in the court*. It says, "If you come across your enemy's ox or donkey wandering off, be sure to take it back to him" (NIV). Now, what enemy is that? That is not a foreign enemy—the Philistines or something. What would their donkeys be doing in Israelite back yards? This is talking about an enemy in a dispute, your legal adversary, somebody with whom you are engaged in some court case before the judges. This law is saying, in effect, "You may have a conflict at law with this other brother, but don't take it out on his animal. It is not the animal's fault that you humans are having a quarrel." The basic injunction here is that, although we may have disputes and quarrels—which we do, as human beings and even as Christians—we should still continue to treat one another with dignity and respect in ordinary human, neighborly relationships. Sad to say, many disputes even among Christians become so vitriolic and so filled with nastiness that people do and say the most despicable things to one another. This passage says, "Even when you are in dispute, love your neighbor as yourself. Remember your covenant obligations."

Finally, verses 6–9 speak also to the *judges*, the elders who had to make decisions when cases were brought before them (as Samuel had done so often in his lifetime): "You shall not pervert the justice due to your poor in their lawsuits. Keep far from a false charge, and do not kill the innocent and those in the right, for I will not acquit the guilty. You shall take no bribe, for a bribe blinds the officials, and subverts the cause of those who are in the right. You shall not oppress a resident alien; you know the heart of an alien, for you were aliens in the land of Egypt" (NRSV). All of these were fundamental rules of justice and integrity, and Samuel's claim was that he had lived and served according to these high standards that were built into Israel's own law. He was saying, "In all my years as a judge, I have followed these laws of integrity, accountability, and transparency, doing what was right and honest in the court."

Deuteronomy 16:18–20 addresses concerns very similar to those in Exodus 23:1–9 and is very emphatic about the integrity of the justice system.

### *Leviticus 19:13–18*

The scope of Leviticus 19:13–18 is even more comprehensive because it describes the whole of Israelite society in various ways. Leviticus 19 is a most remarkable chapter describing the whole of life as the theater of holiness. It told Israel that God wanted them to be holy as God is holy—which meant to be different, to be distinctive from the rest of the nations. Holiness is described in this chapter in relation to life on the farm, in business, in the law court, in the neighborhood, in race relations, in family relations, in sexual relations—the whole of life. In all these areas, Leviticus 19 calls for the ethics of integrity. Look, for example, at verses 13–18, which deal with issues of integrity in employment: "Do not defraud your neighbor. . . . Do not hold back the wages of a hired man overnight" (NIV). What kind of employers we are and how we pay our staff is part of biblical holiness. So is how we treat persons with disabilities: "Do not curse the deaf or put a stumbling block in front of the blind, but fear your God. I am the LORD" (v. 14 NIV). I am very encouraged that the Cape Town Commitment includes a section on persons with disabilities in relation to mission and their needs; it is the first time within the Lausanne documents that that has happened, and I am grateful for it. But in Leviticus 19, a few thousand years before Lausanne was ever thought of, God was speaking about the treatment of the disabled.

Justice in the courts comes in again, in verses 15–16. Then there are the neighborly relations of verses 17–18: "Do not hate your brother in your heart. Rebuke your neighbor frankly so you will not share in his guilt" (NIV). It is interesting that this also is a part of accountability. It tells us that we need to have the courage to speak up when something is being done that is wrong, rather than being complicit in it by silence. This law says that if you do not confront and rebuke your neighbor who is sinning, then you share that guilt. One of the most disturbing things we in the church and in mission may encounter is *abuse*: abuse of power, emotional abuse, sexual abuse, even spiritual abuse. People who inflict such things on others often rely upon the complicity and silence of those they abuse. They get away with it because they believe that people will not expose them. This text is telling us that accountability is not just the obligation of the guilty party to repent and confess his or her guilt; there is also the accountability of those who see and know what is happening, yet fail to speak up.

## THE SOURCE OF SAMUEL'S INTEGRITY:
## OLD TESTAMENT NARRATIVES

These, then, are samples of the kind of laws Samuel would have known. But what about the stories that would have been known to Samuel, stories of people who modeled the kind of integrity and accountability he was professing before the people of Israel? I mention here just two.

## Joseph

Think of the incident in Joseph's life recorded in Genesis 39:6–15. This story of Joseph and Potiphar's wife is what has provided the illustration on the cover of the book *Serving Jesus with Integrity*, through the painting by Sawai Chinnawong, who was an artist in residence at OMSC some years ago.[1]

Joseph was put in charge of the household of Potiphar, who entrusted everything to his care. This is important. Here is a man who is *entrusted* with something. He was expected to be trustworthy and accountable to his master. Now, the Lord blessed the household of the Egyptian because of Joseph; the Abrahamic blessing was reaching the nations because God was with Joseph. Potiphar left everything he had in Joseph's care; he did not concern himself with anything except the food he ate (he did not want to be poisoned!). As far as everything else was concerned, he trusted Joseph.

Then we read, "Now Joseph was well-built and handsome, and after a while his master's wife took notice of Joseph and said, 'Come to bed with me!'" (vv. 6–7 NIV). In Hebrew that is one word: "Lie down with me." It is one word of seduction. But that one word from Potiphar's wife sparks a reply from Joseph that in Hebrew is thirty-four words long! Joseph's statement of integrity and resistance to this seduction is remarkably comprehensive. Read it carefully. He refused, saying, "With me in charge . . . my master does not concern himself with anything in the house; everything he owns he has entrusted to my care. No one is greater in this house than I am. My master has withheld nothing from me except you, because you are his wife. How then could I do such a wicked thing and sin against God?" (vv. 8–9 NIV).

This is a most remarkable statement of accountability and integrity in both the horizontal and the vertical directions. Joseph says, "I am trusted in this household by my master; I am accountable to him, I am trusted by him, and I am not going to betray his trust. But not only will I not betray his trust; if I were to betray *his* trust, I would be sinning against *God*." And so he puts the two dimensions, the human and the divine, into the one statement. That remarkable statement by Joseph

---

1. *Serving Jesus with Integrity: Ethics and Accountability in Mission*, ed. Dwight P. Baker and Douglas Hayward (Pasadena, Calif.: William Carey Library, 2010). Sawai Chinnawong, from Thailand, was the 2003–04 OMSC artist in residence.

would have been known, I assume, by Samuel. It was the way Samuel himself had lived his life.

## Hannah

The second story is that of Samuel's mother, Hannah, and his childhood. Hannah kept her promise to God, even though it must have hurt her to do so. What must it have cost Hannah to give up this little boy, whom she had longed and prayed for, when he was just weaned, to say good-bye to him, and then to be able to visit him just once a year? Some of you know what that is like; that kind of separation from children has been a costly part of missionary life for years. But the point I am making here is that *Hannah made a promise to God, and she kept it.* Samuel would have known that he was a child promised to God and given to God because God had heard his mother's prayer. Even his name, which means "the Lord hears," would have reminded him of this all the time. And so we get a glimpse of the example that Hannah, his mother, was to him. Promises should be kept. Our words are important.

Psalm 15 speaks about the kind of integrity of life that is pleasing and acceptable to God. Verse 4 defines righteousness, among other things, as keeping a promise even when it hurts. This to me is a very important definition of commitment; when you make a promise and then the circumstances change and it is no longer so easy to keep it, you still stick to the commitment rather than break your word. I get very distressed at the number of people who seem to ignore this value, even in Christian circles. So many Christian people seem to have no qualms at all about letting others down, even when they have made a commitment to do something. Hannah kept her promise.

Not only that, but there is also Hannah's understanding of God. If you look at her song in 1 Samuel 2, she has a remarkable grasp of theology. I used to say to my third-year B.D. students at Union Biblical Seminary in Pune, India, "You know, this woman Hannah knows more theology than most of you guys after three years of theological study." What Hannah affirms about God in her song in 1 Samuel 2 is remarkable and comprehensive. Look particularly at verse 3 (NIV; my italics):

> Do not keep talking so proudly
>     or let your mouth speak such arrogance,
> *for the LORD [Yahweh] is a God who knows,*
>     *and by him deeds are weighed.*

Yahweh is the great Auditor. He is the God to whom all books are open and from whom no secrets are hidden. Here is the God who knows and sees and hears and watches, and so there is no point boasting and being arrogant. You cannot conceal anything from God. Even if you can "pull the wool over the eyes" of other people, you cannot deceive God. That conviction should tighten up our commitment to integrity and accountability.

Now if this is the kind of mother that Hannah was (she kept her word), and if this is the kind of theology she taught Samuel (God sees and knows everything), then it is no surprise that Samuel was conscious of his responsibility before the God who is the inspector of all we do. That is why it must also have been so painful for Samuel to have witnessed the corruption of Eli's sons and then the failure of his own sons later on. Those stories of 1 Samuel 1–3 feed into the kind of person Samuel was—the Samuel whom we see standing in his old age in 1 Samuel 12, finishing as well as he had started, as a person of integrity, the child of his mother.

## THE SEQUEL TO SAMUEL'S EXAMPLE

In the centuries after Samuel, we can see a developing tradition within the Old Testament of a demand for integrity in people who are in trusted positions, whether as prophets or judges or kings. When that integrity was lacking, we see very trenchant condemnation and critique.

### David

David had his very serious faults and failings, and we cannot overlook his great sexual lapse into adultery, followed by murder and an attempt to cover it all up—the typical way of an abuser. But when at last it was all exposed by Nathan, David at least was given the grace to confess before God, and we hear his words in Psalm 51.

But I am thinking of another case, one that involved the handling of finances—specifically, funding for a large project. Read the story in 1 Chronicles 29, when there had been a great outpouring of financial generosity. Three things strike me as interesting in this account. First, notice that it was the *leaders* who led by example. Certainly, the people were generous, but they were generous because the leaders were leading in generosity. "The people rejoiced at the willing response of their leaders, for they had given freely and wholeheartedly to the Lord" (v. 9

NIV). This is the opposite way round from most mission organizations and churches, where leaders rejoice at the willing response of the people when the people give wholeheartedly. But here, the leaders start first. What difference would that make to the way we appeal for funding in our churches or mission agencies?

Second, when David responds to all this, in verses 10–19, he says to God, in effect, "Look, Lord, what we are doing here is just giving back to you what belongs to you. It all belongs to you anyway" (vv. 11, 14). Then he goes on, "We are aliens and strangers in your sight" (v. 15 NIV). This is interesting. The words would be better translated "temporary residents." He says, "We are just temporary tenants in your property, Lord." When you are a tenant in a fully furnished house that belongs to a landlord, then everything in the house belongs to the landlord. David says, "That is how it is with us, Lord. We live in your land. Everything we possess belongs to you anyway. So we are only giving back to you what belongs to you." This is his perspective on the outpouring of financial generosity.

Third, this understanding underlies David's sense of integrity and accountability, which he expresses directly to God, "Lord, you test our hearts; you know our motives." This verse, 1 Chronicles 29:17, is one of John Stott's favorites: "I know, my God, that you test the heart and are pleased with integrity. All these things have I given willingly and with honest intent" (NIV).

### Jehoshaphat

In 2 Chronicles 19:4–11, Jehoshaphat led a great legal reform. He appointed judges throughout the land, and he gave clear instructions, stating that he held them accountable for their actions. "Consider what you are doing, for you judge not on behalf of human beings but on the LORD's behalf; he is with you in giving judgment. Now, let the fear of the LORD be upon you; take care what you do, for there is no perversion of justice with the LORD our God, or partiality, or taking of bribes" (vv. 6–7 NRSV). In these verses we see once again the double dimension of horizontal and vertical accountability.

## Daniel

Daniel was a public administrator in a secular pagan government, but he was renowned for his integrity. The king put him in charge, and everybody was accountable to him, and he in turn was accountable to the king:

> It pleased Darius to set over the kingdom one hundred twenty satraps, stationed throughout the whole kingdom, and over them three presidents, including Daniel; to these the satraps gave account, so that the king might suffer no loss. Soon Daniel distinguished himself above all the other presidents and satraps because an excellent spirit was in him, and the king planned to appoint him over the whole kingdom. So the presidents and the satraps tried to find grounds for complaint against Daniel in connection with the kingdom. But they could find no grounds for complaint or any corruption, because he was faithful, and no negligence or corruption could be found in him. (Dan. 6:1–4 NRSV)

The combination is interesting: "no negligence or corruption." In other words, he was neither lazy nor corrupt. Some people are so lazy that it would not matter if they were corrupt, because they never do much anyway. Some people work very hard, but they are corrupt, and much of their work is for their own benefit. But Daniel was *neither* lazy *nor* corrupt. And so he was trusted by the king, the head of the secular government, as a man of integrity.

## Prophets

The prophets have much to say about integrity. Listen, for example, to Amos:

> Hear this, you that trample on the needy,
>     and bring to ruin the poor of the land,
> saying, "When will the new moon be over
>     so that we may sell grain;
> and the sabbath,
>     so that we may offer wheat for sale?
> We will make the ephah small and the shekel great,
>     and practice deceit with false balances,
> buying the poor for silver
>     and the needy for a pair of sandals,
>     and selling the sweepings of the wheat."
>             (Amos 8:4–6 NRSV)

God says that he hears even the thoughts in the hearts of those who desire to exploit the poor and who chafe at waiting to do so, saying "When will the Sabbath be over so that we can get back to all our corrupt practices?" They may not have said this out loud, but it was going on in their hearts and minds. But God says, "I hear it." God calls for integrity even in our thoughts and motives.

Or listen to Jeremiah. In chapter 7 he challenges those who were coming regularly to worship in the temple, but whose lives through the week were lived in complete disregard for God's standards of behavior. "Will you steal and murder, commit adultery and perjury, burn incense to Baal and follow other gods you have not known, and then come and stand before me in this house, which bears my Name, and say, 'We are safe'—safe to do all these detestable things? Has this house, which bears my Name, become a den of robbers to you? But I have been watching! declares the Lord" (vv. 9–11 NIV). God could see what was going on outside the temple. People have come into the temple for public worship, but in the community outside all sorts of social rottenness is happening, and God says, "Don't think I can't see what is going on. I am watching!"

For an even more scathing description of social behavior among God's people who had become totally unaccountable and corrupt, see Ezekiel 22:6–12, 25–29.

### Psalms and Proverbs

There are also psalms that call for personal integrity and that refer to God's seeing and hearing.

> From heaven the LORD looks down
>     and sees all mankind;
> from his dwelling place he watches
>     all who live on earth—
> he who forms the hearts of all,
>     who considers everything they do.
>             (Ps. 33:13–15 NIV)

Many of the proverbs as well speak about integrity, truthfulness, and honesty. See, for example, Proverbs 11:3, 12:22, 19:20, and 21:2–3.

## CONCLUSION

Samuel, it seems to me, is an outstanding model of a core value of the Old Testament: integrity. One of the most important things that the Bible has to say about the LORD God is that he is the God of truth, the God of trustworthiness. He is the God who speaks the truth and who does the truth, the God who himself is incorruptible, and who cannot be bribed. He is the God who sees and knows and acts with complete integrity, trustworthiness, justice, and truth. If those are the qualities of God, then, says the Old Testament Scripture, life that is lived in the way of the Lord must be lived with matching integrity. Our lives must be lived uprightly in the sight of God and in the sight of God's people. This entails accountability. Therefore, Samuel says, "The Lord is my judge, and you are my witnesses." This attitude is the very essence of biblical accountability and integrity.

The danger that underlies some of the problems and issues exposed in this book's case studies comes about when we want to live as if there were no judge and no witnesses, as if what we do could be done in the dark and remain hidden. In reality, the Bible reminds us, what we are and what we do is already known to God. We cannot hide them, and we will never be able to hide them. Ultimately all that we are and do will be exposed. At bedrock we face the chilling pronouncement of Numbers 32:23, "Be sure your sin will find you out" (NRSV). God is not mocked. Whatever we sow, we will reap.

We are safest when what we do in our various ministries is transparent to others; when our actions and transactions are open to their approval or their critique; when we are humble enough to say, "My sister, my brother, let me be your servant, and you be my servant, as we hold one another accountable before the Lord. Let there be nothing hidden in the dark between us."

When I was the principal of All Nations Christian College, in Hertfordshire, England, a time came when issues arose that affected me personally. At that time the chairman of the college's board of directors was a very wise, godly brother whom I greatly respected. I was required to give account of some aspects of how I was running things and decisions that had been made. This was not easy; it is not comfortable to have people poking into everything that is going on. This is true even if you have nothing troubling your conscience. I knew that, in relation to the college, I had done nothing wrong, but still I had to accept the questioning. At one point the chairman of the council said, "Chris, accountability is not a burden; it's a *gift*. It's a gift that we give you. We hold you accountable, and that is for your good; it's for your protection. It's not something we are imposing upon you. It's something we are *giving* to you because we love you, because you are a brother in Christ, and we want to affirm your integrity by expecting proper accountability." I thought that was a very helpful, positive way for me to look at the demanding challenge of accountability. I learned to see being questioned, not as a threat or an insult or something "beneath my dignity," but as something that was honoring to me and also to God.

May we all pray for God to grant us the courage to live and work with complete integrity, and may we honor one another by expecting—and giving—accountability to one another and to the Lord.

# 3

# Paul, a New Testament Model: His Collection for the Poor in Jerusalem

*Christopher J. H. Wright*

IN THINKING OF A New Testament model of accountability, we could not do better than to examine the practice of the apostle Paul. Paul was involved in an active mission movement, and as part of that missionary work he engaged in a collection of money from the churches in Greece (as we would now call it) in the two Roman provinces of Macedonia and Achaia. He oversaw arrangements for this collection to be taken to the believers in Jerusalem, where there seems to have been a great deal of poverty among the believers. Paul saw arranging for financial help from one part of the Christian church to another as a very important thing to do.

Paul's references to this collection of money for the poor in Jerusalem, what he taught in relation to it, and the practical arrangements and safeguards he put into place around the administration of it are revealing and instructive. They show Paul's strong sense of accountability, transparency, and integrity. His example and his teaching are greatly needed in today's churches and missions.

Paul's discussion of his collection for the Jerusalem poor actually occupies more text space in his letters than does justification by faith. This is an interesting thought, in comparison with where we may think the center of Paul's theology lies. Saying this is not in any sense to belittle Paul's doctrine of justification or any of his great doctrinal teaching. But Paul writes much about the collection for the poor in Jerusalem and how it is to be carried out, and he uses the collection as the occasion for a great deal of teaching.

We will look at three major passages and a few shorter ones so as to draw some principles from these texts. The major passages are the end of Paul's first letter to Corinth, chapter 16, where he refers to this collection; 2 Corinthians 8–9, where he devotes a great deal of space to principles of giving; and then Romans 15. In these passages, we see at least six clear principles at work.

## FINANCIAL SUPPORT FOR THE POOR IS INTEGRAL TO BIBLICAL MISSION

Paul's first principle is really the principle that lies behind the collection itself, which is that financial support for the poor is integral to biblical mission. Paul sees no dichotomy between his evangelistic church planting mission and his efforts to bring about the relief of poverty among the believers in Jerusalem. For Paul this is all part of his task, his mission, and his calling.

### Galatians 2

Before turning to 1 Corinthians, let us look at Galatians 2. In Galatians Paul is defending his own apostolic authority, but also his apostolic Gospel and his preaching of the Gospel to the Gentile Christians, the *Galati*, a branch of the great nations of the Celts who had migrated into what is now southern Turkey. Paul had preached the Gospel to them, and they had become believers. Then Paul faced the great theological controversy with the Jewish believers as to how these non-Jewish people could be accepted into the covenant and into the people of God. Some of the Jewish believers had come to Galatia and troubled the Galatian churches, trying to insist that they must become circumcised and observe the Mosaic law.

Paul writes the Epistle to the Galatians against that background in order to defend the fact that his Gospel had been accepted as fully authentic by the apostles in Jerusalem itself. That is what chapter 2 is all about. He states that he had received his teaching from the Lord but had submitted it to the apostles in Jerusalem, and they had accepted that it was authentic and true. In verses 9–10 he states: "James, Peter and John, those reputed to be pillars, gave me and Barnabas the right hand of fellowship [*koinōnia*] when they recognized the grace given to me. They agreed that we should go to the Gentiles, and they to the Jews. All they asked was that we should continue to remember the poor, the very thing I was eager to do" (NIV, used throughout this chapter).

The "right hand of fellowship" in verse 9 is not simply a token of friendship. The word *koinōnia* means much more. It is a sharing in and a sharing of what God has given to us, and this affects the economic dimension as well as the spiritual. In Acts 2 and 4 we read about the *koinōnia* of the early church in Jerusalem. Certainly it was a spiritual *koinōnia*. Believers shared in the apostles' teaching, in the breaking of bread, and in prayers. But it was also a financial *koinōnia* in which they shared with one another in order to relieve poverty. It is clear from what Paul says in Galatians 2 that that spirit of the church in Jerusalem was still operating; the Jerusalem church still cared about the poor in their midst. They saw it as an essential part of Gospel *koinōnia* that, if Paul the apostle was going to be a partner with them and share in their understanding of the Gospel, then he too must be committed to remembering the poor as part of his Gospel credentials. And Paul says, "That was no problem to me. I was eager to do that anyway." We can see that active financial concern for the poor is both the continuing way of operation for the Jerusalem church and the already existing commitment of Paul.

### Romans 15

At the very end of his letter to the believers in Rome, Paul is telling them about his plans. He writes about his lifelong commitment to church planting and evangelistic ministry. Earlier in the chapter he explained how God had given him grace "to be a minister of Christ Jesus to the Gentiles with the priestly duty of proclaiming the gospel of God, so that the Gentiles might become an offering acceptable to God" (v. 16). That is his ministry, and that is what he believes he is called to do. But he has now done it all around the eastern Mediterranean basin, he says, all the way from Jerusalem to Illyricum, which is basically modern Albania. Paul says, "I have fully proclaimed the gospel of Christ. It has always been my ambition to preach the gospel where Christ was not known, so that I would not be building on someone else's foundation. . . . But now . . . there is no more place for me to work in these regions" (vv. 19–20, 23).

So now Paul is longing to go to Rome, and then, verse 24, "I plan to . . . go to Spain." Paul is envisaging and planning a bold missionary project that will take him to the western half of the Mediterranean, out toward Spain. That is his great evangelistic vision. But *at the moment*, says Paul, my priority is that I am on the way to Jerusalem in the service of the saints there. This is verses 26–29: "For Macedonia and Achaia were pleased to make a contribution for the poor among the saints in Jerusalem. They were pleased to do it, and indeed they owe it to them. For if the Gentiles have shared in the Jews' spiritual blessings, they owe it to the Jews to share with them their material blessings. So after I have completed this task and have made sure that they have received this fruit, I will go to Spain and visit you on the way. I know that when I come to you, I will come in the full measure of the blessing of Christ."

Look carefully at what he says a bit later, in verses 31–32: "Pray that I may be rescued from the unbelievers in Judea and that my service in Jerusalem may be acceptable to the saints there, so that by God's will I may come to you with joy and together with you be refreshed."

Paul in effect puts his *evangelistic strategy* on hold in order to carry out his *relief-of-poverty strategy*. It is interesting that at this point Paul does not say, "I've got to go on to evangelize Spain, so I'll dump the responsibility for this financial gift onto somebody else; they can take it to Jerusalem. My job is to preach the Gospel, not to relieve the poor." Paul sees no conflict at all in making his service to the saints through the relief of poverty a priority at this point in his life; this he does by taking collected money to the people in Jerusalem. Not only does he see it as a personal priority, he asks for prayer for it. He asks for prayer just as later he would ask for prayer when he was in prison, asking the people then to pray that his mouth would be open, so that he would be able to preach the Gospel. Just as he called on believers to pray for him in his evangelistic ministry, here he asks the Roman Christians to pray for him in his financial ministry to the saints in Jerusalem.

Then he says, "When I have done that, I will come to you in the full measure of Christ"—not, as it were, "after this unfortunate interruption in my evangelistic career, which I sadly cannot avoid," but "when I have done this," he says, "then I will come to you in the full measure of Christ." That is, by completing this work of poverty relief, he will be fulfilling a Christ-centered calling as much as when he was completing his evangelistic mandate.

So let us take note that Paul sees no dichotomy between the two dimensions of his ministry. Indeed, as one writer has said, "We do not know if Paul achieved this mission [his evangelistic plans to go to Spain], but we do know that he delivered the collection [to relieve the poor in Jerusalem]. *The collection was so vital that its delivery was at that moment a more urgent matter for Paul than his desire to evangelize and plant churches on the missionary frontier.*[1]

In 1 Timothy 6 we see Paul telling Timothy to pass this teaching on to the church. This responsibility of generosity and giving by those who have the means to do so is a fundamental part of Christian commitment and a part of our response to the Gospel. Paul says, "Command those who are rich in this present world not to be arrogant nor to put their hope in wealth, which is so uncertain, but to put their hope in God, who richly provides us with everything for our enjoyment. Command them [the second time he says this] to do good, to be rich in good deeds, and to be generous and willing to share" (vv. 17–18). The English conceals the fact that the last word here is the Greek *koinōnikos*. They are to share their fellowship by their financial generosity, and, echoing the teaching of Jesus, in this way they will lay up treasure for themselves as a firm foundation for the coming age.

Generosity is a Christian duty, says Paul, something that pastors can command. He is probably echoing Deuteronomy 15, where God says to the Israelites, "Give generously to him [the poor person] and do so without a grudging heart; then because of this the Lord your God will bless you. . . . There will always be poor people in the land [or on the earth]. Therefore I command you to be openhanded toward your brothers. . . . Give to him [i.e., the poor person] as the Lord your God has blessed you. Remember that you were slaves in Egypt and the Lord your God redeemed you. That is why I give you this command today" (vv. 10–11, 14–15).

This, then, is the principle that lies behind Paul's efforts in collecting money for the poor. Paul saw generous financial support for the poor, with careful administration of that gift, as an integral part of biblical mission, of Gospel mission. It was part of what he felt he was called to do, as well as the more obviously evangelistic task of preaching and planting churches.

---

1. Jason Hood, "Theology in Action: Paul and Christian Social Care," in *Transforming the World? The Gospel and Social Responsibility*, ed. Jamie A. Grant and Dewi A. Hughes (Nottingham: Apollos, 2009), pp. 129–46; quotation taken from p. 134 (italics in original).

## FINANCIAL ADMINISTRATION IS A STEWARDSHIP
## OF GRACE AND OBEDIENCE

My second point, based mainly on 2 Corinthians 8–9, is that financial administration of people's giving is a stewardship of grace and obedience. That is to say, when we handle money that has been given by God's people, we are handling the fruit of God's grace, the practical proof of human obedience to the Gospel. That is the implication of these two chapters. Money that has been given as an offering to God is not just coins and notes or ledgers or pieces of paper or entries in a journal. When we handle money that has been given by God's people, we are involved in a deeply spiritual matter. Their giving is their response to God, and our involvement is a stewardship of grace and a stewardship of other people's obedience. That is what stewardship means: we are entrusted with something; we are stewards of something that is the fruit of grace and the proof of obedience.

### Grace

This understanding comes from what Paul says at the beginning of chapter 8 and the end of chapter 9. The words are familiar, but notice how frequently the word "grace" occurs. I have marked it with italics.

> Now, brothers, we want you to know about the *grace* that God has given the Macedonian churches. [Macedonia is the northern part of Greece, and Paul is writing to the Corinthians, who were in the southern part of Greece, so a kind of north-south rivalry is going on.] Out of the most severe trial, their overflowing joy and their extreme poverty welled up in rich generosity. For I testify that they gave as much as they were able, and even beyond their ability. Entirely on their own, they urgently pleaded with us for the privilege of sharing in this service to the saints. [The word *koinōnia* is in here again; this desire to give was a mark of their *koinōnia*, or fellowship.] And they did not do as we expected, but they gave themselves first to the Lord and then to us in keeping with God's will. So we urged Titus, since he had earlier made a beginning, to bring also to completion this act of *grace* on your part. But just as you excel in everything—in faith, in speech, in knowledge, in complete earnestness and in your love for us—see that you also excel in this *grace* of giving. (2 Cor. 8:1–7)

Three times Paul uses the word "grace" about the Macedonian believers, and a couple verses later he talks about "the *grace* of our Lord Jesus Christ."

This gift of the Macedonians, Paul writes, was a response to the Lord ("they gave themselves first to the Lord"). Moreover, it was something that they wanted to do. They did not have to be asked to give; they asked for the privilege of giving. Furthermore, Paul says it was because of that grace of God in them that what they did was an act of grace to others. This is reciprocal grace, or grace in action.

Paul then sends Titus to oversee and administer the collection. It is as if Paul were to say, "Because this is such an important evidence of the grace of God and of the fruit of the Gospel in the lives of these believers, I am sending my most trusted senior person to handle this responsibility." He did not send a mere clerk or some young functionary who might be haphazard in dealing with it all. Paul says, "This is a serious matter, so we urged Titus—an important apostolic delegate in the church—to go and make sure that this act of grace is properly handled and treated with the seriousness that it deserves."

## Obedience

This display of generosity was not just an act of grace but also one of obedience. Notice the end of chapter 9, verses 12–15: "This service that you perform is not only supplying the needs of God's people but is also overflowing in many expressions of thanks to God. Because of the service by which you [that is, you Gentiles] have proved yourselves, people will praise God for the obedience that accompanies your confession of the gospel of Christ, and for your generosity in sharing with them [*koinōnia* again] and with everyone else. And in their prayers for you their hearts will go out to you, because of the surpassing grace God has given you." And, Paul adds, "Thanks be to God for *his* indescribable gift!"—which of course is the Lord Jesus Christ.

According to Paul, giving, sharing, and generosity are not just grace; they are also proof of obedience. Why was this important? Precisely because these were Gentiles. We know that the Jewish believers in Jerusalem were still uncertain whether or not these Gentiles who had never been circumcised and were not keeping the Law were really part of the family. Did they really belong to the covenant people of God? Paul responds, in effect, "The fact that you Gentiles have given an offering to meet the needs of Jewish believers is a proof of the fellowship that we have in Christ. Your obedience to the Gospel is a demonstration that you Gentiles, who have been so despised by the Jews historically, are now at one with them; a demonstration that there is no difference, there is no Jew or Gentile, male or female, slave or free." This gift was a proof of obedience to the core meaning of the Gospel.

For Paul, handling such a gift, offered by God's people, was a sacred trust. Administering it was a stewardship of the grace of God and of the obedience of God's people to the Gospel. For that reason he had to take it seriously. His concern with the issues of accountability, integrity, transparency, and honesty was not just because he wanted to satisfy the Roman governors or other officials. His concern arose because he was dealing with something coming from God: the grace of God and obedience to the Gospel.

## FINANCIAL APPEALS REQUIRE
## SYSTEMATIC ADVANCE PLANNING

The third point to be drawn from these passages is a relatively simple one: financial appeals require systematic advance planning. Look how thoroughly Paul prepares the way for the gift. In 1 Corinthians Paul has been answering a lot of questions from the church, and in chapter 16 he comes to something that he has told them about before but wants to raise again: "Now about the collection for God's people: Do what I told the Galatian churches to do. On the first day of every week, each one of you should set aside a sum of money in keeping with his income, saving it up, so that when I come no collections will have to be made. Then, when I arrive, I will give letters of introduction to the men you approve and send them with your gift to Jerusalem" (vv. 1–3). Get ready for this, says Paul. Be prepared.

In 2 Corinthians 9:1–5 Paul shows the same concern for preparedness.

> There is no need for me to write to you about this service to the saints. For I know your eagerness to help, and I have been boasting about it to the Macedonians, telling them that since last year you in Achaia were ready to give [again catch the note of north-south rivalry]; and your enthusiasm has stirred most of them to action. But I am sending the brothers [i.e., some people in advance] in order that our boasting about you in this matter should not prove hollow, but that you may be ready, as I said you would be. For if any Macedonians come with me and find you unprepared, we . . . would be ashamed of having been so confident. So I thought it necessary to urge the brothers to visit you in advance and finish the arrangements for the generous gift

you had promised. Then it will be ready as a generous gift, not as
one grudgingly given [i.e., given at the last moment].

Can you see what Paul is doing here? He does not want this collection to become debased into an emotional appeal in which everybody
is urged to put their hands in their pockets, and the music goes on and
on until everybody has dug deeper, and then the offering buckets are
sent around again. No, Paul is purposely avoiding that type of manipu-
lated, emotional response in giving. He does not want there to be any
kind of on-the-spot pressure or a response that has not been carefully
thought through in advance. Paul wants this collection and the giving by
the church to be something that has been thought about, prayed about,
and prepared for. It should be systematic (you plan what you will give);
it should be regular (week by week setting money aside); it should be
proportionate (according to income, with those who have more, giving more); it should be transparent (the brothers will come and will
oversee it); and it should be public (announced and recorded). All of
this preparation and supervision is built into the arrangement that Paul
makes. Clearly it was something into which he put a lot of thought and
planning.

The lesson to be drawn from this is that accountability is not just an
afterthought; that is, accountability is not something you try to sort out
and tack on after the event—"All this money has come in, how wonderful! Now we'd better decide what we do with it, who is going to count it,
who is going to bank it, and who will keep accounts." Accountability is
not just a matter of reacting when problems arise. It should be planned,
built in from the very start. Paul says, "Look, here is what we are planning. This is what we're asking *you* to do, and this is what *we* will then
do when you have done what we ask." The whole procedure is a matter
of shared responsibility. Paul does not want their giving to be mere op-
portunism: "Paul's come to town again; let's have a quick collection and
give him a love gift." No, Paul wants this offering to be carefully thought
through and planned well in advance so that nobody will be taken by
surprise and nobody can be accused of emotional manipulation. That
is an important way in which he builds accountability into his financial
relationship with the church.

Notice that Paul is concerned, also, about loss of face. In the world
of ancient Greece and Rome he is, I think, in a relational economy, and
so he conducts this offering relationally. He says, "Some of our brothers

will be coming to you, and I will be coming later as well, and we don't want any embarrassment. I don't want you to lose face; I don't want you to be ashamed, and I don't want them to be gloating. So let's do this properly, and let's plan it and have it all out on the table clear and open, so that everybody is satisfied."

Let us learn from Paul's practice, then, that proper planning in advance of financial appeals is important and that safeguards should be set up around financial giving *before* the event, not just tacked on afterward.

## FINANCIAL TEMPTATIONS CALL
## FOR "SAFETY IN NUMBERS"

A fourth point found in these letters from Paul is that wherever there is money, there is temptation. Since this is just as true for Christians as for anybody else, it is wise to protect ourselves from such temptation by having more than one person involved in handling it. We could say that this was true of Paul's ministry in general. Of course, Paul was a great individual minister, preacher, Gospel letter writer, and everything else. But generally he did not operate alone. He was the leader, but he worked with teams that included people like Silas, Barnabas, Timothy, Titus, and many others. Indeed, when Paul did find himself completely alone, he was very distressed about it. In 2 Timothy 4:16 there are some heart-rending words when he says that everyone has deserted him; this was terrible for him. He wanted to be in a team, to belong with others.

Accordingly, 1 Corinthians 16 and 2 Corinthians 8 lay great emphasis on the plurality of people involved in handling the money. Knowing exactly who was involved becomes quite complicated, but there were plenty of them. Look at 1 Corinthians 16:3–4. Paul says, "I will give letters of introduction to the men you approve"—in other words, people whom the Christians in Corinth trusted. Then offering to do the task himself, he writes, "If it seems advisable for me to go also, they will accompany me." So he would not take charge of the money by himself but would involve others.

It is also difficult to know how many people are involved in 2 Corinthians 8:16–24, but we can identify at least one. "I thank God," says Paul, "who put into the heart of Titus the same concern I have for you. For Titus not only welcomed our appeal, but he is coming to you with much enthusiasm and on his own initiative. And we are sending along with him the brother who is praised by all the churches for his service to the gospel [this was a trusted Christian leader]. What is more, he was chosen by the churches to accompany us" (vv. 16–19). So he was someone elected or chosen and appointed to exercise this financial responsibility. "In addition, we are sending with them our brother [Paul does not name him either] who has often proved to us in many ways that he is zealous, and now even more so because of his great confidence in you" (v. 22).

As I noted, it is a bit difficult to know exactly how many persons are involved. But the point is that certainly more than one person was involved, and they were all trusted people. They were accepted and known by everybody. There was no anonymity. Christian accountability is a matter of trust between fellow believers, but Paul shows us the wisdom of building in safeguards of plurality, because even believers are still sinners, and few things are more tempting than money. Paul is well aware that even trusted brothers can go astray. Sadly, we read about a few of them at the end of his letters when he writes that some who preferred the world and the world's ways have gone off and left him (e.g., 2 Tim. 4:10). Paul knew that even the best people need the protection of relational accountability to one another.

Paul thus insists on plurality in the handling of money. It is a very wise principle to adopt in any church or Christian organization. In many churches in the United Kingdom, certainly in my own church at All Souls, gift money is never counted by only one person. When the offering is brought to the vestry, there are always at least two, and sometimes three or four, people in the room. The door is then closed, and they count the offering together. They are a check on one another. Now of course we all trust one another; nobody expects that anybody is going to be doing anything wrong, but there is need for openness and verifiability in handling money. We need to be above suspicion.

Many organizations, including my own, will not allow bank checks to be signed by only one person; there must always be two signatures to manage the bank account and the finances. That is another wise practice.

How do we make that work within a setting where it is culturally unthinkable to question the honor and the authority of the senior leader—least of all by calling him to account over money? I know that in some Asian cultures it is simply not appropriate, and never done, for people to challenge or question a leader, especially if he is older. That would be to break the relationship and cause loss of face. So what can be done to ensure proper accountability? It seems to me that the only avenue available is for the *leader himself* (and it usually seems to be a man, but of course the same would apply to a woman) voluntarily to say, "Please, will you join me as we do this? I request that other people should be involved with me as we arrange our financial affairs, or as we handle these funds, or as we set up this institution. I want other people alongside me to see how the money is handled and how the decisions are made. I want them also to be completely satisfied that all is being done transparently and honorably." In that way the person at the top is able to lead from the top and to set the example, just as the apostle Paul did. Paul could easily have said, "I'm an apostle. Trust me. I'll do this myself." But he did not. He insisted *from the top* that there should be others alongside him to ensure it was all done honestly. If a leader does this *voluntarily*, he is not saying to those under him, "I think you don't trust me." Rather he is saying, "I know you trust me. And because you trust me, I want to make sure that your trust is never betrayed. I want to be completely transparent, and therefore I choose to share my accountability with other trusted Christian friends and brothers." That is the way we may have to begin to introduce higher standards of account-ability. We must lead by example rather than be faced with demands from below. Accountability is something we should *choose* to have, for our own good and for the protection of the Lord's name, not something that is forced upon us.

## FINANCIAL ACCOUNTABILITY DEMANDS TRANSPARENCY BEFORE GOD AND MAN

I love the fact that when Paul has finished talking about all the people that he is bringing into the team to deliver the money to Jerusalem, in 2 Corinthians 8:20–21 he actually explains why he is handling the matter in this plural way. These verses are so important because they express a fifth principle that I believe is transcultural. That is, it provides a bib-lical model for us, whatever our culture or background. After having described all that was going to be done, Paul says, "We want to avoid any criticism of the way we administer this liberal gift. For we are taking pains to do what is right, not only in the eyes of the Lord but *also in the eyes of men* [people; my italics]." This verse is very challenging and very significant. I think it should be hung up on the wall of any room where a Christian organization does its financial business.

All the arrangements that Paul put in place were actually quite complicated. They were also probably quite costly. It would obviously cost a lot more for five or six men to travel from Greece to Jerusalem than for Paul to go there by himself; travel was not cheap in those days either. So the arrangements Paul was building up around this gift could have aroused resistance. People could have criticized and said, "Why send so many people? You are going to waste some of the gift on such expenses"—just as we perhaps complain about the cost of auditing our accounts. But Paul says, "It's worth that cost because I don't want any criticism; I want to be completely transparent before God and people, so that nothing we do can be open to criticism."

Let's be clear that Paul was operating within a culture that in certain respects was quite similar to some non-Western cultures today. The Greek and Roman cultures were very top-down, very hierarchical. The Roman system was patron-client oriented. The men at the top were patrons: they were bankers or politicians, they were wealthy, and people would come to their homes every day wanting favors. Being in favor with the top man was crucially important; that is how Roman politics worked. It was a very relational economy in that sense.

So Paul is acting counterculturally in what he does with this gift. He could have said, "I'm the boss; I'm your patron; I'm the apostle. Give me the money and a single armed guard, and I'll take it to Jerusalem. Just trust me." Instead he says, "No, I want this to be completely transparent, so I must have others with me to make sure all is done properly and above criticism."

I would love for 2 Corinthians 8:21 to become a motto for each of us as Christ's followers, to be something that we could take to heart: "We are taking pains to do what is right, not only in the eyes of the Lord [we all want to do that] but also in the eyes of men." The vertical and the horizontal are both needed. Paul says, "We should be able to trust one another in the Lord, but we want to do what is beyond criticism in the eyes of the watching world as well." To repeat, I would love for that principle to become a motto for each of us and for all our mission organizations. What a difference it could make, and how it could help to prevent some of the tragic scandals of fraud and theft and mismanagement within Christian organizations!

## FINANCIAL TRUSTWORTHINESS IS AN APOSTOLIC HONOR TO CHRIST

When we think about upward and downward accountability, we tend to think that we are *upwardly* accountable to other bodies such as boards, funding foundations, donors, the government, and legal authorities, but that we are *downwardly* accountable to our beneficiaries, that is, to those who actually receive from our ministry, those whom we are serving. Actually, however, the direction of our accountability is the reverse, which is the final transcultural principle I wish to consider from Paul's example. Our *upward* accountability is to those who occupy the position Jesus was referring to when he said, "Whatever you did for one of the least of these brothers of mine, you did it for me" (Matt. 25:40). It is those whom our ministry is serving who actually are Jesus to us. Therefore our accountability to them is really our accountability to him—which is "upward." When we serve others in our ministry, we are serving Christ. We are honoring him in serving them.

Paul says in several passages that discharging this financial responsibility in a trustworthy manner is an honor to Christ, not just a matter of transparency before men. Of course it was important to do the job with honesty and integrity. But even more, it was important to do it for the honor and glory of Christ. Look at 2 Corinthians 8:18–19. Who were these people who were administering the gift? Paul says, "We are sending along with him [Titus] the brother who is praised by all the churches for his service to the gospel. What is more, he was chosen by the churches." Titus was an honored person whose life was already seen to be honoring to the Lord and honoring to the Gospel, and therefore Paul and the Corinthians could trust him with their money. And the way he handles the money will also be honoring to the Lord and to the church. Honest finances are honoring to Christ (with the obvious implication that dishonesty dishonors Christ).

The point is even more explicit in verses 23 and 24. "As for Titus, he is my partner and fellow worker among you; as for our brothers, they are representatives of the churches *and an honor to Christ*. Therefore show these men the proof of your love and the reason for our pride in you, so that the churches can see it" (my italics). The word "representatives," used there, is actually *apostoloi*, apostles. It is used in the weaker sense that occurs several times in the New Testament to refer to others beyond the twelve apostolic pillars of the church (the twelve disciples, minus Judas Iscariot and plus Matthias in the Book of Acts, and then the apostle Paul). In this slightly looser sense the word *apostolos* meant someone who was an emissary or a trusted delegate of the churches. There seem to have been a number of these apostolic delegates going around the churches—Titus, Timothy, and others who are mentioned in 3 John and elsewhere. So, Paul says, these *apostoloi*, these chosen delegates of the churches who are being entrusted with the responsibility of handling finances within the churches, especially this large financial gift to Jerusalem, are an honor to Christ.

What a commendation! What a way to speak of an accountant or treasurer! These persons are entrusted with money. And by being faithful in that trust, not only are they an honor to Christ, but also they should have church approval: "Show these men the proof of your love—because we want them to be seen by all the churches!" (v. 24).

Look at how Paul speaks about Epaphroditus in Philippians 2:25–30: "I think it is necessary to send back to you Epaphroditus, my brother, fellow worker and fellow soldier, who is also your messenger." The last word here is *apostolos*, your apostle. Now, Epaphroditus was not an apostle in the sense that Paul was, but he was the emissary, the representative, the trusted messenger of the church, and hence apostolic. Paul continues, "whom you sent to take care of my needs. For he longs for all of you and is distressed because you heard he was ill. Indeed he was ill, and almost died. But God had mercy on him, and not on him only but also on me, to spare me sorrow upon sorrow. Therefore I am all the more eager to send him [back]. . . . Welcome him in the Lord with great joy and honor men like him, because he almost died for the work of Christ, risking his life to make up for the help you could not give me." What Paul is describing is Epaphroditus's handling of the financial and material gift that the Philippian church had made to Paul when Paul was in need. And Paul says, "That service of Epaphroditus was a work of the Gospel; that was a work born out of love for Christ and for his church. Epaphroditus nearly died doing what he did. Therefore," Paul says, "honor him. What he is doing, he is doing for Christ's sake."

In Philippians 4:14–19 we find another reference to the gift that was sent to Paul through Epaphroditus. Verse 18 reads, "I have received full payment and even more; I am amply supplied, now that I have received from Epaphroditus the gifts you sent. They are a fragrant offering, an acceptable sacrifice, pleasing to God." Epaphroditus's role then, says Paul, was an apostolic honor: serving God and serving Christ by serving the servants of God. In serving the servants of God, people like Epaphroditus are deserving of honor and respect, because they are an honor to Christ himself.

To administer financial affairs with trustworthiness, transparency, and honesty as did Epaphroditus and others in the New Testament is a Christ-honoring thing to do: we do it for him.

In 1 Samuel 2:30, God said through a prophet to Eli, "Those who honor me I will honor." If we want the Lord's honor, then we need to be honorable in the way in which we handle our finances and in the way we are accountable; we need to be transparent men and women of integrity in all that we seek to do for him. Let us make Paul and his teaching on this matter a powerful and authoritative model for ourselves.

# 4

# The Big Picture: Accountability Issues from a Korean Missiologist's Perspective

## Kiho (Timothy) Park

THE KOREAN CHURCH IS one of the most successful outgrowths of the Western missionary movement. From its inception, the church experienced rapid growth, developing into one of the most dynamic missionary churches of the twentieth century. Strengths of the Korean church include its Bible-centered faith and evangelical theology, history of spiritual renewals, experience in indigenous church planting, and long mission experience. The church has also benefited from Korea's growth as a nation, with its booming economy, rise in emigration, widespread diplomatic presence, and developed system of higher education. The Korean church, particularly during Japanese colonial rule and after the Korean War, demonstrated that through the grace of God, even a young, destitute church under persecution can successfully fulfill its missionary responsibilities; in the process, the church learned that mission from a position of weakness is the biblical way of mission.

In its growth, the Korean church has manifested numerous strengths for evangelizing the world, but also a host of weaknesses, including too little attention to issues of the accountability of missionaries, mission-ary-sending bodies, supporting churches, and missionary-receiving bodies.[1] Other aspects of our weakness include an unbalanced mission

---

1. By a "missionary-receiving body" I refer to an agency that "is responsible for ministries in the [mission] fields or the field partner of the mission headquarters at home. . . . This agency is the field administrative organization that invites, trains, de-

theology, a monocultural perspective, a lack of understanding of the various cultures we encounter on the mission fields, unwise deployment of missionaries, inappropriate selection and training of missionaries, competitive individualism, lack of missionary education, administration and training by nonprofessionals, and a lack of cooperation and accountability between sending, receiving, and supporting bodies.[2]

This chapter focuses on the need for greater accountability of Korean mission workers, particularly Korean mission leaders. It first describes biblical accountability, then explains why it is so important, what the problems are, who it applies to, and what the specific points of accountability are. Finally, it lists suggestions for how Korean mission leaders can be more fully accountable in their work.

## WHAT IS BIBLICAL ACCOUNTABILITY?

The parable of the talents in Matthew 25:14–30 teaches us about accountability. God distributes talents to his servants and later checks to see whether they have used the talents in a fruitful manner. According to Min-Young Jung, "Biblical stewardship accountability is doing our best to effectively use the resources God has entrusted to us, doing so according to his intention and with accountability for both the process and the result. All Christians must be faithful before God in maintaining an attitude of accountability for their life and work. . . . If an organization— whether business, church, missions, or any other—has a well-established system of accountability, that organization can be acknowledged as trustworthy and healthy. We cannot expect an organization that lacks a good reputation to be able indefinitely to carry on effective ministry."[3]

Genesis 1:26–28 shows us that God, after creating all things in the heavens, on the earth, and in the sea, created Adam and Eve and gave them the responsibility of taking care of his earthly creation: "Then God said, 'Let us make man in our image, in our likeness, and let them rule

---

ploys, supervises, and cares for the missionaries" (Hwal-Young Kim, "Seongyo Hyeonji Haengjeong System" [Field administrative system], in *Hanguk Seongyo-wa Chaengmu* [Korean missions and accountability], ed. Bangkok Mission Forum Committee [Seoul: Hyebon Publishing, 2006], p. 216, my translation).

2. Timothy Kiho Park, "The Influence of Korean Mission on the World Missionary Movement in the Modern Era," *Global Mission Advance* 46, no. 8: 56–58.

3. Min-Young Jung, "Seongyo-wa Chaegmu" (Mission and accountability), in *Hanguk Seongyosa-wa Chaegmu*, pp. 20–21, my translation.

over the fish of the sea and the birds of the air, over the livestock, over all the earth, and over all the creatures that move along the ground.' So God created man in his own image, in the image of God he created him; male and female he created them. God blessed them and said to them, 'Be fruitful and increase in number; fill the earth and subdue it. Rule over the fish of the sea and the birds of the air and over every living creature that moves on the ground'" (NIV). Sin entered the world because Adam and Eve failed in their responsibility (Gen. 3); as a consequence of sin, God's beautiful, orderly, and glorious creation became ugly, disorderly, and chaotic (Gen. 4–11).

Other biblical examples of individuals who were faithful stewards include Abraham (Gen. 12:1–5), Moses (Exod. 3 and following), Samuel (1 Sam. 12:23), Nehemiah, Job, Jesus (John 17:4, 19:30), and Paul (2 Tim. 4:7). The Bible also tells of poor stewards, such as many of the kings of Judah, the manager who wasted a rich man's possessions (Luke 16:1–2), the wicked and lazy servant (Matt. 25:14–30), and Judas Iscariot (Acts 1:16–20).

In Acts we read that the Antioch church commissioned Barnabas and Paul as missionaries at the instruction of the Holy Spirit (Acts 13:1–3), and later that the two returned to report how God had worked through them (14:26–28). They also reported to the faith community in Jerusalem on how the Holy Spirit worked through them among the Gentiles (chap. 15). Similarly, missionaries today have a responsibility to report to their supporters and sending bodies on how God has used them in their field.

Accountability also extends to the local church. For example, the church in Jerusalem convened a council of leaders to discuss issues their missionaries faced in order to resolve a troubling question (Acts 15:1–2, 28–29).

## WHY IS MISSIONARY ACCOUNTABILITY IMPORTANT?

Missionaries are given both privileges and responsibilities. They are privileged in that God promises blessings to those who obey his directions (Gen. 12:2–3, Matt. 28:20). At the same time, they are responsible for utilizing their God-given gifts (Matt. 25:14–30, John 15:16).

Evangelization cannot be accomplished and God's glory cannot be revealed when mission workers attempt to enjoy privileges but neglect their responsibilities. Therefore, there must be accountability. Whether they are workers in the sending mission, workers in the field, prayer or financial supporters, or workers of the receiving body who deploy, guide, and supervise the field missionaries, each group bears certain responsibilities for its part in the overall work.

According to Min-Young Jung, "It is important to have a leader who is trustworthy in both character and spirituality. However, it is also important to set up an organizational system whose goal will be to protect the selected leader from making mistakes. . . . Instead of trusting in an imperfect person who can never fully get rid of his or her sinfulness, we need to build a system for accountability that will minimize mistakes and wrongdoing."[4]

Jung also comments on the difference between the ideal and the actual. "Separation of powers between legislators, justices, and administrators originated from the concept of accountability. For an ideal democratic society to blossom, each of the three must have a unique role, and there must be a balance of power through mutual checks. The problem and limitation of Korean-style democracy is that the so-called three divisions exist on paper, but in fact power belongs especially to administrators. Likewise, the Korean church has a system of consistory and deacons, but actual power rests with the consistory or the senior pastor. No matter how good the system, if the actual exercise of power is not balanced, operations will become nominal and ineffective."[5]

Leaders of all parts of the total missionary enterprise must therefore voluntarily establish a system of accountability and try their best to abide in it out of fear of the Lord. "To reject a system of accountability is not a matter of Christian freedom, but it is to reject a solemn responsibility before God and the community. In reality, it is a shortcut to downfall."[6]

## WHAT ARE THE PROBLEMS OF THE KOREAN CHURCH IN RELATION TO ACCOUNTABILITY?

On November 23, 2010, a group of Korean missionaries studying at Fuller Seminary's School of Intercultural Studies gathered at a café in Pasadena, California, to discuss these topics. Belonging to the Global Mission

4. Ibid., p. 22.
5. Ibid., p. 23.
6. Ibid.

Society of Korea, they worked in China, Ethiopia, India, Philippines, Sri Lanka, and Vietnam. I asked them, "What do you see as the problems of Korean church missions in relation to mission accountability?" The group shared an abundance of comments and insights, which I list here under the following four categories:

### *Missionaries*

1. Missionaries tend to select mission fields based on personal preference or on the recommendation of their mission sending body, instead of upon invitation from the receiving body.

2. Missionaries tend to be involved in ministries they prefer versus responding to unmet needs of the field.

3. Missionaries tend to conduct independent ministries instead of collaborating with local people and the local church, thus wasting energy and funds.

4. Missionaries tend to plant denominational churches or establish denominational seminaries in the fields, instead of helping ministries of existing local churches and agencies.

5. Missionaries go to mission fields without proper training.

6. Many missionaries are not successful in language acquisition and culture training.

7. Missionaries are not held accountable for time management. A missionary who worked in China confessed that he had a guilty conscience for not using time wisely, except for the time he was learning the language. A missionary to the Philippines said that he became a tour guide for visitors and went to a tourist site more than three hundred times. Quite a few missionaries, particularly among senior missionaries, leave their field for private travel, apart from their regular vacation or furlough times.

8. Missionaries are not transparent in fund-raising and the use of funds.

9. Missionaries are not completely honest in making missionary reports. In some cases they have taken credit for the work of national coworkers.

10. Missionaries tend to work in the same place until they retire, becoming stagnant in their ministry and leadership development.

### Sending Bodies

1. Objectives of sending bodies are often not clear; they sometimes appear to be only an extension of the work of the home church.

2. Sending bodies must have a right understanding of the fields they serve, based on research and reliable information, before sending out missionaries.

3. Missionaries are sent to a field without invitation from, or consultation with, the host country church or agency. Sending bodies tend to send missionaries to places that have no missionaries from their own denominational mission.

4. Missions launch new ministries on their own instead of working with existing ministries of the host country churches or agencies.

5. Missions tend to send missionaries based on availability instead of on gifts that can help meet the existing needs.

6. Missions lack professionalism in selecting and training missionaries.

7. Missions are not doing well in deploying, redeploying, and withdrawing missionaries.

8. Missions tend to foster the dependency of local churches through the use of financial support and intervention.

9. Missions are weak in developing mission policies and strategies.

10. Most missions have no missionary-care system in place.

11. Missions are neglectful in developing missionary leaders.

12. Missions do not have a crisis management system.

### Receiving Bodies (Field Missions)

1. Receiving bodies lack sufficient knowledge of the fields they serve.

2. They do not have workable strategies.

3. They lack programs for proper orientation, language acquisition, and culture learning.

4. They do not responsibly deploy missionaries.

5. Receiving bodies do not supervise missionary life and work closely.

6. They are weak in team and cooperative ministry.

7. They do not have missionary care systems.

8. They do not have crisis management systems.

### Supporting Bodies

1. Missionary-supporting bodies do not have accurate knowledge of their mission fields. A missionary who worked in India reported that, during his fourteen years there, he received no visit from his supporting church.

2. Missionary-supporting bodies, and particularly local churches, think that missionaries' financial support should not exceed the salary of the senior pastor of the supporting church.

3. Missionary-supporting bodies do not take responsibility for the education of missionary kids (MKs). Missionaries therefore must take full responsibility for educating their own children, which becomes a hindrance to their missionary work. For example, more than 200 Korean missionaries to the Philippines live in homes around Faith Academy, an MK school near Manila, and do not leave the city where the school is located.

4. Missionary-supporting bodies are not satisfied with their role as prayer and financial supporters and try to control missionary work, even though they lack professional knowledge to do so.

5. Missionary-sending bodies like to send money directly to missionaries who are connected to them personally, instead of through their missions organizations. The consequence is that there have been cases of funds being misused.

6. Missionary-supporting bodies often promote themselves and do ministry in their own name.

7. Individuals and agencies that support missionary work through prayer and finances have concerns about unreasonable use of finances by mission agencies, unreasonable fund-raising, misuse of funds, and nontransparency of missionaries.

## WHO HAS ACCOUNTABILITY IN MISSION?

Who is accountable for the work, for relationships, and for attitudes in mission? The short answer is that *each Christian is!* How much more, then, those who are called to specific roles and ministries in the work of passing on the Good News of Jesus Christ and his salvation! Consider Romans 12:3–11, which gives wonderfully comprehensive teaching on Christian accountability:

> For by the grace given me I say to every one of you: Do not think of yourself more highly than you ought, but rather think of yourself with sober judgment, in accordance with the measure of faith God has given you. Just as each of us has one body with many members, and these members do not all have the same function, so in Christ we who are many form one body, and each member belongs to all the others. We have different gifts, according to the grace given us. If a man's gift is prophesying, let him use it in proportion to his faith. If it is serving, let him serve; if it is teaching, let him teach; if it is encouraging, let him encourage; if it is contributing to the needs of others, let him give generously; if it is leadership, let him govern diligently; if it is showing mercy, let him do it cheerfully. Love must be sincere. Hate what is evil; cling to what is good. Be devoted to one another in brotherly love. Honor one another above yourselves. Never be lacking in zeal, but keep your spiritual fervor, serving the Lord. (NIV)

In the whole area of missionary work, every segment—missionaries, sending bodies, supporting bodies, and receiving bodies—both collectively and each person individually, is equally responsible and should be accountable for their work. According to this passage, each should respect and love one another equally, and each should carry out his or her responsibilities thoughtfully and faithfully.

## WHAT ARE MISSIONS LEADERS ACCOUNTABLE FOR?

In this section we spell out more broadly ways that missions leaders, in whatever capacity they serve, must be accountable for their life and work.

### *Missionaries*

1. Missionaries are accountable for their personal and family devotional life, for physical and emotional health, and for maintaining moral standards. Not a small number of Korean missionaries fail in maintaining their own and their family members' spiritual, physical, and mental well-being.

2. In order for missionaries to fulfill their proper role, they must have a correct understanding of the mission field and must participate in ministry that fits their own gifts. Missionaries must not perform work that nationals or other missionaries are already doing well, but should be involved in other work that such persons cannot or do not do. Korean missionaries are commendable for their commitment to go to hard-to-evangelize areas to preach the Gospel, but they often go to such mission fields without a proper understanding of them.

3. Missionaries are accountable for preaching the Gospel faithfully and without distortion. They should present the Gospel by the power of the Holy Spirit, not using deceit or argumentative confrontation as they witness to people of other faiths.

4. Regardless of their possible involvement in other important activities, missionaries should not neglect to preach and teach the Gospel, which brings reconciliation between God and men.

5. Missionaries should be involved directly or indirectly in planting churches that are true communities of Christian faith among the various nations, peoples, and languages.

6. Missionaries should avoid bringing people of existing churches into their own church.

7. Missionaries are accountable for their use of time. Because, compared with workers at home, they receive less oversight and su-

pervision on the field, missionaries sometimes have problems with using time responsibly.

8. Missionaries are accountable for being knowledgeable about the overall work in their country. In one instance, a missionary to the Philippines did not know the population of the Philippines, the percentage of Christians there, the greatest needs of the country, the number of churches and educational institutions that were planted and established, or the number of baptized members.

9. Missionaries are accountable for transparent fund-raising and use of funds; they should report this information to their supporters.

10. Missionaries are accountable for honest missionary reporting. There must not be exaggeration in missionary reports. "Two special groups of people to whom missionaries must give account are people in the sending churches and the mission agency. . . . Well-informed people can be more effective in prayer."[7]

11. Missionaries are accountable for their life in the local society. They should not follow wrong sociocultural practices such as exchanging money on the black market or using bribes.

12. Missionaries are accountable for following mission policies. They "must support the policies and procedures of their mission agency with a cooperative spirit."[8]

13. Missionaries are accountable for working within legal boundaries and for being blameless and without deception, even for hard-to-enter countries that require "creative access."

14. Missionaries should not use the local people for personal benefit, but must love them and seek to promote their happiness.

15. Missionaries are accountable for their own leadership development. They should expect their leadership capacity to grow, which their work should reflect.

7. Paul E. Beals, *A People for His Name*, rev. ed. (Pasadena, Calif.: William Carey Library, 1995), pp. 157, 167.

8. Ibid., p. 167.

## Sending Bodies

The various mission sending bodies are accountable for the following:

1. Having a clear purpose and mission, which is the coming of the kingdom of God, not merely a fulfillment of the goals of their denomination or mission.

2. Field research in cooperation with those already in their field.

3. Planning strategies for effective ministry.

4. The selection and training of missionaries who will meet the needs identified in their fields.

5. Strategic deployment of missionaries and supervision for their work.

6. Communication between missionaries and supporting bodies.

7. The care of their missionaries. "Mission agencies should be prepared to provide for the care and well-being of dependents of mission workers serving in the field. The agency and its administrators, supervisors, and boards of trustees assume legal as well as moral responsibility for the protection, health, and basic needs of dependents, particularly the safety and education of dependent children."[9]

8. Fund-raising and the management of funds.

9. Having a plan in place for crisis management for their missionaries.

## Receiving Bodies (Field Missions)

Most missionaries, except those who serve in fields where there is no responsible national church or organization, have receiving bodies—the field missions of their home church or denomination and/or missions of the host countries. These receiving bodies are accountable for the following:

9. Douglas Hayward and Paul E. Langenwalter, "Holding Missionaries Accountable: A Proposed Code of Ethics for Missionaries Based upon the Code of Ethics of the American Anthropological Association," in *Serving Jesus with Integrity*, ed. Dwight P. Baker and Douglas Hayward (Pasadena, Calif.: William Carey Library, 2010), p. 367.

1. Providing information about the field to mission headquarters and supporters.

2. Planning strategies for mission in that field.

3. Requesting needed missionaries.

4. Knowing and protecting the legal status of the missionaries.

5. Orientation and field training of new missionaries.

6. The missionaries' language acquisition and learning of their new culture.

7. Assigning missionaries to the ministries according to their gifts and, when appropriate, reassigning existing missionaries for new ministry.

8. Developing new field ministries.

9. Guidance and supervision of missionaries and their ministries.

10. Cooperative and partnership ministries with local denominations or missions.

11. Missionary care and crisis management.

12. Use and maintenance of properties obtained in the fields.

13. Deciding on the amount of money for missionary living allowances, education of children, housing, and so forth.

### Supporting Bodies

Supporting bodies are accountable for:

1. Prayer and financial support, which are their two greatest responsibilities.

2. Having a correct understanding of the field. Leaders of supporting bodies need to visit the fields that they pray for and support in order to obtain practical knowledge of their missionaries' day-to-day situation.

3. The education of their missionary children.

4. Understanding and providing practical help for the leadership development of their missionaries.

## SUGGESTIONS FOR A HIGHER LEVEL
## OF ACCOUNTABILITY IN MISSION

In summary, I list a dozen points that all partners in the total mission process need to be aware of and support. Overall, mission leaders of the Korean church must strive to be more fully accountable in their work, which can lead to more efficient and effective ministry. This accountability includes the following actions:

1. Conduct thorough missions research of the mission fields.

2. Analyze the gifts of individual missionaries.

3. Pursue closer cooperation between missionaries, sending bodies, supporting bodies, and receiving bodies.

4. Have continuing education programs for missionaries, sending bodies, supporting bodies, and receiving bodies.

5. Make detailed policies for all areas of missions.

6. Organize a new level of mission board, one consisting of representatives of missions, supporting bodies, receiving bodies, and senior missionaries.

7. Hire leaders who have both knowledge of and experience in missions administration, education, and training.

8. Create missionary care systems that are detailed and workable.

9. Have written moral standards for missionaries.

10. Develop professional mission leaders.

11. Have periodic audits by internal and professional external auditors.

12. Have knowledgeable and competent agencies conduct evaluations of each of these points.

# 5

## Response to Kiho (Timothy) Park, "The Big Picture"

*Geoffrey W. Hahn*

MULTIPLE STRANDS OF ACCOUNTABILITY have coexisted through-out the modern and current mission eras. Recent mission trends, however, raise new questions with regard to the processes and procedures for administrative and fiscal accountability in missions. In relations between the Korean church and international mission agencies, questions of accountability frequently center on clarifying to whom in the partnership the missionary is accountable. The missionary has natural relational connections both within the home church community and within the mission agency community. With healthy collaboration, both partners offer differing strengths to help provide the various accountability mechanisms necessary for effective cross-cultural ministry.

Numerous Korean churches are exemplary as proactive, highly engaged, missional churches. As Timothy Park notes, "From its inception, the [Korean] church experienced rapid growth, developing into one of the most dynamic missionary churches of the twentieth century" (p. 53). The Korean church has been a blessing to the nations, and Korean missionaries have strengthened the ministries of international mission agencies, increasing their effectiveness for the kingdom of God.

## AN IMPORTANT TENSION

Timothy Park superbly highlights the different accountability roles the partners provide in missions. He also lists in detail the various accountability problems commonly encountered in collaborative missions effort. Many of the problems described in Park's analysis arise from a tension between two core values in mission, which in the table below I identify as the "contextualization value" and the "ecclesiology value." Churches and mission agencies, as do all organizations, have values that may be good, yet when these different organizations work together, their particular values can come into tension, even into a paradoxical relationship with each other. When this occurs, it does not necessarily signify that one of the two values is in error, or that one should be discarded, or even that one should be given priority. At times, they both need to be upheld simultaneously. A discussion of the paradoxical relationship between these two mission values may provide a helpful framework for considering the issues that Park raises.

Two essential values

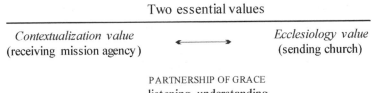

| *Contextualization value* | | *Ecclesiology value* |
|---|---|---|
| (receiving mission agency) | ←——→ | (sending church) |

PARTNERSHIP OF GRACE
listening, understanding
dialogue, negotiation
time, patience, mutual submission
journeying together

**Table 5.1.** Essential values for mission

For missions a key value is that of mission contextualization, of seeking to understand the local context and to adapt appropriately. As a community the mission agency tends to be highly focused on issues of contextualization, on appropriate adaptation of the Gospel message to the culture where the mission is doing ministry. Over time, international mission agencies have gained wisdom about contextual realities that they are able to bring to bear on the missional task. This wisdom plays an important role in accountability. Is the ministry the missionary wants to do wise to carry out at this time? How does the local church see the Spirit of God moving? What are the legal parameters in the country? What are the felt needs of the community? Who are potential local ministry partners in that country? Those living in the context of the ministry are best positioned to understand the current contextual realities and accordingly are best placed to make wise ministry decisions. Proximity matters.

Another key missions value is a strong ecclesiology. To me this means that mission agencies should not bypass the church but rather should be an extension of the church. The agencies need to have a robust ecclesiology, from which cross-cultural mission emanates and which itself is continuously nourished by the church. As for the churches, it is hoped that those engaged in cross-cultural mission are strong, proactive, and missional in their ethos. Ideally, as George Peters writes, "missions flows from the inner constitution, character, calling and design of the church."[1] Churches need, in the words of John Oak, to see themselves as "the gathering of believers who have been called by God and sent out into the world as the witnesses of Christ. Spreading the gospel to the ends of the earth is the most important responsibility of the church."[2] An active sending church provides many natural accountability mechanisms through its relationship with missionaries: the church knows the missionaries, with their strengths, weaknesses, and history; it will have determined their suitability for a mission assignment and will be praying regularly in response to the missionaries' correspondence.

What happens when these values collide? For example, in determining vision and strategy, determining personnel placement, and launching major ministry initiatives, the international mission agency naturally focuses on the contextualization value and may find it annoying when a church in another country wants to join the dialogue. Were the agency, however, to ignore the voice of the sending church in the decision-making process, the ecclesiology value would be diminished. Conversely, the sending churches may diminish the contextualization value by insisting that their missionaries conform to their own designs for ministry. The danger is in not recognizing that a values paradox exists. The tension in the paradox cannot be resolved logically. When the role of either the sending church or the mission agency is undervalued in the partnership, the neglected party's functions of wisdom and account-

---

1. George W. Peters, *A Biblical Theology of Missions* (Chicago: Moody Press, 1984), p. 200.

2. John H. Oak, *Called to Awaken the Laity* (Glasgow: Bell & Bain, 2009), p. 91.

ability in the missions effort are significantly diminished, and ministry effectiveness is reduced.

## MAINTAINING BOTH VALUES

How does one resolve this type of dilemma occasioned when two good values function paradoxically in relationship yet in opposition to each other? A possible solution is found in following a core principle associated with successful, healthy partnering, namely, that *both partners must function and be treated as equals, with both being consulted in important decisions.* When both the contextualization and the ecclesiology values are held strongly, with both partners being able to bring their strengths to the mission endeavor, then the accountability gaps are greatly lessened, and each partner's understanding is sharpened in the dialogue. In such a context Park's recommendation to "pursue closer cooperation between missionaries, sending bodies, supporting bodies, and receiving bodies" (p. 65) can actually be followed.

It is a mistake to focus on one value and ignore the other. International mission agencies often err by focusing predominantly on the contextualization value, while ignoring the corresponding ecclesiology value and giving the sending church neither voice nor vote in the decision-making processes. When these two partners, with their parallel accountability mechanisms, do not provide similar goals or advice, Korean missionaries find themselves in the difficult situation of having to make either-or choices between respecting the authority of their sending church or respecting the authority of the international mission agency. Placing missionaries in such a predicament is unhelpful and unhealthy.

Tension in the partnership between sending churches and mission agencies does not arise only in the Korean context. The experience of South Korean churches engaged in sending missionaries, however, highlights the weaknesses that result if cooperation and accountability between the different partners are lacking. Failure of church and agency partners to acknowledge and give due respect to each other's important roles leads to an inability to fully benefit from each other's strengths. Highly engaged sending churches need to be keenly aware that they are not well positioned to understand contextual realities in the quite different countries and cultures where their missionaries serve. Conversely, if international mission agencies fail to listen receptively to proactive sending churches, they lose the benefits of the initiative, momentum, and creativity generated by the Korean church. Reducing or brushing aside ownership by the sending church also inhibits the powerful, communal, holistic support of missionaries and ministries (including prayer, financial giving, emotional support, encouragement, and wisdom) offered by the church, along with all the accompanying accountability mechanisms naturally flowing from that relationship.

Despite the tension, neither value should be dismissed or diminished. In the past, highly engaged sending churches could not, even if they wished to, give direction to missionaries on the field, for communication took months and was unreliable, and travel to the field was prohibitively expensive and/or time-consuming. In this era of globalization, however, highly engaged churches are able to communicate with their missionaries regularly via the Internet, make regular on-site visits, and be more aware of the reality on the ground than at any time in the past. These now-possible contacts create a blurring of the lines of responsibility and accountability that will not go away. Mission systems must adapt to the new reality, rather than try to make sending churches conform to the realities of a past era. Having highly proactive, engaged sending churches is what all believers should hope to see all around the world.

Both the contextualization value and the ecclesiological value can remain strong if the paradox is addressed through a partnership of equals *characterized by grace*. Grace allows the partners to listen to and understand each other's perspective. Grace is necessary during dialogue and the negotiation of major decisions, including developing overall vision and strategy, placing the missionary, and determining the missionary's primary ministry role. Time, patience, perseverance, and mutual submission are indispensible if all involved are to journey together in grace.

Park notes that "Korean missionaries are commendable for their commitment to go to hard-to-evangelize areas to preach the Gospel" (p. 61). Around the world, we indeed notice a clear pattern of Korean missionaries faithfully serving in some of our planet's most austere and rugged living and ministry environments. It is humbling to visit these Korean missionaries as they persevere with hope and joy in such difficult settings. The global church, as well as international mission agencies, stands to be further blessed by the increased integration and impact of Korean missions in the global missions movement.

# 6

## Mission, Missionary, and Church Accountability That Counts: Implications for Integrity, Strategy, and Dynamic Continuity

*Stanley W. Green*

*Nonprofits have historically operated in what was referred to as "the sanctified sector," a sector that was above criticism, but times are changing.*

—Rachel Atkin Christensen

### ACCOUNTABILITY MECHANISMS
### AND MISSION-BASED ACTIVITY

MICHAEL McCUBBINS HAS WRITTEN: "Mission boards will often tout accountability as one of the chief reasons for their existence. . . . Accountability is not really a big worry to mission boards. . . . Remember that missions exist to . . . protect their own futures."[1] The figures for the amount of money entrusted to mission agencies, baldly considered, suggest that McCubbins's indictment is not universally endorsed. That this view exists, however—and indeed that it is held by a local congregational

---

1. Michael D. McCubbins, "Missionary Accountability," www.biblebaptistarleta .org/b_missionary_accountability.pdf. The epigraph at the head of this chapter is from Rachel Atkin Christensen, "Accountability Mechanisms and Mission-Based Activity: A Nonprofit Agency Serving Immigrants and Refugees" (Master's paper, Virginia Polytechnic Institute and State Univ., 2002), http://scholar.lib.vt.edu/theses/available /etd-04262002-105015/unrestricted/MajorPaperChristensen.pdf, p. 4.

leader—is troubling. In the same article McCubbins contends that "missions were not started by churches to provide accountability, but rather by missionaries to provide a conduit for moneys to be sent to them on the foreign fields" and asserts that this situation remains true for most modern missions. "No thought," he writes, "was really given to accountability." We are left wondering whether his assessment really holds true. Is it even remotely possible that mission agencies have little interest in being accountable and exist simply to "protect their own futures"?

If accountability is about giving account, about answering to others for our actions, then accountability is fundamental to who we are as part of the Christian community. Accountability is not merely an onerous burden that must be tolerated; correctly understood, it is of critical (and strategic) concern. As the children of God, we believe that we are not only responsible to others but also primarily and ultimately responsible to God for our actions, thoughts, and words. Alignment with God's purposes and following in the way of Jesus are our yardsticks. The first goal of our mission is God's glory and the advance of his kingdom. This objective is at the heart of our undertaking to be accountable. Our mission is centered on God's redemptive purposes and reconciling love for all nations. Additionally, our mission is to be patterned after Christ's mission in the world, for this responsibility is the thrust of Jesus' commission: "As the Father has sent me, even so I am sending you" (John 20:21 ESV). Jesus' words mean that we are accountable not only for the task of proclaiming the Good News in word and deed but also, and equally importantly, for the way in which we carry out this task. Our mission is to be modeled after the pattern left to us by Jesus. Perhaps the strongest indictment by Jonathan Bonk in his book *Money and Missions* is of our failure to live and witness incarnationally.[2] This failure, Bonk laments, has occasioned enormous harm and hindered the Gospel. If we are to be faithful to our call, our attitudes and words must be a "sign, instrument and foretaste" of the kingdom of God, as Jesus was its embodiment.[3]

---

2. Jonathan J. Bonk, *Missions and Money: Affluence as a Missionary Problem—Revisited*, rev. and expanded ed. (Maryknoll, N.Y.: Orbis Books, 2007).

3. Lesslie Newbigin, *The Gospel in a Pluralist Society* (Grand Rapids: Eerdmans, 1989), p. 233.

## ACCOUNTABILITY IN THE BIBLE

Accountability is neither a modern invention nor a foreign presence in the biblical text; accountability is an essential biblical principle that characterizes humanity's relationship with its Creator. The narrative of faith is grounded in relationship. The relationship of God the Creator with the created order presumes accountability: the Creator God fashions humanity after his own image for a particular purpose (i.e, relationship); Yahweh identifies a chosen people with a peculiar responsibility (to be a blessing to the nations); a messiah comes to restore God's purposes for humanity. Jesus opens up all creation to God's reign, thus infusing the created order with the seeds of God's restorative purposes and inviting us to be instruments of these purposes. The Bible's rendition of this narrative is suffused with the notion of accountability.

Accountability is at the heart of the Old Testament. The Hebrews believed they had a special relationship with God and that therefore the worship of any other gods was proscribed. The evolving relationship between God and this chosen people came to be based on mutual obligations and formalized criteria—in other words, on a covenant. Included in the covenant initiated by God with Abraham were duties and promises by both parties. The overall goal was to bless all of the families of the earth through this family of Abraham (Gen. 12:3). This covenant, like other Old Testament covenants, is framed within an expectation of accountability—a framework that included the acknowledgment of mutual responsibility. Tragically, the Jews were unable to fulfill their responsibilities under the Abrahamic covenant. They failed to acknowledge and enter into the promise of being a blessing to all the families of the earth. The entire prophetic canon in the Old Testament emerges as an impassioned plea to the people of God to account for their failure to fulfill their obligations under the covenant and as a call to turn toward God and God's purposes for the nation.

In the New Testament, and in the ministry and teachings of Jesus in particular, the notion of accountability is pervasive. Again and again Jesus makes statements like the following: "I tell you, on the day of judgment people will give an account for every thoughtless word they have uttered" (Matt. 12:36 ISV). Moreover, in the parables Jesus reiterates the idea of accountability. In the parable of the Talents, or Minas, for example, those who have received "talents" are called to give account of how they have exercised stewardship over the resources with which they have been entrusted (Matt. 25:14–30; Luke 19:12–27).

After the birth of the church, issues of accountability became particularly germane. Paul is careful to counsel the believers at Corinth (2 Cor. 8) about the appropriate care to be exercised in the collection and distribution of church funds. He is at pains to reassure the Corinthian church, which has collected a substantial offering for distribution to the poor in distant Jerusalem, that Titus, whom they know to be a man of integrity, and another highly regarded man (unnamed in the text) have been "chosen by the churches to accompany us as we carry the offering" (v. 19 NIV); a third companion, a man of integrity and trust, will also watch over the carrying of the funds (v. 22). Paul does not want sole responsibility for these funds. Titus and these two men who join Paul and his group constitute a team that can be trusted to handle and distribute the offerings. The presence of these trusted men is clearly welcomed by Paul and gives him a sense of freedom from suspicions; it is likely that Paul himself has invited their involvement, for he attests, "We want to avoid any criticism of the way we administer this liberal gift" (v. 20 NIV). He affirms that he is "taking pains to do what is right, not only in the eyes of the Lord but also in the eyes of men" (v. 21 NIV). Paul is careful to preserve his own integrity and prevent harm to the church. He acts to avoid any suspicion, pursuing transparency and making himself accountable.

## SEEKING A DEFINITION AND GRAPPLING WITH RELATED ISSUES

Beyond gaining a collective sense of what accountability means, we need to explore the variety of meanings attached to the concept and a wide range of issues related to making accountability effective. Accountability is often framed in terms of holding someone responsible and exercising a right to impose sanctions for unsatisfactory performance. More recently a broader perspective has emerged that encompasses both "being held responsible by others" and "taking responsibility for oneself." On this view, accountability is seen as being more than merely a "reactive response to overseers; [it is] also a proactive one linked to ensuring that the public trust is served."[4]

4. Alnoor Ebrahim, "Making Sense of Accountability: Theoretical Perspectives and

Accountability manages the power relations between persons who interact with or affect each other directly or indirectly. It can be understood as "giving an account" to another party who has a stake in what has been done. It evokes a sense of taking responsibility, but it also includes the meaning of being held responsible by others—being "held to account."[5] The notion of being held to account is not something that is positively embraced across the board. Because of unfortunate ways in which accountability has sometimes been exercised, many people have a negative view of being held to account. Accountability, however, has some very positive dimensions.

For example, accountability can be a means through which an agency exercises responsibility internally for refining its organizational mission and values. Additionally, accountability can be an instrument for allowing objective external scrutiny and for assessing performance in relation to the organization's goals. The exercise of giving account can thus have beneficial outcomes not only for the stakeholders of an agency but also for the agency itself. There is strategic value in promoting a culture of compliance with fiscal responsibilities and organizational policies. Furthermore, doing so advances learning and innovation, enables an agency to maximize its trust, and builds confidence among both insiders and external stakeholders.

Recent research and reflection on accountability offer a model that contains four essential or core dimensions:

- transparency in the gathering and sharing of information

- answerability/justification that includes the opportunity to provide clear reasoning for actions and decisions, including lines of action not pursued, so that these steps may be fairly assessed

- evaluation

- enforcement/sanctions (including complaints and redress) when performance is unsatisfactory in terms of compliance, justification, or transparency.

---

Practical Mechanisms for NGOs" (working paper no. 2002-1, Global Accountabilities: Center for Social Monitoring Analysis, Virginia Tech, 2002), p. 3; quoted in Christensen, "Accountability Mechanisms and Mission-Based Activity," p. 11.

5. Andrea Cornwall, Henry Lucas, and Kath Pasteur, "Introduction: Accountability Through Participation; Developing Workable Partnership Models in the Health Sector," *IDS Bulletin* 31, no. 1 (2000): 1–13, see esp. p. 3.

When these dimensions are rooted in an agency's policies, processes, and practices, it is more likely that an organization will experience "giving account" as a positive and strengthening exercise.

Accountability is routinely framed positivistically as a technocratic or administrative matter. Problems are generally easy to identify: financial mismanagement, fraud, misleading reporting, inflation of outcomes, and other forms of malfeasance. The solutions to these problems are simple, if not easy, and may call for tougher regulation, revised codes of conduct, and appropriate sanctions. This understanding of accountability is built on the presumption that more "truthful" information and greater transparency elicit higher levels of compliance and render corrective action straightforward.

An approach that is increasingly gaining currency sees accountability as a social phenomenon in which the impact of accountability is the result of relationships of power and interactions among the principals (those requiring accountability) and the agents (those called to give account). Recognizing the social nature of accountability raises important questions: Whose metrics are used? What kinds of information, knowledge, and expertise are valued—or devalued? How do the mechanisms of accountability serve to reproduce, or alter, existing configurations of power? Metrics thus become linked to concerns about power: why certain metrics are selected over others, who decides what metrics are important, who collects the data, who interprets it, and who decides how to use it.

Compliance-driven accountability, on the one hand, is a reactive response to concerns about public trust. It is about doing what one has to do, such as complying with the law, disclosing whatever information is necessary in order to account for resource use, and taking fiduciary responsibility seriously in order to prevent fraud or malfeasance. Under this approach, nonprofit leaders share information about their performance or operations largely because funders or regulators demand it. Strategy-driven accountability, on the other hand, is a proactive approach to addressing concerns that can strengthen trust and confidence by increasing transparency, improving performance, and achieving the stated mission.

## ADDRESSING ACCOUNTABILITY MYOPIA—COUNTING WHAT REALLY COUNTS

The accountability that we have been primarily addressing so far is focused upward to those (donors, constituents, supporters, and governing boards) who have the power to influence an agency's capacity to accomplish its mission. A second tier of accountability is lateral, or inward, and addresses the issue of congruity between an agency's performance and its mission, vision, and values. This focus is critical for organizational alignment and staff/stakeholder empowerment. A third vector of accountability is directed "downward" and focuses on those who are deemed to benefit from the agency's intervention.

In a thoughtful chapter in a book he coedited with Edward Weisband, Alnoor Ebrahim talks about "accountability myopias."[6] While most agencies have had a long history of engagement with upward accountability, I believe that downward accountability to those who are impacted by our initiatives is, indeed, an accountability myopia that hampers and mars our best efforts. If our benchmark is the kingdom of God as it was personified in the incarnation of Jesus, then our regard for those whom we seek to impact, our attitudes toward and characterization of these intended beneficiaries, is central to our mission. Indeed, the very nomenclature of downward accountability, taken from secular NGO parlance, is problematic. In God's economy those who are considered "the least of these" are equated with Jesus himself. This equation is a mystery of cosmic proportions and ought to have profound implications for our accountability. Taken seriously, it might engender critical questions such as, What is the impact of our actions on the humanity of those we seek to affect? Whose interests are being served in the engagement? Who really benefits through the initiative? If we are sincere in our inquiries, then we will take care to ensure that the response to these questions is given not by the agency but by those affected by the agency's activity.

Unfortunately, in most cases the need for accountability is driven by the concerns of the more affluent partner (usually from the North), which has control over resources. This situation often exacerbates imbalances of power. The "receiving" partner is forced into a vertical relationship of dependency upon the partner with greater financial

---

6. Alnoor Ebrahim, "Towards a Reflective Accountability in NGOs," in *Global Accountabilities: Participation, Pluralism, and Public Ethics*, ed. Alnoor Ebrahim and Edward Weisband (Cambridge: Cambridge Univ. Press, 2007), pp. 193–234.

resources and is unable to maintain horizontal relations with other actors as equals. These dynamics inevitably lead to feelings of humiliation because of their lesser financial resources, or of loss of dignity and self-esteem among those who are on the receiving end of the relationship. By contrast, kingdom values require that North-South engagements be driven by the needs, priorities, and potentials of both the "senders/givers" and the "recipients." The recipients should be jointly engaged in discerning not only the vision for any initiatives in their context but also how the outcomes are to be evaluated. This assertion is particularly applicable to restricted-access countries and to those regions where the church is forced to remain invisible and can be gravely harmed by ill-considered interventions. In the absence of mutual accountability the church in the South is unlikely to value its own important resources of local knowledge, contextual acumen, and strategic relationships. In the words of Rachel Christensen, "Downward accountability, then, refers to the responsibility of [agencies] to 'be accountable to the needs and aspirations' of those it intends to benefit."[7]

A kingdom-oriented approach in mission must foster healthy, interdependent relationships between sending and receiving partners that are sustained by willingness to learn from each other and to grow together in obedience to God while serving him together. The primary focus in the relationship must be on the needs of the receiving partners, open communication, humility, mutual trust, and accountability, leading to outcomes that benefit all participants and the kingdom of God. A dictum frequently ascribed to Albert Einstein is here most pertinent: "Not everything that counts can be counted, and not everything that can be counted counts."

## MODELING AN INCLUSIVE, PARTICIPATORY ACCOUNTABILITY IN THE SPIRIT

The story of the Jerusalem council, in Acts 15, shows us that New Testament mission eschews arrogance and triumphalism. Rather than seeking to wield power, however benignly or beneficently, the council models voluntary surrender of power to the leading of the Spirit among the whole people of God. Paul and Barnabas, freshly back from their

7. Christensen, "Accountability Mechanisms and Mission-Based Activity," p. 17, quoting Adil Najam, "NGO Accountability: A Conceptual Framework," *Development Policy Review* 14 (1996): 345.

first journey to Cyprus and Asia Minor, are called to the "partnership council" in Jerusalem to answer questions regarding the need for Gentile circumcision. Here the early church leaders faced one of their greatest challenges. Would those who had the power (the leadership in Jerusalem) issue a fiat based on Jewish religio-cultural understandings without regard to what the Spirit was doing among the Gentiles? This critical issue had interethnic and international overtones. It required a theological consultation—sitting around Jerusalem's partnership table. The council dealt with the issue in a calm and careful manner, under the leading of the Holy Spirit. As *equal partners* in the mission of Jesus, the various groups within the early church had to be flexible and allow for shared discernment under the Spirit's leading. The Jewish believers, the leading group, had to surrender their assumed prerogative to determine the direction in which the new church would go. Their willing commitment to do so led, ultimately, to a position different from their preferred interest. Partnership in the Gospel thus came to mean sharing power, becoming open to new traditions, and allowing the Spirit to direct the decision-making process. And this decision apparently was unanimous (Acts 15:22).

ActionAid International provides one example of an agency that is working intentionally at mutual accountability and shared discernment with the people who are impacted by the agency's interventions. In a document entitled *Alps: Accountability, Learning, and Planning System,* the agency affirms that it lives by these values:

> Mutual respect, requiring us to recognise the innate worth of all people and the value of diversity. . . .
> Solidarity with the poor, powerless and excluded will be the only bias in our commitment to the fight against poverty and injustice.[8]

The agency further states:

> In ActionAid we have multiple accountabilities—to the poor and excluded people and groups with whom we work, supporters, volunteers, partners, donors, governments, staff and trustees. Alps emphasises accountability to all our stakeholders—but most of all to poor and excluded people, especially women and girls.

8. ActionAid International, *Alps: Accountability, Learning, and Planning System,* www.actionaid.org/sites/files/actionaid/actionaids_accountability_learning_and_planning_system.pdf, p. 2.

Alps is a framework that sets out the key accountability requirements, guidelines, and processes in ActionAid International. Not
only in terms of organisational processes for planning, monitoring, strategy formulation, learning, reviews and audit but also
personal attitudes and behaviours.

Alps defines our standards, not only about what we do but also
how we do it.[9]

The Alps document declares:

Alps can only be effective if our staff, volunteers, activists, trustees and partners hold attitudes and behave in ways that fit with
our shared vision, mission and values. These include:
• Behaviour that is not domineering or patronising but that
genuinely shares power with others rather than keeps it for
oneself.
• Behaving in a way that genuinely supports those who are
excluded to fully participate, bringing poor and excluded people
into the heart of decision-making, rather than simply informing
and consulting them.[10]

Just as NGOs such as ActionAid International are taking seriously the dignity and humanity of the people they seek to serve, so new
models for mission and accountability are critically needed today if we
are to be faithful to our charter delineated by the kingdom of God. The
world is different and the global church is different. Such change calls
for new models for mission engagement, new models for relationships,
and new models for managing accountability. During the period from
the late eighteenth century to the midpoint of the twentieth century,
mission initiative flowed *from* congregations *through* agencies *to* what
was called the (mission) field. Vision was shaped in the West and was
implemented elsewhere. In the period following the Second World War
(roughly 1950–95), mission engagements were increasingly pursued not
by missionaries going into situations where the Gospel was completely
unknown, but in cooperation with maturing national churches or local
Christian nongovernmental organizations. During this period mission
was generally performed *by* the agencies *with* field partners *supported
by* congregations, businesses, and individuals in the West. Consultation,

9. Ibid., p. 4.
10. Ibid., p. 9.

not common discernment and planning with the non-Western church or communities in the Global South, was the modus operandi.

In the closing decades of the past century, particularly as many former colonies gained their independence, the older paradigms were increasingly seen to be no longer sufficient to account for the growing mission initiative and awareness in the churches in the South. Communities of believers in the South assumed involvement in decision making or launched their own mission initiatives. Increasingly, attention came to be focused not so much on subject-object relations (described by the relative power and capacity of the "senders" and "recipients") but more on the joint initiative of the two groups and the integrity of the relationship between them.

Inspired by trends like those that were influencing ActionAid International, Mennonite Mission Network, the mission agency for the Mennonite Church USA, along with other partners, felt challenged in the last decade of the twentieth century to make a shift to a new form of accountability. The agency was discovering anecdotally, as well as in the writings of respected commentators on the trends in the church in Africa, such as Lamin Sanneh, Andrew Walls, Philip Jenkins, and David Barrett, that a shift in the nature of mission relationships was occurring. It was clear that the time had come to move away from past assumptions that mission initiative and vision emerged solely, or even primarily, from the North Atlantic churches. For the sake of the global church and its mission, the agency felt called to imagine a way of being together in mission that is rooted in the conviction that the whole church in every part of the world is called to be missional subjects. To move away from the ugly dependencies and awkward paternalisms of the past required deliberate effort. The agency acknowledged that, given the world's economic imbalance, the North Atlantic or Global North churches may continue to have greater financial resources to share. This imbalance was a matter for concern, for in the past, control of resources had bedeviled relationships and had made authentic sharing nearly impossible.

Mennonite Mission Network participated with its African partners in creating Partnership Councils, which were intended to transform the relationship between former subjects and objects of mission with the intent that initiative and vision for mission would be relocated to those within whose context a mission initiative was to be undertaken. The role of Western agencies would be that of invited partners who might assist in making the locally discerned vision a reality. The goal was to strengthen local ownership and to ensure that accountability rested primarily with those most deeply affected by a particular initiative. The Partnership Councils, which were created in all of the former "mission fields," are African led and owned. Western agencies participate as guests and committed partners. Mennonite Mission Network believes that this arrangement will deepen local ownership and thus not perpetuate the perception that the people in that region are "having something done *for* them" or "on their behalf," or worse yet, that they are "having something done *to* them." Unless the local church community discerns enough of a need for a particular initiative that it is willing to direct energy and local resources to the undertaking, it may endure the intervention, but it will not have sufficient ownership of the project for a good outcome. It may yet be too soon to make an informed assessment of the effectiveness of this new paradigm, but the agency is learning as it goes what it means to surrender its dominance and need for control. We are discovering together with our African partners what authentic partnership and respectful relationships require.

## CONCLUSION

Finally, the most common mechanisms of accountability, such as were addressed earlier in this chapter and that involve disclosure statements, reports, and project evaluations, serve mainly to ensure compliance. They tend to focus on accounting for funds and by and large report short-term results. The complex challenges before mission agencies make more strategic processes of accountability requisite for lasting transformative change. Most protocols that serve funding and regulatory purposes tilt toward easily measurable indicators of progress. They routinely ignore or undervalue adaptive assessments that are essential for understanding how an agency might improve its work. Strategy-driven accountability requires that we build internal capacity in non-profits for adaptive learning. We will never arrive at the place of perfect accountability. The journey that leads to new insights, altered practices, and transformed relationships—and thus to more effective mission—is the "road less taken." If we dare to travel down that road, potentially new and liberating possibilities may be unleashed among us.

# 7

## Response to Stanley W. Green, "Mission, Missionary, and Church Accountability That Counts"

### *Nam Yong Sung*

STANLEY GREEN'S WRITING IS rich and addresses accountability comprehensively, like a textbook on the subject. Historically, our concern has tended to be with so-called upward accountability; Green, however, calls attention to lateral and downward accountability, while pointing out many other areas that we are prone to overlook. Those who are involved in the work of mission agencies have a responsibility to the people visible around them, but much more are they responsible to the invisible God. He has called us as a church and sends all of us out into the world. And he expects us to be channels of blessing to all the people we meet along the way. These people include the powerless and weak, whom we can choose to ignore at no immediate disadvantage to ourselves. As Green asserts, however, we will account for all we have done when we stand before the judgment seat of the Lord. This kind of *coram Deo* consciousness is what missionaries need to have as their basic ethos for accountability. Green ably covers the various areas or forms of accountability. I do not need, therefore, to expand on what he has written but will offer several reflections stimulated by his comments.

Michael McCubbins is not alone in harboring negative feelings about mission agencies. Nevertheless, support for mission agencies and missionaries continues because God's people deem missions to be more important than the problems agencies present. Still, mission agencies cannot afford to be complacent and ignore this distrust. For the sake of transparency, agencies must do their utmost to find ways for churches and supporters to participate directly and indirectly both in financial matters and in the content and procedures of their ministry. The churches should be able to recognize that the ministries of the mission agencies are truly their own ministries as well. Nor can we forget that formulating good mission policies is essential if missionaries are to be equipped to handle their obligations of accountability. It is not that certain ethnic or cultural groups are inherently more honest than others; instead, some groups have established good structures that help to ensure greater honesty. Good structures aid honesty. To foster accountability, it is more effective for agencies to rely on specific structures than on specific people.

## SOUND FINANCIAL POLICIES

Two kinds of policies are central to good accountability. First, sound financial policies are essential. In most mission agencies missionaries raise their own support, and therefore good fund-raising policies need to be well established. Support of missionaries includes basic salaries, housing expenses, retirement funds, administration fees, travel expenses, medical expenses, children's education expenses, and more. Missionaries can also raise ministry funds and special project funds. It is extremely important that mission agencies recognize the basic missionary salary as "private property" required by missionaries in order to plan their own futures. The unfortunate reality is that most Korean missionaries spend their salaries on their ministries and are thus unable to prepare financially for their future. At the same time, certain missionaries have wrongly privatized their semipublic ministry funds and their public project funds, neither of which is a personal possession.

Mission agencies typically collect an administration fee of 10 percent of a missionary's basic support and also take a certain percentage from ministry and project funds. Some missionaries and supporters prefer to have separate accounts in order to avoid paying the administration fee, but the creation of two support accounts is dishonest. Churches and supporters come to distrust mission agencies because they do not fully understand the various administration fees. To avoid such problems, mission agencies need to raise funds separately for administrative expenses. Above all, it is essential that using project funds to purchase property be completely disclosed; such information should be fully available to the public. Lack of a clear policy in this area can lead to problems with the ownership and transfer of property. Good policy prevents confusion and dishonesty, whether inadvertent or intentional, and it increases the level of missionary accountability.

## CLEAR MINISTRY POLICIES

The second area essential for good accountability is a clear ministry policy. If missionaries leave their field and stay away without the approval of their agencies, they are not being faithful in terms of accountability to their supporters. National partners may come to regard such missionaries as mere wage earners and not as servants of Christ. For the sake of accountability, mission policy needs to properly address matters such as vacations and official trips, doing so in a manner that is acceptable to national partners and that enables missionaries to fulfill their ministerial responsibilities.

Green urges that mission recipients be engaged from the start both in discerning the vision for any ministry and in evaluating its outcome. Any kind of relationship structure between missionaries and national partners that benefits only one side is not healthy in itself. It is best if national partners consistently participate in the raising of funds. The high dependency of certain national churches on overseas funds may be the result of both missionaries and local leaders deciding that a unilateral relationship is more convenient. It is obviously right for all churches to help each other, but each church should grow independently in capability and in ability to contribute. As Green indicates, support of independent church growth is motivated by the desire to move away from "the ugly dependencies and awkward paternalisms of the past" (p. 81). The early Korean church, for example, was very weak financially. Missionaries working in Korea, however, were determined to apply the Nevius Method—with its goals of self-support, self-propagation, and self-government—to their ministries. The missionaries were aware that, while use of outside resources might have short-term benefits, those gains would come at the detriment of long-term effectiveness.

The early Korean church sought to have each church take responsibility at least for the salaries of pastors, church management, and construction of places for worship. According to Myung Soo Park, of the

188 Presbyterian churches in Korea in 1908, 186 were self-supporting.[1] In light of the situation of both the country and the church at that time, this achievement is nothing short of a miracle. Church members put forth their best efforts in giving offerings, which were used to build their own churches. With an outside power encroaching upon and taking control of their country, they did not want to lose their church as well. Thus they emphasized self-support, self-reliance, and independence. As discussed recently by Dong Min Jang, it is significant that traditional religious customs were transformed into Christian traditions in a way that increased the accountability of Korean churches.[2] Koreans regarded the early dawn (*InShi*, the time from 3:00 a.m. until 5:00 a.m.) as sacred, a belief that was brought into Christian practice in the form of the early morning prayer service, of which the Korean church is rightfully proud. The respect with which Koreans regarded the books of Confucianism— holding them to be sacred, and loving to read and recite them—came to be applied to Bible study, memorization, and recitation. The Korean *PumAcii* system—a communal sharing of labor—gave birth to "day offerings," which in turn led to the tradition of self-propagation evidenced by Korean evangelizing. *SungMi*—which traditionally was offered to the house guardian "spirit" (also translated as "ghost")—became the church tradition of *SungMi*, whereby Christians took responsibility for the pastors' support and became self-supporting. It is important to wait patiently for churches that are not self-supporting to be able to stand on their own. Unidirectional support helps neither the giver nor the recipient.

## RESPECTING LOCAL MINISTRY PARTNERS

Green acknowledges that the North Atlantic churches have greater financial resources to share. The consequent economic imbalance between missionaries and local partners must be handled carefully. Most, if not all, missionaries serving in developing countries feel burdened by the fact that they are far wealthier than their local partners. In many cases the financial gap is wide enough to create undesirable tension between them. In 1991 David Barrett predicted that this disparity would continue to grow: "In 1980, the absolutely poor numbered 975 million (22.3% of

1. Myung Soo Park, *Hanguk Gyohoesa-ui Gamdongjeogin iyagi* (Moving story of Korean church history), (Seoul: KookMinIlBo, 2006).

2. Dong Min Jang, *Daehwaro Puleoboneun Hangukgyohoesa 1* (Korean church history opened through dialogue 1), (Seoul: Revival and Reformation, 2009).

the world). By 1991 this has risen to 23.4%. It is now calculated that global warming will speed up this process until by the year A.D. 2050 some 50% of the world will be living in absolute poverty."[3]

When I was a missionary working in Nigeria, a missionary couple with two children received a living allowance at least fifteen times greater than that of local partners. While this amount was low in comparison to the size of the allowance received by pastors working in Korea, most missionaries in the country felt understandable uneasiness. Missionaries need to try very hard to overcome such disparities by imitating the incarnation of our Lord Jesus Christ. I believe that the incarnation of Jesus Christ must be the model for all missionaries to adopt. We need to learn the humility of Jesus Christ and find ways in which both (comparatively) affluent missionaries and poor local partners can work together without feeling economic disparity. SIM Nigeria has a housing policy that encourages missionaries to maintain their houses in a manner that is acceptable to local partners, thereby reducing the potential for disharmony between the two groups. Missionaries are likewise encouraged to keep their standard of living within the bounds of the social norms around them, avoiding, for example, excessive nonessential travel.

Stanley Green hints that the role of Western agencies should be limited to that of invited partners and assistants, citing ActionAid International as an example of how contemporary missionaries might operate. The problem is that missionaries today, wishing to be considerate of locals, are oftentimes too passive and may therefore be regarded as wage earners. Missionaries are no longer going into unreached areas. Out of fear of being regarded as patronizing, they have lost their passion to find new and creative ministries. It is good for missionaries to be humble and to regard local partners as equals. It is not good, however, for them to lose their missional passion and limit their ministries. Whatever ministry God has entrusted to us, it is right for us to do our best to redouble it—this is what a ministry with accountability before the true God should look like!

3. David B. Barrett, "The Status of the Christian World Mission in the 1990s," in *Mission in the Nineteen Nineties*, ed. Gerald Anderson et al. (Grand Rapids: Eerdmans, 1991), p. 72.

# 8

# Accountability in a Local Church's Ministry of World Mission: SaRang Community Church as a Case Study

## Seung Kwan (David) Yoo

THE THEME OF THE 2011 Korean Global Mission Leadership Forum, hosted by OMSC, with its focus on issues and examples of the three-way accountability between mission organization, missionary, and local church, is timely and meaningful. The whole study and discussion is simply to help us all carry out more faithfully the Great Commission of our Lord Jesus Christ (Matt. 28:19–20).

This case study considers the foreign and domestic mission ministries of the SaRang Community Church, located in Seoul, the capital of South Korea. In particular, we look at how the church has handled matters of accountability during the past ten years. After summarizing SaRang's overall ministry and the ministry vision of its World Mission Department, we examine SaRang's mission accountability in three areas: administration, finance, and recruitment.

All Christians today ought to know clearly their identity as God's people who are called to be separate from this world. At the same time, all Christians need to grasp that they are Christ's disciples who are sent into the world. It is critical for each Christian to understand these two aspects of Christian life in order to be assured of his or her newly created status in Jesus Christ, and also to obediently live out his or her faith in this world. Christians must view the place where they are as the very place of their own mission field, as their end of the earth, living a life *there* in obedience to the Lord's Great Commission.

The first Protestant missionaries arrived in Korea in the 1880s, a little over 125 years ago. Not long after, in 1907, the great Pyongyang Revival began.[1] And now, more than ever, the Korean church, including the SaRang Community Church, sees itself as part of the global church, needing to share globally in a greater level of communication and co-operative networking. We believe it is especially critical for the Korean church to establish better communication channels with the Western church and its mission organizations and mission research institutes, all of which can encourage a healthy synergy in our collective commitment to world mission.

It is SaRang's sincere wish that this forum may contribute to the pursuit of integrity in our mission work, ultimately encouraging many churches to deepen their model and experience of missions.

## UNDERSTANDING SARANG COMMUNITY CHURCH

SaRang Community Church, whose senior pastor now is Rev. Dr. Jung-hyun Oh, was founded in Seoul in 1978 with nine members. Even as a newly planted house church, it had three ministerial emphases: laity training, youth evangelism, and "northern region" evangelism (i.e., evangelism in the Communist nations). SaRang also has had three ministry philosophies, expressed in the slogans that it should be a propagating church, a training church, and a healing church.

Under the leadership of SaRang's founding pastor, Rev. John H. Oak, who passed away on September 2, 2010, the seed of discipleship training was sown from the outset. During the past three decades, SaRang has kept intentional disciple-making at the core of its ministry, with a constant emphasis on the value of one soul and the urgency of developing that soul through training. The result has been the growth of a very successful, dynamic, and healthy church.

As of December 2010, SaRang had an average Sunday attendance of 43,500 people: roughly 6,000 children, 4,500 youth and college-age, and 33,000 adults. In addition, SaRang supports 117 smaller and financially dependent churches outside the Seoul metropolitan area, as well as 159

1. The great Pyongyang Revival began on January 14, 1907, in Jangdaehyun Church in Pyongyang. It was started by Western missionaries and was triggered by the public repentance of church leaders. This phenomenon was followed by explosive church growth in the region. The effect of this repentance movement spread widely throughout Korea, and church growth exploded nationally.

missionary families or missionary units (see table 8.1), with a total of 502 persons including children, serving cross-culturally in 54 countries. In all, 87 percent of SaRang's appointed missionaries are non-clergy, lay professionals.

Missionaries of SaRang Community Church (December 2010)

| Families | Missionary Category |
|----------|---------------------|
| 65 | Cooperative: not appointed by SaRang but partially supported by SaRang |
| 22 | Overseas volunteers: appointed by SaRang as agency administrator to experience the mission field before long-term commitment |
| 42 | Appointed: long-term commitment, full-time missionary with mission organization membership, financially supported by SaRang |
| 30 | Appointed professional: long-term commitment with professional tentmaking career, may receive financial support from SaRang |
| 159 | TOTAL |

**Table 8.1.** Breakdown of SaRang Church's missionaries by category

SaRang Community Church believes that, in order for a disciple-making ministry to be fruitful, the leaders of a church must themselves possess a strong faith, a deep passion, and a clear vision of their ministry philosophy. When such elements are lacking in church leadership, it will be very difficult to carry out an effective disciple-making ministry.

SaRang Community Church is famous as a local church that trains laity and raises them up as coworkers in all church ministries. Based on the biblical definition of local church and apostolic vision mentioned in Ephesians 4:11–12, SaRang's theological review of what is needed for the church in the twenty-first century has led to its current emphasis on the "Maniac Theory," which stresses the importance of the pastor's role, and "Ecclesiology," which at SaRang Church focuses on disciple making and lay empowerment for ministry. We believe this emphasis will allow the church to fully concentrate in disciple making on helping each member actually to "become mature, attaining to the whole measure of the fullness of Christ" (Eph. 4:13 NIV).

SaRang Community Church recognizes the value of each soul, seeing each person as a potential lay leader who can be raised up through training. In turn, such a lay leader can become, in effect, a little pastor who cooperates with the clergy. In order to train such lay leaders, SaRang spends thirty-two weeks each year in discipleship and leadership training. As of November 2010, SaRang had 3,000 functioning small groups, called "Upper Rooms," each led by a lay leader who had successfully finished this training.

Overall, SaRang can express its ministry vision in the acronym HEART:

Healing our nation

Equipping disciples

Assisting the global Christian network

Raising up the next generation

Transforming society and culture

The World Mission Department of SaRang Community Church assists the global Christian network through our domestic ministries, as well as through our worldwide network of global ministries.

## VISION AND MINISTRY
## OF THE WORLD MISSION DEPARTMENT

The spiritual slogan of SaRang's World Mission Department is "Sowing seeds of discipleship training, blossoming in world mission." The mission department also firmly believes in what it has called the "missionaryhood of every believer."[2] The department takes its responsibility and ministry goal to be to encourage, disciple, and train SaRang's lay members so they can maximize their discipleship-trained spirituality, along with their professional skills, in mission fields.

---

2. The term grew out of Martin Luther's emphasis on the priesthood of every believer. According to Matthew 28:19–20, the Gospel is not restricted to the twelve apostles, but the entire church inherits the apostolic vision as its mission. This point was notably claimed by Adrianus Saravia, who was a Reformed minister in the Netherlands and later dean of Westminster in London (Alan Neely, "The Teaching of Missions," in *Toward the Twenty-first Century in Christian Mission*, ed. James M. Phillips and Robert T. Coote [Grand Rapids: Eerdmans, 1993], p. 271). The theoretical background of "the missionaryhood of every believer" is mentioned in Seung-Kwan (David) Yoo, "Lay Professional Mission Leadership and the Mission Strategy of the Local Church in the Viewpoint of Every Believer Missionaryhood" (doctoral thesis in Christian missiology, Baekseok Theological Seminary, 2008), pp. 6–17.

The World Mission Department has defined a fourfold vision, the first three points of which we consider in more detail in the subsections below.

- Globalization of discipleship training

- Promotion of lay tentmaking mission

- Practice of holistic mission

- Pursuit of biblically based missions model

In pursuing this fourfold vision, SaRang Community Church has established cooperative partnerships as shown in figure 8.1.

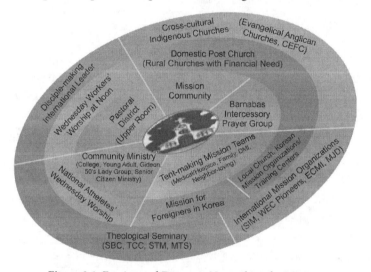

**Figure 8.1.** Foreign and Domestic Networking for Mission

Figure 8.1 represents SaRang Community Church's cooperative network in concentric circles, including foreign and domestic. At the center of the diagram is the church itself, which has pastoral care for its congregations in each district, lay tentmaking mission communities, mission intercessory prayer groups operated by the World Mission Department, its ministry to handicapped persons, its "Forever Ministry" (senior member care), hospice, Gideon ministry (for singles over thirty-three years of age), and more.

The second concentric circle represents SaRang's domestic mission network with regional churches in various provinces, especially with 117 local churches, Korean indigenous mission organizations, foreign workers ministry, Taeneung Olympics Athletes ministry, a Wednesday noon service for professionals, and so forth.

The outermost circle represents SaRang's global networking for world mission, including its work with the evangelical Anglican Church network, international mission organizations (SIM, Interserve, Pioneers, ECMI, MJD, WEC), theological seminaries (SBC in Singapore, TCC in Singapore, STM in Malaysia), as well as numerous international leaders (e.g., Dr. U. Obed and Rev. Edmund Chan) in disciple-making.

## Globalization of Discipleship Training

The first element of the vision of the World Mission Department is to globalize the training of Christian disciples. To this end the church has published the book *Called to Awaken the Laity*, by founding pastor John H. Oak. Originally published in Korean, the book was first translated into English and then, in 2006, into French and later also Spanish, Portuguese, and Estonian. German and Dutch translations are now in progress.

Over the past several years, SaRang has invited leaders of local churches around the world and of international mission organizations to events of cooperative networking.[3] These events include SaRang's Called to Awaken the Laity (CAL) Seminar.[4] Many influential mission leaders from SIM, Pioneers, WEC, and ECMI have come to attend the CAL seminars, which has strengthened the common vision for implementing discipleship training. Through SaRang's vision and efforts, a total of 254 church and mission leaders from twenty-three different countries have attended the CAL seminar since 2005 and are reaping fruitful results after implementing the teaching in their own ministries (see table 8.2).

SaRang has also formed cooperative networking arrangements with numerous Anglican Church leaders from Malaysia, Singapore, Australia, and other parts of the Pacific region, plus South American and African

---

3. In 2008 SaRang participated in leaders' meetings of international mission organizations. One such was in Pattaya, Thailand, January 14–15, at the invitation of John Fletcher, international director of Pioneers, where a lecture was given on SaRang's disciple-making ministry and lay tentmaker missions. SaRang leaders also had an interview with the executive chairman of Lausanne, Doug Birdsall (March 10), and with Johan Lukasse of European Christian Mission International (April 25). Lukasse also attended SaRang's CAL Seminar.

4. From 2005 to 2010, a total of 254 international leaders from twenty-six countries attended SaRang's CAL Seminar.

indigenous church leaders.[5] SaRang is also promoting discipleship training and lay missions through a cooperative network with leaders of the
Chinese diaspora in the Asian evangelical Anglican Church. In order to
strengthen this partnership, SaRang's leaders have been regularly visiting
the churches in Singapore and Malaysia that are implementing discipleship training. They also attended the centennial celebration of the Diocese
of Singapore (November 2009), as well as the diocesan mission conference
in Kuala Lumpur, Malaysia (August 2010).

CAL attendance by country, 2005–10

| No. | Country | No. | Country | No. | Country |
|---|---|---|---|---|---|
| 89 | Malaysia | 4 | Nigeria | 2 | Mauritius |
| 67 | Australia | 4 | United States | 2 | Pakistan |
| 33 | Singapore | 3 | Ghana | 2 | Paraguay |
| 9 | Dominican Rep. | 3 | United Kingdom | 2 | Ukraine |
| 7 | Indonesia | 3 | Zambia | 1 | Argentina |
| 6 | India | 2 | Cambodia | 1 | France |
| 5 | China | 2 | Ethiopia | 1 | Macedonia |
| 4 | Brazil | 2 | Hong Kong | 254 | TOTAL |

Table 8.2. Called to Awaken the Laity Attendance

### Promotion of Lay Tentmaking Mission

In order for SaRang's small-group lay leaders who have completed training
in discipleship and in leadership to participate in world mission, SaRang
offers various mission schools. In particular, these mission schools put
strong emphasis on helping members utilize their spiritual gifts from discipleship training and their professional skills for world mission.

The Lay Tentmaking Mission School includes the Elementary
Training Course (ETC), the Intensive Training Course (ITC), and the
very practical Mission Practice (MP), which is a year-long curriculum.
This school builds competence and the level of commitment of serious-
minded and devout trainees.[6] In order to provide opportunities for

5. On June 21, 2008, SaRang was involved in the After Discipleship Training
Launching Service, held at Orchard City Church; on June 24, 2008, a seminar was held
for introducing SaRang's discipleship training to Archbishop John Chew and his clergy,
of the Diocese of Singapore; and in August 2010 SaRang's disciple-making ministry was
introduced during the Diocesan Mission Conference in the Diocese of West Malaysia
Anglican Church.

6. ETCs and ITCs are offered four times annually. In 2009 a total of 603 members

more substantial training and equipping, short-term mission trips are highly encouraged during vacation seasons.[7] These are one of the "Go" ministries of the World Mission Department; such ministries encourage members of SaRang to commit themselves as future missionaries. The trainees for the Leadership Training Course (LTC) are carefully selected from ITC graduates and are given the opportunity for up to six additional months of education. Also during LTC, SaRang offers training in various languages and cross-cultural adaptation, including SIM's SIMTI English course and Global Awareness Program (GAP) in Canada.

Through these mission training opportunities future missionaries learn the importance of financial management, children's education, communication with the sending church, cross-cultural adaptation, networking with healthy mission organizations, the importance of intercessory prayer for missionaries, and other issues. As of December 2010 a total of 4,333 graduates had completed the Lay Tentmaking Mission training at SaRang Community Church. (See table 8.3.)

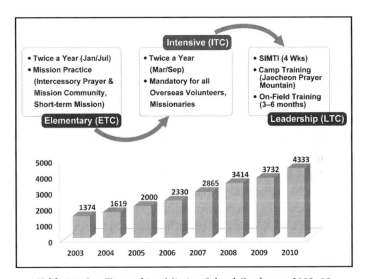

**Table 8.3.** Lay Tentmaking Mission School Graduates, 2003–10

took the ETC, and 121 took the ITC. In addition, 89 members committed themselves to become short-term missionries (i.e., for 1–2 years). Of the 121 graduates of the ITC, 32 (26.4 percent) committed themselves to become long-term missionaries. In 2010 there were 525 graduates of ETC and 76 graduates of ITC. The number of those committing to specific missionary service in 2010 was 48 short-term (out of 76) and 32 long-term (out of 76).

7. A total of 6,800 members have participated in summer short-term mission trips (5,796 to Korea, and 1,004 overseas to twenty countries).

In 2010, a total of 6,800 SaRang members participated in summer short-term mission trips, 5,796 domestic and 1,004 overseas (see table 8.4, also appendix 2). Short-term mission trips are offered each year in order to give church members a *brief* taste of missionary life. SaRang Community Church holds a commissioning service at the beginning of each year's short-term season and a concluding service at the end of each short-term season, to thank and to praise God. Each short-term team is custom-designed according to each mission field's needs and wants. In advance, it prepares ministry tools such as Sunday School camps, street evangelism, taek won do, crafts, cooking, beauty care, music, worship dance, IT service, opera, art, balloons, and so forth. In order to properly equip each member, the World Mission Department offers short-term mission academies to teach such skills to novice members for up to a six-week period prior to departure.

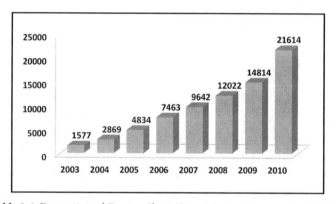

**Table 8.4.** Domestic and Foreign Short-Term Mission Participants, 2003–10

As of December 2010, twelve Lay Tentmaking Mission Communities were operating within the World Mission Department at SaRang Community Church.[8] In addition, four NGOs (OM Korea, His International in Cambodia, FOV in Russia, FOK in Kyrgyzstan), operated and managed by the World Mission Department are utilized as strategic bases for reaching out to sensitive regions that require "creative access."

8. The Lay Tentmaker Mission Communities meet monthly for encouraging church members to participate in mission-related functions by utilizing their professional skills. At SaRang this group includes professors, teachers, artists, IT personnel, people in foreign diplomacy, trade, and the media, the Korean military, short-term mission supporters, protocol volunteers (SAPAiers), the Salight Dance Team, and the Salight Men's Choir.

## Practice of Holistic Mission

In practicing holistic mission, it is very important that lay members have the opportunity to use their professional skills. Especially for providing education, SaRang Community Church has been supporting the Y university in C country which serves as a strategic base.

Also many projects are in progress to promote exchange between Korean and Chinese Christians so as to set a new trend in relations between the two nations.[9] Also, through SaRang's S Cultural Center in Russia, SaRang is mobilizing lay professionals to utilize their professional skills—such as art, music, and entrepreneurship—for mission.[10] Many lay members are in the process of preparing themselves as future lay tentmaking missionaries, not only for Russia but also for Central Asia and North Korea.

In 1998 SaRang Community Church adopted nine unreached people groups (Uzbek, Azeri, Kyrgyz, Khalkha-Mongol, Uyghur, Acehnese, Burmese, Khmer, Cho-sun). Furthermore, SaRang is looking to engage more proactively in holistic missions through NGO networks of the International Operation Charity in Korea, Inc., encompassing OM Korea,[11] S Cultural Center in Russia, Kyrgyzstan, and Hischild International of Cambodia.

For Korea's domestic mission, SaRang has set up a mission network with various local churches throughout Korea, from farming villages to remote islands.[12] In addition, the church has ministries for the Korean Armed Services and ministries to foreign workers in Korea.[13] On every

9. Examples from 2008 include a visit on May 6 to official Chinese church headquarters in Shanghai for a Christian exchange between the two nations; a visit June 16–19 to the Schechwan region damaged by earthquake, with a donation given; and an initial meeting on October 6 for the Korea-China Christianity Exchange, with Rev. Gau Feng plus six official Chinese church leaders.

10. Contacts during 2008 include the opening ceremony for the Solnechny Cultural Center (June 6), a Korean food seminar (July 2–3), a handicap seminar (July 14–18), a vision trip (July 21–27), a wildflower seminar (August 2–9), and a classic guitar seminar (August 2–9).

11. OM Korea, the Korean branch of OM International, has trained and sent 300 missionaries to forty countries. Its missionaries include both short-term and long-term workers; some are engaged in ship ministries with *Doulos* and *Logos Hope*.

12. SaRang strengthens its network with major churches in each province through the members of Barnabas Intercessory Prayer. And SaRang's seniors are organized in various groups that reach out to others.

13. Discipleship training has been introduced into the Korean Army Deputy Officer Training Camp, and there is close networking with numerous foreigner ministry centers and the Christian leadership of the Taeneung Olympic Athletes camp.

third Wednesday evening, SaRang sends preachers and praise teams to serve the Taeneung Athletes' Village Olympic training camp, where they lead worship and prayer meetings for Korea's national athletes. SaRang's Sports Mission Community specializes in ministries involving soccer, ping pong, badminton, and tae kwon do. It follows a Mission Practice curriculum, which each year is developed and improved.[14] On Wednesdays, noon services are conducted for company workers who are on the job in the Gangnam Station area of Seoul, not far from the SaRang center.

SaRang also designates and cooperates closely with "post churches" in the governmental administrative center of each province of Korea for more effective rural evangelism.[15] These post churches often serve as networking vehicles in carrying out SaRang's domestic mission throughout the Korean peninsula. For local churches of each province, SaRang financially supports and sends evangelism teams and short-term mission teams to help out rural ministers who are serving within the eight provinces. As of November 2010, SaRang was supporting 117 local churches throughout all eight provinces.

In its program called Barnabas Intercessory Prayer, the SaRang Community Church has divided the world into ten regions in order to be better focused in its mission intercessory prayer.[16] During these meetings, SaRang members intercede for each prayer request submitted by SaRang's missionaries. The church also publishes monthly prayer guides containing each missionary's prayer requests, for distribution to the church's 3,000 small groups. Through the small-group system the entire church actively intercedes for each and every missionary's prayer requests on a regular basis. Also, on every third Tuesday evening the church has a joint prayer service for world missions, where any SaRang

14. During 2008 the domestic program Mission Practice for Korea included helping in the clean-up of the Tae-an oil spill (January 19–March 8), serving as a choir during SaRang's dawn service (March 29), leading the commissioning service for the summer short-term mission team (July 9), officiating at baptisms at various military bases (7th and 27th Army Divisions, Jin-hae Navy vessel base, Navy east coast fleet HQ), and leading the discipleship training graduation ceremony of the Army Deputy Officer Training Camp (October 26).

15. SaRang's post churches include the Joo-hyang Church in Choonchun, Kangwon Province (Rev. Byung-chul Lee); the Gwangyang Daegwang Church in Junra-nam Province; and the Pal-bok Church of Junra-Book Province (Rev. Kwang-hoon Cho).

16. In 2009 Barnabas Intercessory Prayer had an average attendance of 274 members, with all ten of the world regions being prayed for.

member can participate in intercessory prayer for missionaries. This joint prayer service also allows missionaries to come and give a mission report directly to the SaRang congregation.

## ACCOUNTABILITY IN MISSION

SaRang's World Mission Department operates in four ministry teams: Planning, Domestic, Overseas, and External Cooperation. Each is led by a full-time pastor, and there are five full-time staff members serving these four teams.

### *Administration*

The World Mission Department oversees a broad span of ministries, equivalent to a good-sized independent mission organization. To effectively carry out this large-scale mission ministry requires a high level of professionalism and efficiency in administration. For this reason the department employs a team of experienced full-time pastors and workers, who use a "plan, do, see" approach in all aspects of mission ministry.

The World Mission Department starts each day with prayer and a devotional time together. It then begins its staff meetings, conducted according to the goals of clear communication and cooperation, using a "cross-check" framework. This calls for each member of the team to openly and clearly communicate with the other members in making mutually-agreed-upon decisions, even for matters that do not directly concern the ministry of one's own team. Issues at hand are constantly shared, and feedback is gathered on ways of improving the management of the department.

#### MID-TERM AND LONG-TERM STRATEGIZING

The World Mission Department develops a three-year plan of ministry, as well as an annual plan and budget, all of which are consistent with its fourfold vision, outlined above. The yearly budget is based on each year's specific plans.

In order to carry out its ministry plan and to budget more transparently and effectively, the department holds mission strategy meetings twice a year. Every pastor and staff member of the World Mission Department actively participates to evaluate the past year's ministry and to set the ministry direction of the following year.

Every quarter the World Mission Board meets to make decisions on ministries involving substantial financial expenditure. This sixteen-member board consists of the senior pastor of SaRang Community Church, the four World Mission Department pastors, the overseeing elder, and the ten lay leaders of the Barnabas meetings for intercession.

### Missionary recruitment

During its quarterly meetings, the World Mission Board reviews the qualifications of each missionary candidate. The selection process for new missionaries includes the following steps:

- Individual interview (the "first examination")
- Submission of the application
- Application screening and second interview ("second examination")
- Approval of the candidate as a cross-cultural missionary ("third examination")
- Final confirmation and approval by the World Mission Board
- Sending out

After missionaries have served a four-year term, the status of each as an approved and sent missionary is individually considered for renewal.

During the selection process each missionary, according to the following categories, is required to present a variety of documents, as listed below:

A. Appointed missionary

  1. Application (for each adult, married or single). Refer to appendix 3.

  2. Letter of recommendation from senior pastor or assistant pastor. Refer to appendix 4.

  3. Missionary oath, with applicant's signature. Refer to appendix 5.

  4. Ministry plan. Refer to appendix 6.

  5. Résumé (for each adult).

  6. Confession of faith (for each adult).

7. Letter of petition from the head of the mission organization the applicant has chosen.

8. Proof of acceptance from the applicant's mission organization.

9. Proof of the completion of training from the applicant's mission organization.

10. Proof of education: highest level of education or diploma received.

11. Mission field research report on the applicant's mission field of interest (at least eight typewritten pages).

12. Proof of counseling and personality testing (for each adult).

13. Proof of foreign language proficiency.

14. Korean national ID certificate, physical examination results, family photo, passport copy.

15. Any additional documentation requested by the World Mission Department.

B. Lay tentmaking missionary
   Documents 1–6, 13–14.

C. Overseas volunteer missionary
   (i.e., short-term, for one or two years)
   Documents 1–6, 10, 14.

D. Cooperative and mission organization missionary
   Documents 1–8.

As part of its overall ministry, the World Mission Department of SaRang Community Church offers its Lay Tentmaking Mission School to members interested in overseas missionary service. The church also provides various language programs. The purpose of its Overseas Volunteer program is to motivate members wishing to explore their calling as cross-cultural missionaries through a short-term (of one or two years) missionary commitment.

All SaRang members who wish to become missionaries, whether full-time or short-term, need to become members also of a sound mission organization. This means that each missionary serves in what we may call a relationship of "holy triangle tension" between the receiving body (RB: the mission organization that oversees the cross-cultural mission work), the missionary (M), and the sending church, or sending body (SC/SB: the missionary's home church). See figure 8.2.

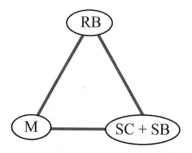

**Figure 8.2.** The "Holy Triangle Tension" Relationship

### MISSIONARY MINISTRY REPORTS

SaRang missionaries are required to submit a ministry report at least once a month, by surface mail or e-mail. The Overseas team compiles them and distributes the information to the ten Barnabas prayer meetings, as well as to the 3,000 "Upper Room" small groups for 24/7 intercessory prayer. Every December the World Mission Department sends out annual Christmas gifts to all missionaries. With this mailing the department includes the "Ministry Report and Future Ministry Plan" form and the "Request Form for Summer Short-Term Mission Teams." By utilizing such a reporting process, the World Mission Department can ascertain each missionary's ministry schedule, prayer requests, plans for upcoming sabbatical leaves, and so forth. (See appendix 7 for "Form for Ministry Report and Future Ministry Plan" and appendix 8 for "Request for Summer Short-Term Mission Team.")

### INTERCESSORY PRAYER FOR MISSION

SaRang Community Church currently has sent out and cooperates with 277 missionaries (159 families) in fifty-four countries. As of November 2010, for each of the ten regions—Korea, Southeast Asia, Middle East/Africa, Europe/Latin America, Y University in C country/North Korea, China, Central Asia, Mongolia/Russia, Japan, and India/Southwest Asia—Barnabas intercessory prayer meetings gather on the second and fourth Sundays of each month. The ten leaders of these regions, who lead these Barnabas prayer meetings, are in close contact with missionaries to receive and relay their urgent prayer requests to SaRang's intercessory prayer personnel. The Barnabas leaders also take summer short-term mission teams to visit their designated region's mission fields to assist and encourage their missionaries.

On the third Tuesday evening of each month, SaRang Community Church holds its joint intercessory prayer meeting for world mission, which is open to every SaRang member who wishes to intercede for the church's missionaries. Also SaRang's 3,000 small groups—the "Upper Rooms"—are strategically connected with SaRang's missionaries for more effective intercessory prayer support. It is very important for each missionary to be connected to SaRang's small groups for prayer support, the fruits of which have been a great blessing. While the World Mission Department mainly provides administrative support to missionaries, each small group can look after a missionary more personally, including praying for the requests of the missionaries' children. Twice a year the World Mission Department publishes a list of the connections between the small groups and the missionaries.

### Finances

The 2010 annual budget for domestic and overseas mission of SaRang's World Mission Department was 4.8 billion won (approx. US$4.4 million), or 7.89 percent of the church's entire annual budget. However, if we include the budgets of other departments involved in short-term mission and similar activities, then the overall mission budget of SaRang is 21.25 percent of the entire annual budget. The World Mission Department's annual budget is set from its previous year's actual monies spent and the coming year's projected expenses, after review by the session Board of Elders and the congregational General Assembly. Refer to appendix 9. Once a week, spending amounts are released from the church's general account into the World Mission Department account, but only after each expenditure item is drafted and signed by each team's staff and pastors. Also, the monies spent by the department are closely examined by periodic audits, with the goal of maximizing financial transparency and wisdom in the use of all funds.

Financial support for missionaries and mission organizations, whether paid out on a monthly basis or in periodic lump sums, is managed reasonably and transparently. The World Mission Department sets personal and family support policy based on analysis of the financial support policies of other churches and mission organizations. It takes into consideration the different regions of the world, including the price indexes of major cities. Please refer to table 8.5 for the regular support figures for SaRang's missionaries. For ministries involving large lump-sum items, each case is approved separately at a meeting of the World Mission Board.

Amount of regular monthly financial support for SaRang's missionaries[a]

| Amount | Type of missionary or mission work |
| --- | --- |
| 800 | Appointed, single |
| 1,000–1,500 | Appointed, married, plus 100/child |
| 500 | Lay tentmaker |
| 400 | Overseas volunteer |
| 300 | Cooperative |
| 300–900 | Mission organization |

[a] All figures in US$. A conversion rate of $1 = ₩1,100 is assumed.

**Table 8.5.** Missionaries' monthly financial support by category

The World Mission Department sends ministry account funds to each missionary's bank account as designated by his or her mission organization. This arrangement allows for more transparent financial dealings. It allows all three parties involved—missionaries, sending churches, and the mission organizations—to know clearly how and when funds are sent and received. The World Mission Department discourages church members from sending personal mission offerings directly to missionaries. Instead, the Barnabas Mission Offering account has been set up to serve as a common channel for all personal missionary support funds received and sent. Through this Barnabas account, gifts from SaRang's 3,000 small groups, as well as other contributions from individuals, can be clearly tracked.

SaRang missionaries receive additional benefits such as medical care support (refer to appendix 10), in addition to the regular personal support shown in the table.[17]

17. Missionary financial benefits include an initial settling-in allowance (less than US$2,000), a support fund for the education of missionary children ($100 per child, with college education support for one child), airfare (round-trip airfare for the entire family at the time of the sabbatical), literature support (subscription to periodicals), medical support (regular physical examination, medical expense support), support for

*Recruitment*

### CULTIVATING FUTURE MISSIONARIES

The local church can serve as a rich human resource for mission work, and especially as a source for mission workers. The World Mission Department puts great emphasis on identifying and recruiting future missionary candidates by challenging SaRang members to participate in short-term mission trips, the Lay Tentmaking Mission School, leadership training, the Overseas Volunteer program, and other opportunities. From the time of preparing for a short-term mission trip, to the trip itself, to submitting a report of the experience, to the thanksgiving service for the short-term missions, SaRang participants become motivated toward mission and naturally come to be obedient in receiving a call as future missionaries. At SaRang, a great many members become missionaries through the experience gained during short-term mission trips.

Providing the opportunity to reside temporarily as a short-term missionary in a mission field is very important in cultivating future missionaries. Through this time of direct experience, future missionary candidates may be led to commit themselves as long-term missionaries. For this reason SaRang sends out missionaries for a one- or two-year term in cross-cultural environments, allowing them to experience the mission field and to examine themselves as to their possible calling as overseas missionaries.

SaRang Community Church has adopted the Overseas Volunteer Service program offered by the Korean International Cooperation Agency (KOICA), a government agency within the Korean Ministry of Foreign Affairs and Trade. Many future missionary prospects are sent during and after college education or after completing their required military service. Through this agency they are sent for one or two years. In order to receive financial support from the church, they must have finished SaRang's Lay Tentmaking Mission School. Year by year, we are seeing the number of long-term missionary commitments increasing because of younger church members successfully completing the Overseas Volunteer Program.

---

lifelong education, and other benefits (e.g., celebration and condolence gifts for the members of the missionary's immediate family).

## COOPERATIVE NETWORKS

SaRang Community Church increases its mission synergy through coop-eration with various local churches, mission organizations, and mission research organizations, both domestic and overseas. As of November 2010, SaRang is contributing to the support of ninety-seven local churches, mission organizations, and mission research organizations.

SaRang Community Church, as a megachurch, has enough resources of its own that it could easily carry out its own mission work. It is com-mitted, however, to guiding its members to become members of healthy mission organizations. SaRang believes that a local church will see more abundant harvests in mission fields when it relies, not only on its own human and financial resources and the intercessory prayer it can provide, but also on the abundant ministry experience and skill in mission strat-egizing of mission organizations and mission research institutes.

## CONCLUSION

Emil Brunner once said, "The church exists by mission as fire exists by burning."[18] Every local church must have a missional ecclesiology, neces-sary for carrying out our Lord's Great Commission by fulfilling our role as salt and light for the world. We can never overemphasize the respon-sibility of the local church to use every possible human and financial resource to this end.

As noted above, the SaRang Community Church was planted with three ministerial visions: laity training, youth evangelism, and "northern region" evangelism. Of these three emphases, two are directly related to mission. In order to effectively carry out these missional responsibilities, the World Mission Department has been implementing a "plan, do, see" strategy since its founding. It has been making a constant effort during the last ten years to carry out its role of mission administration more efficiently and logically. It pursues financial transparency and a realistic annual budget, recruits and prepares future missionary prospects, and seeks to increase the number of its missionary applicants, the number actually sent out, and the level of its care for missionaries.

The explosive growth of the Korean church and its influence worldwide is unlike that of any other church. It has been very successful

---

18. Emil Brunner (1889–1966) was a Swiss Protestant theologian who served as professor of theology at the University of Zürich (1924–53) and at the International Christian University, Tokyo (1953–55). "Emil Brunner," *Columbia Encyclopedia*, 6th ed. (2008), www.encyclopedia.com/doc/1E1-Brunner.html.

in mobilizing financial and human resources for domestic and cross-cultural missions, to the point that it now sends out more missionaries than any other nation except the United States. In addition, the Korean church has developed strong traditions of small-group Bible studies, evangelism, discipleship training, and church music. It has been a major influence in areas of the Two-Thirds World, especially China, as well as Africa and Latin America. Many church denominations and mission agencies have sought to learn about the Korean church's spirituality and theology, and reasons for its explosive numerical growth.

The Korean church clearly has its responsibility and its role to play in the Lord's harvest field in the near future. It must give back the blessings it has received by contributing spiritual assistance to other nations. After Western missionaries introduced the Gospel to Korea 125 years ago and contributed to the 1907 Pyongyang Revival, the Korean church now must join with other nations in forming a united front for world mission.

Strengthening its communication channels through global networking with Western churches, mission organizations, and mission research institutions will enable the Korean church to work more effectively in the Christian world mission. SaRang Community Church sincerely hopes that the Korean Global Mission Leadership Forum at OMSC might serve as the catalyst for such a trend.

## ADDENDUM

In this section, we consider nine comments and/or questions raised by Sherwood Lingenfelter in the various sections of his response (see chap. 9), summarized loosely, followed with answers by David Yoo.

### *Recruitment and Training*

#### COMMENT 1

SaRang's application process for full-time missionaries includes fifteen different steps of documentation, including their formal education and their pre-field experience. However, there was no evidence of how each candidate's emotional and cultural aptitude is evaluated for ministry.

#### ANSWER 1

This is a very good comment. We agree that the process of collecting documents from applicants and interviewing them has limitations in objectively evaluating their emotional and cultural aptitudes. SaRang relies on other sources, however, for verifying an applicant's health in these areas.

1. *Feedback from SaRang Community Church pastors.* The church offers one year of discipleship training, one year of leadership training, plus three to four years of various nurturing and pastoral programs overseen by the pastors. The network of multiple pastors on the staff is in a position to objectively verify the life and character of missionary candidates; these pastoral evaluations are crucial.

2. *Feedback via evaluation from field leaders in the mission fields.* SaRang Community Church receives emotional and psychological information from field missionaries who spend one to two years with SaRang's potential long-term missionary candidates during the Overseas Volunteer Program. Also, during each short-term mission project, the pastors in charge are required to evaluate and submit reports on the character of the team members under their supervision.

3. *Feedback from mission organizations.* SaRang consults with mission organizations that accept SaRang's missionary candidates. During the mission organizations' training process, the emotional stability and character of candidates can be further evaluated. As needed, SaRang and/or the mission organization can further evaluate and provide professional counseling and psychological tests.

Cross-cultural training is handled through various programs, including overseas short-term missions, the Overseas Volunteers Program (one or two years), and field training of the various mission organizations. During these ministries, evaluations by the leaders of mission organizations and various tools of self-evaluation are also gathered by SaRang. Missionary candidates can utilize these opportunities for self-examination, helping them to ascertain whether making a commitment for long-term mission is appropriate for them. During the past seven to eight years, these methods have proven to be very effective for SaRang.

## COMMENT 2

What criteria are used in evaluating the character and quality of the applicants and their preparation?

**ANSWER 2**

SaRang relies on the following means, both inside and outside of the structure of the church itself, for ascertaining the readiness of applicants for missionary service.

1. Within SaRang, applicants must have successfully completed the church's rigorous Discipleship Training and Leadership Training, each one year in length. They also must have served as a small-group leader or in any other church ministries that provide opportunity for careful evaluation by their training pastors and pastoral care pastors, as well as by the senior lay leader group, including elders and senior small-group leadership.

2. Also within SaRang, applicants must have successfully completed the Lay Tentmaking Mission School, comprising the Elementary Training Course (ETC), Mission Practice (MP), and Intensive Training Course (ITC). They must receive a "qualified" recommendation by SaRang's World Mission Department pastors and experienced field missionaries who teach them in ETC and ITC courses.

3. For standards outside of SaRang, applicants must be willing to respect and abide by the rules and selection process of healthy and reliable mission organizations. (Membership in a mission organization is required for all who wish to be sent out from SaRang.)

4. After meeting all the requirements set by SaRang and by its cooperating mission institutions, applicants present their full documentation to a quarterly meeting of SaRang's World Mission Board, where the board members make the final decision regarding the status of each candidate.

**COMMENT 3**

There is no evidence in the report of a set of standards of achievement for ETC/ITC graduates. Does the church periodically make improvements to the curriculum to better prepare missionaries who graduate from these schools? Does SaRang collect data from the mission fields on the performance of their full-time missionaries?

## Answer 3

The main purpose and goal of SaRang Community Church's Professional Mission School is to allow the entire congregation to obey the Lord's Great Commission, to consider where they live and work to be the ends of the earth, and to live out their missional life as Christians, wherever they are.

Only those who have successfully completed the two-year-long Professional Mission School, including ETC, MP, ITC, and LTC, are considered qualified as "going missionaries." All others who financially and spiritually support with intercessory prayers are considered as the "sending missionaries," who may also participate in short-term mission trips.

In looking back over the past ten years, we can say that the Professional Mission School has reaped much fruit and had successful results. Graduates who become missionaries have received very positive and encouraging feedback from many mission organizations.

Trainees who participate in the Professional Mission School submit anonymous evaluation forms at the end of each school term, which helps the World Mission Department to continually make adjustments and improvements to the program curricula. Also, each participating trainee's information and data are kept up to date via the Missionary Administration Program (MAP), developed by SaRang's IT department. The information accumulated in the system is utilized for keeping feedback from the leaders of mission organizations, and also in preparation for the evaluation of the status of each permanent missionary at the time of his or her four-year sabbatical.

## Comment 4

Does SaRang have a process in place by which it evaluates mission organizations to be sure that the issues of missionary success are adequately addressed and managed for the missionaries sent out by the church? Normally, the local church sending out missionaries is not equipped to provide extensive missionary care such as coaching, physical health management, interpersonal relationship issues, and so forth. Thus, local churches usually leave these responsibilities to mission organizations. How is SaRang checking mission organizations for these functions?

## Answer 4

This is an excellent question. I believe that every local church must be concerned with this issue and must attempt to find a solution. Personally,

I have always believed in the "holy triangle tension" relationship, which refers to the healthy and appropriate tension between the missionary-sending local church, the missionaries, and mission organizations.

Thus it is SaRang's policy not to try to overly regulate or exercise influence on mission organizations, which have their own policies of missionary coaching, missionary member care, and resolving interpersonal conflicts among missionaries. In another words, the local church serves only as a pool of competently qualified missionaries that provides human resources to mission organizations, followed by intercessory prayer support, financial support, and sending out of short-term mission teams. Mission organizations must primarily focus their resources and energy on mid- and long-term mission strategies and execution, evaluation of missionaries' performance, coaching, caring for the spiritual and physical well-being of missionaries, care of missionaries' children, and so forth. Finally, missionaries must send their prayer letters to mission organizations and to sending churches, clearly communicating with them using all possible channels of communication. When this type of healthy triangular tension exists, much synergy will result for world mission.

SaRang Community Church makes extensive efforts to discover and develop each missionary candidate's gift, professional skills, ministry vision, mission field (or country) of interest, language, and cross-cultural adaptation capabilities, and then it tries to match them to the most appropriate mission organization. For this purpose, the World Mission Department hosts Mission Organization Exhibitions, where the candidates and officials of mission organizations can meet each other. Through these encounters, candidates may participate in the initial level of training offered by various mission organizations before having to make a final decision. As various ministry issues arise in finance, health, specific mission projects, sabbatical breaks, or MK education, SaRang Community Church attempts to communicate with mission organization headquarters, as well as with mission organization field leaders, in seeking a resolution. At the end of each year, SaRang invites leaders of every mission organization in Korea to host a meeting for more effective communication with SaRang. SaRang continues to look for ways to more efficiently and substantively increase communication with mission organizations.

*Finance and Property*

## COMMENT 5

One possible weakness of the SaRang financial system is the difficulty of tracking expenses by the individual missionary in his or her field of ministry. SaRang has no structures of financial accountability for missionaries who are deployed to other organizations. The mission organization is responsible for auditing field expenses of missionaries, and the church has no way of reviewing or verifying these records. Field audits are not part of the SaRang financial system.

## ANSWER 5

Personally, I cannot deny that this is a weak aspect of the financial policy of the Korean church and the Korean missionary. In this regard the Korean church must learn from the systems of well-experienced Western churches and mission organizations.

As for SaRang, we have attempted to cope with this problem in two ways. First, SaRang established NGOs in four different regions of the world. Second, each missionary must deal individually with his or her own mission organization's financial regulations.

The four NGO organizations are under the umbrella of International Operation Charity in Korea, Inc., a nonprofit NGO establishment officially registered under the Ministry of Foreign Affairs and Trade of the Korean government. Each of the four regional mission bases includes various real estate properties and a mission fund; each is periodically audited and submits financial and ministry reports for transparency and accountability. Once every year, each of the four NGOs' financial reports are closely examined by a CPA and then approved by the board, prior to being officially submitted to the Korean government.

For individual missionaries, SaRang trusts their mission organizations' internal auditing functions and does not enforce individual audits. However, the World Mission Department requests copies of annual financial reports from all its missionaries in order to ascertain each missionary's financial management.

SaRang looks forward to receiving further advice on these issues from various organizations in the future.

*Policies*

## COMMENT 6

SaRang seems to have financial policies that relate to missionaries' support levels and to gifts for missionaries and mission-related workers. However, the system seems to manage only church offerings used for mission expenditure. SaRang must devise additional policies for both domestic and field fund management in order to achieve higher transparency. For example, when it is decided to build a school on a foreign mission field, who oversees the purchase of the real estate property and the hiring of local workers?

## ANSWER 6

I appreciate your excellent comment, and I believe SaRang will have to continue to work on this issue. According to 1 Timothy 6:10, "the love of money is a root of all kinds of evil" (NIV), an observation that is relevant also to every missionary. More than anything, the transparent use of mission funds is absolutely necessary. Accountability systems therefore need to be devised so that no missionary can claim mission funds for their private use or possession.

SaRang Community Church has been trusting and respecting missionaries and their organizations' systems for their mission projects, including purchase of real estate, property renovations, and so forth. However, for certain projects involving large sums of money from mission donations and contributions, missionaries are required to draft and submit a project planning proposal for approval by the World Mission Department. In regard to employment of local workers, SaRang locally delegates all employment matters to NGO organizations and their missionaries under the umbrella of the International Operation Charity in Korea, Inc.

*Assessment of Ministry Effectiveness*

## COMMENT 7

SaRang Community Church follows a "plan, do, see" system, which involves annual planning. But what kind of standards does the World Mission Department use to evaluate its ministry efficiency and progressiveness? Such standards seem to be missing from this paper. Perhaps, through the globalization of discipleship training mentioned by David Yoo, one's gifts can be discovered and developed for appropriate ministry, although the paper does not clearly specify the standards. The numbers of trainees and participants are mentioned and emphasized, but not their efficiency in ministry. Many people may have attended the CAL seminar and returned home, but has there been any assessment of ministry effectiveness? Does the World Mission Department have a clear statement of criteria used to determine when a ministry is "stagnant or ineffective"?

### ANSWER 7

The World Mission Department annually concludes each year of missionary work with a careful evaluation of each task, team, and ministry. Twice a year, the World Mission Department holds retreats to evaluate the past year's ministry and to plan for the following year's ministry, all in line with the "plan, do, see" framework.

In addition, in order to strengthen networking among foreign spiritual leaders who come to SaRang to attend the CAL Seminar, SaRang is constantly strategizing for new ways to follow up on their needs for successful implementation of the disciple-making ministry philosophy. So far, the leaders of the Southeast Asian Anglican Church (in Singapore, Malaysia, and Indonesia), as well as Chinese church officials, have been receiving SaRang's follow-up consulting, and the World Mission Department expects to more closely cooperate with the Disciple-Making Ministries International (DMI) at SaRang.

### COMMENT 8

SaRang Community Church's small-group system seems to be very effective because ministry opportunities are given not only to pastors but also to laity. Also, Barnabas Intercessory Prayer group leaders are serving as board members of the World Mission Board, which also seems to be an excellent arrangement. However, what would be SaRang's standards of evaluation for such intercessory prayer efforts? I am asking this question because, in personal communication, David Yoo noted that some prayer groups are more effective and proactive than others in communicating with and supporting missionaries.

**ANSWER 8**

This is a very important question. So far, we have not had any solid ministry evaluation standards for Barnabas Intercessory Prayer leaders and their group ministries. However, the World Mission Department pastors attend each Barnabas group session and observe the entire scope of ministry. Each meeting comes under the pastors' close scrutiny. Also, the World Mission Department hosts an annual departmental retreat for all the mission-affiliated personnel and members, which gives another opportunity for the World Mission Department to verify each group's integrity and direction of ministry. As the Barbanas ministry is continually growing in size, it would be commendable for us to adopt objective evaluating measures for ascertaining the effectiveness of the intercessory prayer gatherings for missionaries.

*Missionary Retention*

**COMMENT 9**

The matter of missionary attrition is one of major issues that faces world mission nowadays. Especially in Islamic regions, where it is costly to train, send, and maintain missionaries, missionary retention has greatly suffered in recent years. And this is not simply due to a lack of financial support for missionaries. Many missionaries return home for what are said to be reasons of physical illness, but in reality, most suffer from emotional, interpersonal, and psychological imbalance in their mission fields. Korean churches seem to be quite good at fostering a global vision and in sending out their missionaries with manageable tasks to accomplish, but proper personal care that goes beyond those measures has been quite ineffective. Even megachurches in Korea are lacking in this aspect, and we simply have not done the necessary research in order to understand the problem. SaRang's report seems to be missing this aspect of the overall missional effort.

**ANSWER 9**

I agree with Lingenfelter's opinion. As he mentions, many Korean missionaries have left their ministries and returned home prematurely. Several years ago a mission report, *Too Valuable to Lose: Exploring the*

*Causes and Cures of Missionary Attrition*, was published.[19] The biggest reason for Korean missionaries quitting their mission work is tension in relationships on the mission field. As Lingenfelter points out, most Korean missionaries have left their fields because of emotional, psychological, and interpersonal frictions.

Even among SaRang's missionaries, quite a few have become "burned out" in such ways, especially in Central Asia and the Middle East. The number seems to continually be on the rise. When the cause of burn out is due to unstable conditions, the church has at times been able to intervene and assist the mission in relocating missionaries to a ministry in a more stable country. Such cases serve as a good example of how the mission organization and the local church can cooperate in greatly reducing potential missionary attrition.

Just as healthy church members make up healthy churches, so healthy missionaries make up a healthy mission. For this reason, SaRang Community Church has been providing substantial medical benefits, including a physical exam during sabbatical breaks at reputable Korean hospitals and service by well-regarded dental groups. The World Mission Department has worked out special deals with these fine establishments for better medical, dental, and psychological coverage.

Recently, more missionaries, especially the older ones, have become more vulnerable to cancers, and the World Mission Department is actively looking into proper insurance coverage. Especially in dealing with these kinds of issues, we need close cooperation between mission organizations and local churches.

In conclusion, I would like to express my deepest gratitude to Sherwood Lingenfelter for his very thorough analysis and response to SaRang Community Church's missional accountability report.

---

19. William D. Taylor, ed., *Too Valuable to Lose: Exploring the Causes and Cures of Missionary Attrition* (Singapore: WEF Missions Commission, 1997).

# Appendix 1

## SARANG COMMUNITY CHURCH MISSIONARIES
## (AS OF FEBRUARY 2011)

1. By missionary category

| Missionary Category | Families | Individuals |
|---|---|---|
| Appointed: Short/long-term | 42 | 68 |
| Appointed: professional | 29 | 55 |
| Cooperative: family | 66 | 129 |
| Cooperative: organization | 5 | 8 |
| Overseas volunteers | 16 | 17 |
| **TOTAL** | **158** | **277** |

2. By region

| | Missionary category | | | | | | | |
|---|---|---|---|---|---|---|---|---|
| | Appointed | | Cooperative | | Overseas | Total | |
| Region | Short/Long-Term | Professional | Family | Organization | Volunteers | No. | % |
| Middle East/Africa | 7 | 3 | 14 | 0 | 5 | 29 | 18 |
| Europe/Americas | 4 | 5 | 10 | 0 | 2 | 21 | 13 |
| China | 6 | 6 | 6 | 0 | 1 | 19 | 12 |
| Central Asia | 11 | 1 | 5 | 0 | 0 | 17 | 11 |
| India/SE Asia | 4 | 2 | 5 | 0 | 3 | 14 | 9 |
| Mongolia/Russia | 3 | 4 | 3 | 0 | 4 | 14 | 9 |
| SE Asia/Indochina | 2 | 1 | 10 | 0 | 0 | 13 | 8 |
| Y Univ. | 2 | 6 | 5 | 0 | 0 | 13 | 8 |
| Japan | 1 | 0 | 8 | 0 | 1 | 10 | 6 |
| Korea | 2 | 1 | 0 | 5 | 0 | 8 | 5 |
| **TOTAL** | **42** | **29** | **66** | **5** | **16** | **158** | **99** |

*[Appendix 1 continued]*

3. By mission organization

| Mission Organization | Missionary category: Appointed Short/Long-Term | Professional | Cooperative Family | Organization | Overseas Volunteers | Total |
|---|---|---|---|---|---|---|
| YUST | 2 | 6 | 5 | 0 | 0 | 13 |
| WEC | 12 | 1 | 2 | 0 | 1 | 16 |
| OM | 5 | 0 | 6 | 0 | 1 | 12 |
| Interserve | 5 | 4 | 5 | 0 | 0 | 14 |
| GMP | 4 | 3 | 5 | 0 | 1 | 13 |
| Denomination | 1 | 0 | 11 | 0 | 0 | 12 |
| GBT | 3 | 0 | 4 | 0 | 1 | 8 |
| HOPE | 1 | 1 | 2 | 0 | 1 | 5 |
| SIM | 1 | 0 | 1 | 0 | 1 | 3 |
| OMF | 0 | 0 | 3 | 1 | 0 | 4 |
| GP | 0 | 0 | 2 | 0 | 0 | 2 |
| FMnC | 0 | 0 | 3 | 0 | 0 | 3 |
| CCC | 1 | 0 | 2 | 0 | 0 | 3 |
| YWAM | 1 | 0 | 1 | 0 | 0 | 2 |
| KOICA | 0 | 0 | 0 | 0 | 3 | 3 |
| PIONEERS | 1 | 0 | 0 | 0 | 0 | 1 |
| ECMI | 0 | 0 | 1 | 0 | 0 | 1 |
| Others | 5 | 1 | 8 | 4 | 5 | 23 |
| Independent | 0 | 0 | 4 | 0 | 2 | 6 |
| Tentmaker | 0 | 13 | 1 | 0 | 0 | 14 |
| **TOTAL** | **42** | **29** | **66** | **5** | **16** | **158** |

## *Appendix 2*

## SARANG COMMUNITY CHURCH SHORT-TERM MISSION
## TEAM PARTICIPANTS
## (DOMESTIC AND OVERSEAS)

1. By overall totals

| Item | 2000 | 2001 | 2002 | 2003 | 2004 | 2005 | 2006 | 2007 | 2008 | 2009 | 2010 | TOTAL |
|---|---|---|---|---|---|---|---|---|---|---|---|---|
| No. of countries | 13 | 12 | 9 | 11 | 17 | 19 | 19 | 19 | 24 | 20 | 31 | 194 |
| No. of teams | 17 | 18 | 14 | 12 | 42 | 44 | 61 | 51 | 53 | 61 | 61 | 434 |
| Participants | 203 | 354 | 313 | 150 | 729 | 1,058 | 1,004 | 875 | 951 | 1,087 | 1,004 | 7,728 |

2. By department

| Department | 2000 | 2001 | 2002 | 2003 | 2004 | 2005 | 2006 | 2007 | 2008 | 2009 | 2010 | TOTAL |
|---|---|---|---|---|---|---|---|---|---|---|---|---|
| Youth | 0 | 0 | 0 | 0 | 40 | 85 | 82 | 0 | 0 | 93 | 113 | 413 |
| College | 66 | 141 | 117 | 52 | 171 | 209 | 185 | 258 | 235 | 203 | 184 | 1,821 |
| Young Adult | 30 | 50 | 128 | 87 | 186 | 216 | 272 | 197 | 223 | 252 | 221 | 1,862 |
| Gideon | 0 | 0 | 0 | 0 | 32 | 32 | 45 | 38 | 72 | 60 | 74 | 353 |
| Adult | 0 | 16 | 24 | 0 | 26 | 50 | 57 | 15 | 70 | 35 | 64 | 357 |
| Medical Missions | 0 | 50 | 42 | 0 | 76 | 83 | 70 | 113 | 130 | 151 | 156 | 871 |
| Foreigners Ministry | 0 | 0 | 0 | 0 | 32 | 50 | 77 | 108 | 86 | 65 | 32 | 450 |
| World Miss. Dept. | 0 | 18 | 2 | 11 | 84 | 68 | 96 | 129 | 124 | 179 | 105 | 816 |
| Misc. (Joint) | 107 | 79 | 0 | 0 | 82 | 265 | 120 | 17 | 11 | 49 | 55 | 785 |
| TOTAL | 203 | 354 | 313 | 150 | 729 | 1,058 | 1,004 | 875 | 951 | 1,087 | 1,004 | 7,728 |

**Note:** Table 3, Participants by region, is located on the following page.

4. By ministries

| Ministry | 2000 | 2001 | 2002 | 2003 | 2004 | 2005 | 2006 | 2007 | 2008 | 2009 | 2010 | TOTAL |
|---|---|---|---|---|---|---|---|---|---|---|---|---|
| Street evangelism | 3 | 4 | 1 | - | 4 | 8 | 8 | 6 | 10 | 4 | 3 | 51 |
| Children | 0 | 1 | 1 | - | 3 | 9 | 9 | 8 | 10 | 9 | 10 | 60 |
| Culture/sports | 3 | 4 | 1 | - | 2 | 9 | 5 | 3 | 11 | 9 | 6 | 53 |
| Intercessory prayer | 0 | 0 | 0 | - | 1 | 2 | 2 | 1 | 3 | 5 | 2 | 16 |
| Campus | 0 | 2 | 2 | - | 4 | 6 | 11 | 8 | 8 | 5 | 6 | 52 |
| Locals care | 2 | 3 | 2 | - | 5 | 5 | 11 | 8 | 5 | 11 | 5 | 57 |
| Medical care | 1 | 1 | 2 | - | 4 | 4 | 4 | 6 | 6 | 7 | 4 | 39 |
| Survey trip | 7 | 3 | 1 | - | 4 | 4 | 6 | 7 | - | 5 | 9 | 46 |
| Other | 1 | 5 | 5 | - | 15 | 9 | 9 | 13 | 11 | 10 | 4 | 82 |
| TOTAL | 17 | 23 | 15 | - | 42 | 56 | 65 | 60 | 64 | 65 | 49 | 456 |

*Note:* Figures showing the various ministries for 2003 were not available for the purposes of this table.

*[Appendix 2 continued]*

3.  Participants by region, showing number of *teams* (before the hyphen) and number of participants (after the hyphen)

| Region | 2000 | 2001 | 2002 | 2003 | 2004 | 2005 | 2006 | 2007 | 2008 | 2009 | 2010 | TOTAL |
|---|---|---|---|---|---|---|---|---|---|---|---|---|
| Mid. East/Africa | 0 | 0 | 1-23 | 1-2 | 3-35 | 2-42 | 3-21 | 0 | 4-45 | 3-31 | 3-44 | 20-243 |
| Europe/Americas | 0 | 0 | 0 | 1-7 | 2-28 | 0 | 0 | 2-36 | 5-60 | 4-83 | 3-72 | 17-286 |
| NE Asia | 3-40 | 5-130 | 2-40 | 1-2 | 6-100 | 10-153 | 15-258 | 13-255 | 8-128 | 14-223 | 15-190 | 92-1,519 |
| SE Asia/Indo. | 7-101 | 5-129 | 2-66 | 1-6 | 9-234 | 7-215 | 11-192 | 6-107 | 10-155 | 7-134 | 15-300 | 80-1,639 |
| Mong./Russia | 2-14 | 3-28 | 1-65 | 0 | 5-139 | 9-332 | 6-103 | 7-122 | 7-170 | 9-197 | 4-51 | 53-1,221 |
| Central Asia | 3-25 | 3-26 | 5-61 | 4-51 | 8-70 | 4-51 | 7-81 | 6-96 | 4-62 | 5-49 | 2-14 | 51-586 |
| Japan | 1-13 | 1-7 | 1-11 | 1-20 | 3-50 | 4-101 | 8-165 | 6-100 | 7-154 | 11-231 | 11-209 | 53-1,061 |
| India/SW Asia | 1-10 | 2-34 | 2-47 | 3-62 | 6-73 | 8-164 | 11-184 | 11-159 | 8-177 | 8-139 | 7-124 | 67-1,173 |
| TOTAL TEAMS | *17* | *18* | *14* | *12* | *42* | *44* | *61* | *51* | *53* | *61* | *60* | *433* |
| TOTAL MEMBERS | **203** | **354** | **313** | **150** | **729** | **1,058** | **1,004** | **875** | **951** | **1,087** | **1,004** | **7,728** |

# Appendix 3

## SARANG COMMUNITY CHURCH MISSIONARY
## APPLICATION FORM

1. Personal

| Last Name: | First Name: | □ Male <br> □ Female | □ Married □ Single |
|---|---|---|---|
| DOB: | | Korean National ID #: | |
| English Name: | Passport #: | Expiration Date: | |
| Address 1. <br> 2. <br> 3. | | Telephone 1. <br> 2. <br> 3. | |
| E-mail: | | Homepage: http:// | |
| Appointed | □ Long-term | □ Short-term | □ Lay tentmaker |
| Other | □ Overseas Volunteer | □ Cooperative | □ Mission Organization |
| Last Name: | First Name: | □ Male <br> □ Female | □ Married □ Single |
| DOB: | | Korean National ID #: | |
| English Name: | Passport #: | Expiration Date: | |
| Address 1. <br> 2. <br> 3. | | Telephone 1. <br> 2. <br> 3. | |
| E-mail: | | Homepage: http:// | |

2. Family Members

| Name | DOB | Relationship | Occupation | Church Attended | Position |
|---|---|---|---|---|---|
| 1. | | | | | |
| 2. | | | | | |
| 3. | | | | | |
| 4. | | | | | |
| 5. | | | | | |
| 6. | | | | | |
| Address of Parents or Supporters: | | | | | |
| Telephone: <br> Emergency Contact Information: | | | | | |

## *[Appendix 3 continued]*

7. Missionary supporters _____

| Name: | Telephone<br>Home:<br>Mobile: | E-mail: |
|---|---|---|
| Address: | | |

| Name: | Telephone<br>Home:<br>Mobile: | E-mail: |
|---|---|---|
| Address: | | |

8. Spirituality and personality _____

| How long do you pray daily? | How many times have you read through the entire Bible? |
|---|---|
| What are your strengths? | What are your weaknesses? |

Please rate your own personality

| | Excellent | Higher than avg. | Avg. | Lower than avg. | Low |
|---|---|---|---|---|---|
| 1) Heart for serving | 5 | 4 | 3 | 2 | 1 |
| 2) Getting along with others | 5 | 4 | 3 | 2 | 1 |
| 3) Individual tasking ability | 5 | 4 | 3 | 2 | 1 |
| 4) Creativity | 5 | 4 | 3 | 2 | 1 |
| 5) Responsibility | 5 | 4 | 3 | 2 | 1 |
| 6) Communication skills | 5 | 4 | 3 | 2 | 1 |
| 7) Ability in cross-cultural<br>adapting (food) | 5 | 4 | 3 | 2 | 1 |
| 8) Mental stability | 5 | 4 | 3 | 2 | 1 |

I hereby pledge that all the above information given is true to the best of my knowledge.
Signature:

Date : _____

           Month       Date       Year

## *[Appendix 3 continued]*

7. Missionary supporters _____

| Name: | Telephone<br>Home:<br>Mobile: | E-mail: |
|---|---|---|
| Address: | | |

| Name: | Telephone<br>Home:<br>Mobile: | E-mail: |
|---|---|---|
| Address: | | |

8. Spirituality and personality _____

| How long do you pray daily? | How many times have you read through the entire Bible? |
|---|---|
| What are your strengths? | What are your weaknesses? |

Please rate your own personality

| | Excellent | Higher than avg. | Avg. | Lower than avg. | Low |
|---|---|---|---|---|---|
| 1) Heart for serving | 5 | 4 | 3 | 2 | 1 |
| 2) Getting along with others | 5 | 4 | 3 | 2 | 1 |
| 3) Individual tasking ability | 5 | 4 | 3 | 2 | 1 |
| 4) Creativity | 5 | 4 | 3 | 2 | 1 |
| 5) Responsibility | 5 | 4 | 3 | 2 | 1 |
| 6) Communication skills | 5 | 4 | 3 | 2 | 1 |
| 7) Ability in cross-cultural adapting (food) | 5 | 4 | 3 | 2 | 1 |
| 8) Mental stability | 5 | 4 | 3 | 2 | 1 |

I hereby pledge that all the above information given is true to the best of my knowledge.
Signature:

Date : _____
          Month       Date       Year

## *Appendix 4*

## LETTER OF RECOMMENDATION

APPLICANT

Name _____

Address _____

Telephone _____ E-mail _____

RECOMMENDER

Name _____ Telephone _____

Address _____

Position:    ☐ Sen. Pastor      ☐ Asst. Pastor (_____Ministry)
            ☐ Mission Organization Leader      ☐ Elder        ☐ Other

How long have you known the applicant?_____

▸ Please evaluate the applicant:

| | Excellent | Above average | Average | Below average | Lacks | Do not know |
|---|---|---|---|---|---|---|
| Mental stability | 5 | 4 | 3 | 2 | 1 | 0 |
| Competency | 5 | 4 | 3 | 2 | 1 | 0 |
| Capacity for accepting criticism | 5 | 4 | 3 | 2 | 1 | 0 |
| Intellectual ability | 5 | 4 | 3 | 2 | 1 | 0 |
| Communication skill | 5 | 4 | 3 | 2 | 1 | 0 |
| Commitment in church ministry | 5 | 4 | 3 | 2 | 1 | 0 |
| Financial responsibility | 5 | 4 | 3 | 2 | 1 | 0 |
| Leadership | 5 | 4 | 3 | 2 | 1 | 0 |
| Cooperating ability | 5 | 4 | 3 | 2 | 1 | 0 |
| Flexibility | 5 | 4 | 3 | 2 | 1 | 0 |

▸ Please answer below in as much detail as possible:

1. How much do you think the applicant has prepared himself/herself for emotional readiness in a cross-cultural environment?

_____

_____

_____

_____

*[Appendix 4 continued]*

2. How much do you think the applicant has prepared himself/herself for academic readiness in a cross-cultural environment?

_____
_____
_____
_____

3. How much do you think the applicant has prepared himself/herself for professional readiness in a cross-cultural environment?

_____
_____
_____
_____

4. What talents do you think God has given the applicant?

_____
_____
_____
_____

5. What would be the applicant's weakest point?

_____
_____
_____

6. Can you tell us what else we need to know about the applicant?

_____
_____
_____

7. What would be your overall recommendation regarding the applicant being considered as a cross-cultural missionary?

☐ I strongly recommend   ☐ I partially recommend   ☐ I do not recommend

Month _____ Day _____ Year _____

Signature _____

Please mail this recommendation letter to:

The World Mission Department
SaRang Community Church
Han-il You&I Building #208
1303-10 Seocho-dong, Seocho-gu
Seoul, Korea 137 - 074

*Appendix 5*

## MISSIONARY'S OATH

Name (English): _____ (_____)

Korea National ID#: _____

Sending Church: _____ (_____)

Field (Country/City): _____ (_____/_____)

I, as _____ of SaRang Community Church, solemnly pledge to pursue Jesus' incarnational and holistic mission according to the mission policy of the World Mission Department. In case of failing to fulfill my duties as missionary as mentioned below, I will gladly accept the ruling of the World Mission Department Board's decision on the termination of my status as a missionary.

- Term Expiration:
     Appointed (long-term), 4 years
     Appointed (short-term/lay tentmaking), 2 years
     Cooperative, 2 years
- Failure to fulfill responsibilities as a cooperative missionary, including regular mission report, financial support report, sending prayer requests, etc.
- Unacceptable change in ministry without proper notification, including departure from mission field, discontinued membership from mission organization, marriage, studying abroad, etc.
- Unacceptable because of failure in personal ethics, character, sincerity in ministry, etc.

Month _____ Day _____ Year _____

Signature _____

Return signed form to:
The World Mission Department
SaRang Community Church

# Appendix 6

## MINISTRY PLAN

| | |
|---|---|
| Region | Country:                    City: |
| Period of ministry | |
| People ministered to | |
| Purpose of ministry | |
| Goal of ministry | |
| Content of ministry | |
| Detailed plan | |
| Cooperating partner (organization) | |

## *Appendix 7*

## **MINISTRY REPORT AND FUTURE MINISTRY PLAN**

### *(Appointed, Cooperative, Lay Tentmaking, Overseas Volunteer)*

Date: _____

| Name | | Country | | City | |
|---|---|---|---|---|---|
| Contact info. | Address | | | | |
| | E-mail | | | | |
| | TEL | | FAX | | |
| Ministry report | | | | | |
| Future ministry plan | | | | | |
| Ministry cooperation | | | | | |
| Prayer requests | | | | | |
| Future plan for sabbaticaland study abroad | | | | | |
| Other | Struggles and suggestions (other than for financial support) | | | | |
| | Any change taking place either personally or in your family? | | | | |

# Appendix 8

## REQUEST FOR SUMMER SHORT-TERM MISSION TEAM

| | |
|---|---|
| 1. Ideal time of visit | Month   Day   Year 201 , (   total days) |
| 2. Ideal group size and gender make-up | How many?   Age group:<br>Gender ratio (male/female): (   /   ) |
| 3. Ministry programs | |
| 4. Accommodation/meals | |
| 5. Precautionary measures needed at immigration | |
| 6. Other | |

\* To better serve your needs in the future, please fill in the bottom parts:

| | |
|---|---|
| 1. What are the benefits of having a short-term team visit your ministry field? | |
| 2. Precautionary measures a short-term team should take during a visit to your ministry field? | |
| 3. How should your short-term team prepare in Korea before its arrival to your ministry field? | |

Submission deadline by __/__/201_
(If not submitted by the above date, the World Mission Department will not consider sending a short-term mission team.)

Submission by e-mail to hypark@sarang.org or haruae26@sarang.org
or by fax at +82-(0)2-3489-1327
or by mail to the address provided below:
The World Mission Department
SaRang Community Church
Han-il You&I Building #208
1303-10 Seocho-dong, Seocho-gu
Seoul, Korea 137 - 074

*Appendix 9*

## 2011 ANNUAL BUDGET ORGANIZATION

We present on the following pages the line-item breakdown of the SaRang 2011 annual budget. It is divided into 12 activities (numbered with whole numbers); the activities are divided into categories (decimal numbers), which in turn are divided into subcategories (unnumbered). For each subcategory, figures are entered in the following eight columns:

| 2010 Budget | | 2010 | 2011 Budget | | Comment | | |
|---|---|---|---|---|---|---|---|
| Total | 2010 Budget | Actual (Jan–Sep) | Total | 2011 Budget | % Dec. | % Inc. | Reason |

The first two show the total spent and the amount budgeted for 2010. The third column shows the money spent between January and September 2010. The fourth, fifth, and sixth columns show the amount spent and the amount budgeted in 2011, and the percentage of decrease (if any). The seventh and eighth columns show, where appropriate, the percentage of increase, followed by the reason for the change.

## [Appendix 9 continued]

| Activity | Category | Sub-Category | 2010 Budget | | 2010 Actual (Jan~Sep.) | 2011 Budget | | Comment | | Reason |
|---|---|---|---|---|---|---|---|---|---|---|
| | | | Total | 2010 Budget | | Total | 2011 Budget | % Dec. | % Inc. | |
| 1.Missionary and Mission Organization Support (Regular Periodic Support) | 01.01 Missionary Periodic Support | Existing Support | | | | | | | | |
| | | New Missionary — Appointed | | | | | | | | |
| | | Lay Prof. | | | | | | | | |
| | | Overs. Vol. | | | | | | | | |
| | | Cooperative Organization | | | | | | | | |
| | | Ind. Leader | | | | | | | | |
| | 01.02 Overseas Org. | Existing | | | | | | | | |
| | | New | | | | | | | | |
| | 01.03 Domestic Org. | Existing | | | | | | | | |
| | | New | | | | | | | | |
| | 01.04 Domestic Org. Special Support | Korean Church Volunteers | | | | | | | | |
| | 01.05 Overseas Org. Special Support | SEED International | | | | | | | | |
| | Total | | | | | | | | | |
| 2.Missionary Care and Special Support Fund | 02.01 Missionary Airfare/Settling | Appointed | | | | | | | | |
| | | Lay Prof. | | | | | | | | |
| | | Overs. Vol. | | | | | | | | |
| | | On Sabbatical | | | | | | | | |
| | | Airfare Support (Celeb/Condol & Special) | | | | | | | | |
| | | Settling Fee Support | | | | | | | | |

*[Appendix 9 continued]*

| | | |
|---|---|---|
| **2. Missionary Care and Special Support Fund** | 02.02 Missionary Education & Welfare | Missionary & MK Educ. |
| | | MK Retreats |
| | | Missionary Recharging |
| | | Medical Cost Support (Exams & Treatment) |
| | | Mission Home Maintenance |
| | | Counseling |
| | 02.03 Miscellaneous Special Support | Encouragement |
| | | Equipment Support Request |
| | | Christmas Presents for Missionaries |
| | | Magazine Subscription |
| | | Sermon Tapes Support |
| | | Mission Bulletin Board Maintenance |
| | Total | |
| **3. Mission Project Support** | 03.01 Special Project Support | Solnechny Cultural Center Support |
| | | Bible Translation & Literature Distribution(NLL, DT Material) |
| | | Special Mission Project Support |
| | | FOK Additional Support |
| | | Solnechny Residence Construction |
| | Total | |
| **4. Mission-related Network Support** | 04.01 Discipleship Training Globalization | CAL Protocol for Participants from Overseas |
| | | Lodging |
| | | CityTour/HomeStay |
| | | CAL Participant Airfare Support |

*[Appendix 9 continued]*

| | | | |
|---|---|---|---|
| 4. Mission-related Network Support | 04.02 International Mission Leader Network | Protocol and Ministry Support | |
| | | Gifts for International Leaders | |
| | 04.03 Korea-China Christian Exchange Network Support | Korea-China Christian Exchange Network Support | |
| | 04.04 YUST Support | Graduation | |
| | | Appointing/Soccer Team/Faculty Support Encouragement | |
| | | PAUA conference support | |
| | 04.05 Overseas Mission Conference/Event Support | MJD retreat | Conference support |
| | | OMSC Forum | Conference support |
| | | Transform World | Conference support |
| | | Diaspora | Conference support |
| | | KIMNET | Conference support |
| | | Chinese Diaspora | Conference support |
| | | PGM | Conference support |
| | | Ephesus Joint Prayer Conf. | Conference support |

*[Appendix 9 continued]*

| Category | Item | Details |
|---|---|---|
| 4. Mission-related Network Support | 04.06 Domestic Mission Conf. | NCOWE<br>Ephesus Joint Prayer Conf.<br>Int'l Islam Forum<br>GEMS in Korea<br>Mission Organization & Local Church Network |
| | 04.07 Northeast Asia Mission Strategy Conference | Event and Conference support |
| | 04.08 Visiting Missionaries | Visits to SaRang's Missionaries<br>Regional Retreats for SaRang Missionaries |
| | 04.09 Mission Strategy Meeting & Mission Seminars | Mission Community Seminar |
| | Total | |
| 5. Short-term mission support | 05.01 Overseas Short-terms support | Winter<br>60 teams during summer(Salight Team, Family Mission Team, Sunday School, NHM, Overseas Evangelism) |
| | 05.02 Domestic Short-terms support | Domestic Short-term Teams (Farming Villages, Remote Islands)<br>Domestic Evangelism |
| | Total | |
| | 06.01 Mission School | Twice a Year |

*[Appendix 9 continued]*

| | | | | | | | | | | |
|---|---|---|---|---|---|---|---|---|---|---|
| 6. Mission Training | 06.02 Mission Education Cost | Various mission training program support (Mission Korea, GPTI, DTS, OM, Canaan Farmer's School, LTC, ITC, Homecoming Day) | | | | | | | | |
| | Total | | | | | | | | | |
| 7. Mission gathering | 07.01 World Mission Department Meetings | Meeting Expenditure | | | | | | | | |
| | | Barnabas Intercessory Team support(twice per year) | | | | | | | | |
| | | WMD Joint Retreat(400 attendance) | | | | | | | | |
| | | The World Mission Board Meeting (Quarterly) | | | | | | | | |
| | | Joint Prayer Service for World Mission | | | | | | | | |
| | | Retreat for Mission Leadership | | | | | | | | |
| | | World Mission Department work shop | | | | | | | | |
| | Total | | | | | | | | | |
| 8. Domestic local Church support | 8.01 Domestic Cooperating Church Support | Existing Support | | | | | | | | |
| | | New Support | | | | | | | | |
| | | Pastor Seminar Support | | | | | | | | |
| | 08.02 Domestic cooperating church special support | Ministry content support (sermon tapes, books) | | | | | | | | |
| | | Christmas gifts for domestic pastors | | | | | | | | |
| | | Domestic Mission Network (Post churches in each province) | | | | | | | | |
| | | Struggling church pastors' retreat | | | | | | | | |
| | | Sanctuary remodeling and automobile support | | | | | | | | |
| | Total | | | | | | | | | |

*[Appendix 9 continued]*

| | | |
|---|---|---|
| 9. Military Mission Support | 09.01 Korea Military Service | Baptism Ceremony/Service |
| | 09.02 Military Mission Network | Military mission non-regular support |
| | | Military church construction and infrastructure support |
| | | Military base QT seminar & QT material support |
| | | Discipleship Training and CAL Seminar support |
| | | Military chaplaincy support |
| | | Military outreaching event support |
| | Total | |
| 10. Foreign Workers Ministry | 10.01 Foreign workers/Int'l students Ministry | Foreign students support |
| | 10.02 Multi-cultural Home Ministry | Multi-cultural family ministry & event support |
| | Total | |
| 11. Tent-making Mission | 11.01 Tent-making Mission | Mission Communities by Professions |
| | | Meetings support |
| | | Mission Community event support (twice per year) |
| | | Mission Community education & retreat |
| | | Culture Mission Teams |
| | | Salight Dance |
| | | Salight Men's Choir |

[Appendix 9 continued]

| | | | | | | | | |
|---|---|---|---|---|---|---|---|---|
| **11. Tent-making Mission** | 11.01 Tent-making Mission | Wednesday Noon Service for Workers | | | | | | |
| | | EBM Open Forum | | | | | | |
| | | Taerueng Olympic Athlete's Wed. Service support | | | | | | |
| | | Special Ministry support | | | | | | |
| | 11.02 Mission DVD Production | Mission Ministry DVDs and Promotion Material Production | | | | | | |
| | Total | | | | | | | |
| **12. Operating Cost** | 12.01 Operating Cost | | | | | | | |
| | 12.02 Reserve Fund | | | | | | | |
| | Total | | | | | | | |
| | Grand Total | | | | | | | |

*Appendix 10*

## POLICY ON MEDICAL CARE SUPPORT

The medical care policy of the World Mission Department for appointed missionaries (including during the sabbatical period) who are returning and receiving medical examinations and treatment at medical facilities in cooperative contract with SaRang Com munity Church (including Yonsei Medical Center and all its affiliates, Gang -nam Severance Hospital, Shin-chon Severance Hospital, Dental Clinic, Yong-in Severance Hospital, and Severance Psychiatric Hospital) is as follows:

I. Eligibility: Appointed missi onaries at home during regular ( 4-year) sabbatical. Appointed missionaries or overseas volunteers with illness and temporarily visiting home for treatment. (Must have Korean medical insurance.)

II. Financial Support
Physical Examination (B asic)
*Cost:* Appointed missionaries during regular (4-year) sabbatical are fully supported. Overseas volunteers are not included.

For any two additional examinations beyond the Basic package, the World Mission Department will pay 50% of the cost. All other additional procedures are to be personally paid by missionaries. (http://sev.iseverance.com)

*Treatment Cost*
For treatment at the Yonsei Medical Center, the World Mission Department will pay 50% of treatment cost below 1 million KWN. For other medical facilities, the Wo rld Mission Department will cover up to 50%.

For treatment cost over 1 million KWN, the World Mission Department will cover 50% exceeding cost above 1 million KWN at Yonsei Medical Center. In any other facilities, however, only 30% of the cost above 1 million KWN will be covered.

*[Appendix 10 continued]*

2-1) For general illnesses, the above conditions will apply for missionaries and their families.
2-2) For cancer and all other rare diseases, the above condition will apply for 1 year starting from the time of initial treatment.

*Appointed Missionary's (spouse included) Death or Serious Injury*
The above conditions will apply plus additional support provided as below:
3-1) Death: 3 million KWN (5 million KWN in the case of a couple)
3-2) Serious Injury: 2 million KWN (hospitalized for over 2 months)

# 9

## Response to Seung Kwan (David) Yoo, "Accountability in SaRang Community Church"

### *Sherwood G. Lingenfelter*

THE MISSION PROGRAM OF SaRang Community Church is impressive by any measure. The pastoral leadership of a single congregation of approximately 45,000 adults has successfully mobilized the church's members to engage in local and global mission that has impacted the nation of Korea and the world through a diversity of evangelism, discipleship, and holistic ministries. The scope of ministries (159 families in full-time mission work and nearly 20,000 participants in domestic and foreign short-term mission) matches or exceeds the efforts of many denominational and parachurch mission organizations in the United States and Europe.

My task is to provide a critical review of the accountability systems described by Seung Kwan (David) Yoo in his overview of the SaRang World Missions Department and its ministries. My review will focus on the following areas: structures, recruitment and training, finance and property, policies, and assessment of ministry effectiveness. Throughout this response I raise questions that I hope every Western and every Korean church will seriously consider.

### STRUCTURES OF ACCOUNTABILITY

The SaRang Community Church is an extremely complex organization that defies simple analysis. Furthermore, after a careful reading of David Yoo's paper and then our conversations at OMSC, it is clear that SaRang has more systems in place than he had space to describe in his report. As I reviewed the paper, I could see that SaRang clearly has a very highly developed system of structures that are designed to mobilize its pastoral staff and laity for the extremely complex mission of the church. His figure 8.1 ("Foreign and Domestic Networking for Mission"; see page 92) well illustrates the complex concentric network of relationships that exists. The World Mission Department is the primary structure that oversees a global network of relationships.

In summary, the World Mission Department has appropriate planning structures and appropriate management structures for both domestic and overseas workers. The church also has a well-defined structure for managing finances for both the church and its world mission program. My review will raise questions that implicitly ask about how these and similar structures work in all mission sending churches worldwide.

## RECRUITMENT AND TRAINING

> *Question:* What criteria does your church use in evaluating applications for mission support? How are decisions made to accept or reject an applicant? Is it just a checklist of the application details, or are other qualitative criteria employed, such as evidence of character and spiritual and emotional stability?

SaRang's application process for full-time missionaries includes fifteen different steps of documentation that are required for candidates. Staff in the World Mission Department review these documents and make decisions on applicants. As I look at the documents that are used by the church to decide whether or not to support a missionary, it is clear that formal education and pre-field training are required for professional mission ministry. Yoo further reported that church pastors who are part of the missionary training process seek to verify a candidate's life and character. And the World Mission Department expects that these variables will be reviewed by the mission-sending organization to which the church will second these missionaries. Since success in the mission field is dependent in large part on the missionary's character and emotional and cultural maturity, SaRang relies upon both its staff review and its external partners in mission to conduct this aspect of screening for missionary candidates.

The challenge for most churches is that their missionaries are part of dual relationships. A SaRang missionary must first be accepted as a member of a mission organization (a Korean mission or a Western agency such as SIM or Pioneers) to be supported by SaRang as one of its professional missionaries. SaRang requires each candidate to obtain a letter of petition for support from the head of the mission organization, proof of acceptance, and proof of training completion from that organization.

SaRang Community Church has its own professional missionary training school, which has an extensive yearlong curriculum and six months' additional training in leadership for those who qualify after completing the yearlong program. This is a rigorous program, more rigorous than most, which is very commendable. And SaRang solicits anonymous evaluation forms from its missionary trainees at the end of each school term, which the pastoral staff uses to adjust and improve the program curriculum.

However, like most Korean and American churches, SaRang does not yet have a process to solicit feedback from experienced field missionaries about the strength or weaknesses of the training they received before going to the field; furthermore, most missionaries would be very careful not to criticize the training program of their major supporting church. To be fair to SaRang, most North American training programs also lack these assessment processes. Most training programs focus on what they pour into students, but very few examine how students take this material and apply it, whether successfully or unsuccessfully. And few, if any, seriously use feedback from graduates to revise their training programs.

One other factor that is a challenge for the church is that the graduates of their professional missionary training school are deployed to other organizations. While the church may continue to provide support for these graduates, it does not have direct control over their field ministry. Instead, it relies upon outside mission organizations to evaluate missionary performance in a field of ministry, provide coaching for missionaries who are in trouble, manage interpersonal conflict between missionaries, and do crisis intervention with missionaries who are struggling with health, ministry, or other issues. It would be inappropriate to expect the sending church to manage all of these issues with so many missionaries in so many different organizations.

*Question:* Does your church have a process in place by which it evaluates mission organizations to be sure that the issues of missionary success are adequately addressed and managed for the missionaries sent out by the church? If the church does not review this, they have no assurance that the missionaries they send out will in fact receive the support essential to be effective in ministry.

I was particularly impressed with SaRang's overseas volunteer service program, which deploys short-term missionaries into cross-cultural environments. One- or two-year assignments allow volunteers to experience mission work and evaluate whether they are gifted and called to longer-term cross-cultural ministry. To help these volunteers find direction, the staff seeks feedback from the veteran missionaries under whom they have served. Occasionally the staff approves extending the time of a volunteer, when requested by veteran missionary supervisors. The volunteer service program seems a very positive strategy by the church to continue to recruit longer-term missionaries.

## FINANCE AND PROPERTY

*Question:* Does your church have processes in place to evaluate the financial accountability structures of its mission partners to whom you deploy professional missionaries? Do these partners do field audits? Do they provide assurance that missionaries use funds as intended by the sending church and donors?

SaRang Community Church clearly has systems in place for regular budgeting and auditing of its mission finance program. The strength of the church's financial system is the auditing of its own financial management and the budgeted allocation of resources to its diverse mission outreach programs. One important innovation is the "Barnabas mission offering," whereby donors and church members give directly to missions through bank account transfers. In this way, the church avoids the potential problems of handling cash outside of the general church offerings and provides receipts for tax purposes to donors. In addition, funds are transferred directly to missionary field accounts.

SaRang is dependent upon its partner organizations to provide structures of financial accountability for missionaries who are deployed to them. The partners are responsible for auditing field expenses of missionaries, and the church does not, and should not, have a process whereby they review or check these organizations. As Yoo notes, the local church serves primarily to provide qualified people to serve in mission organizations and supports them with intercessory prayer, financial support, and short-term missionary team encouragement.

## POLICIES

> *Question:* Do your partner organizations have policies about funds used to employ national church workers, to purchase property in international settings, and to build church or educational buildings? Who oversees these funds when they are donated and accounts for these expenditures?

SaRang has financial policies that define the support level of missionaries, as well as the practice of receiving gifts or celebrations for missionaries and mission-related personnel. Like most churches, they have respected and trusted missionaries and their organizations to manage funds for the purchase of property, building projects, and employment of national workers. Yet this area has potential for significant abuse and mismanagement. SaRang has seen this problem, and for projects that entail sizable funding, they require draft proposals and project planning for approval by the World Mission Department.

## ASSESSMENT OF MINISTRY EFFECTIVENESS

> *Question:* Does a church like SaRang, with such extensive programs and supporting over 150 missionary families, have a clear statement of criteria used to determine when a ministry is stagnant or ineffective?

The SaRang World Mission Department has a well-defined process of assessment called "Plan, Do, See." The "plan" process is annual and includes the evaluation of the ministry work in the previous year and proposals to seek to improve each area of ministry according to the goals of the World Mission Department. It seeks to evaluate each task, team, and ministry it supports.

Pastor Yoo states that the key mission of the church is the globalization of discipleship training. This is defined in terms of the "apostolicity of the laity." He then identifies three criteria: (1) trained, (2) gifted to serve, and (3) a lived life of ministry and service. These are excellent criteria, which have defined the purpose for both recruitment and the evaluation of effective or stagnant ministry. The "do" step in ministry effectiveness is evaluated in terms of the "schedule" that is defined in the annual plan. "See" refers to the ministry evaluation done during the annual evaluation meeting. The world mission staff gathers feedback from the participants in the mission programs and evaluates it in these annual meetings.

SaRang has a specific program called "Upper Rooms," which is the organization of 3,000 small prayer groups for SaRang's missionaries. This is a very impressive, positive, and powerful way to mobilize laity in support of SaRang's missionaries. SaRang's small-group leaders, who are thoroughly trained in discipleship and leadership training, serve as quasi-pastors who are very proactive in their small-group contexts. They connect their small groups directly to field missionaries, receiving information from them, praying for them, and sharing this information more broadly with the entire congregation. This decentralized process of missionary prayer support is an exceptional aspect of SaRang's missions program.

SaRang also has a program called "Barnabas Intercessory Prayer," meeting on the second and fourth Sundays of every month. These meetings, which are led by ten members of the World Mission Departmemt of the church, result in board members keeping in close contact with each missionary deployed by the church through the exchange of letters and e-mails. These same board members also lead short-term mission teams to their designated region's mission fields to assist and encourage missionaries. Once again, the church has a great process of connecting with and supporting missionaries.

> *Question:* Does the World Mission Department make explicit the criteria that are used to evaluate the effectiveness of these "Barnabas Intercessory Prayer" leaders and groups?

In personal communication, Yoo noted that some groups are more effective and proactive in communicating with and supporting missionaries than others.

## CONCLUSION

As I review the report prepared by Seung Kwan (David) Yoo, I conclude that SaRang Community Church is one of the most innovative and effective local-church sending bodies in Korea and in the world. In each of the areas where I have posed questions, I found that the World Mission

Department of SaRang has taken these issues very seriously and has established effective accountability structures and processes to assure the effectiveness of its mission programs.

My concluding comments are not about SaRang per se but focus more generally on the Korean missions movement and on what I have learned from the reports and experiences of Korean missionaries who have come to study with me and the mission faculty of Biola University and Fuller Theological Seminary.

As an outside observer of the Korean mission movement, it has grieved me to see this powerful movement of the Spirit of God attacked, often successfully, by Satan, as I have seen it afflicted by the same human weaknesses that threatened the postwar missions movement out of the United States. The very attributes of the Korean missions movement—its commitment to follow leaders, its sacrificial giving, and its mobilization of people engaged in mission—not only are the blessings of the movement but also may become its liabilities.

In the Korean mission movement, as in the Western mission movement, we find that interpersonal conflict among missionaries is one of the continuing liabilities and challenges. The inability of missionaries to work together in unity causes division and confusion in every mission field of the world. Furthermore, conflict between Korean missionaries and national church leaders is pervasive. This conflict often arises out of the "hungers" of individual missionaries to control the ministry's outcomes, to use power and resources to force people to comply with the missionary's goals, and to achieve recognition and significance.

In the West we have not adequately addressed these issues in our systems of accountability. We have been very strong in managing financial accountability, but we have labored and often failed in dealing with interpersonal conflict and conflict between nationals and missionaries. Western and Korean missionaries alike are motivated by their internal needs and weaknesses that fuel these conflicts and that undermine the credibility of the work of Christ in our ministry efforts.

Some of the Western mistakes replicated in Korean missions:

- *Ethnocentrism.* I have found that Korean doctoral students are most interested in thinking about and studying Korean culture in Korean churches, and only a handful desire to study the peoples and cultures to which they have been sent to minister. Many report that they do not listen to the nationals or seek to learn from them how better to minister in a local context.

- *Focus on doing.* As the Western mission force was in the twentieth century, so the current Korean mission force seems to be focused on doing, without adequate time being given for listening and reflection. Korean missionaries report that they do not listen to one another, nor do they reflect together on how best to do ministry in their local contexts.

- *Training for skills rather than character.* Most Korean churches have very high expectations for missionaries to learn mission work and skills. Yet they—and we—struggle with how to develop character along with knowledge. How should a church and mission assess the character of the missionaries they are sending into the field? Do we ask the missionary, How do you live and work when no one is watching? Do we ask nationals, How does the missionary live and work when no one is watching?

- *Failure to address conflict and difficulties.* In classes at Fuller and Biola, returned Korean missionaries testify that there is no "safe place" for missionaries to talk freely about their problems. In Confucian cultures it is shameful even to acknowledge that one has a problem or difficulty in the field. As a consequence, even if a person has difficulties, he or she is not able to discuss them, and certainly would not want to share these with his or her supervisor. The missionary who has lived with conflict experiences both fear and shame about these difficulties. As a consequence, people return to their home churches, tell the stories that will earn them approval, and bury the issues that cause them shame deep in their subconscious. Such unresolved emotions and pain sometimes become so severe that individual missionaries can no longer continue in their field of ministry.

It is incumbent upon us as mission leaders to create "safe places" where missionaries may deal with unresolved emotions, pain, and ministry challenges. Questions to explore in these "safe places," where people can open their hearts, include:

- What are the blessings and the sufferings that you have experienced?

- What are the frustrations that have made your ministry difficult and your family situation challenging for you?

- What are the kinds of temptations that Satan uses to challenge you and to disrupt and to derail your ministry in this context?

- What level of pain have you experienced during your last term in the mission field?

In my experience, I have found that many missionaries have very high levels of emotional, spiritual, and physical pain at certain times in their ministries. We rarely ask them about their level of pain, and we have very few strategies for helping them to deal with the pain that they have experienced through their work. We might conclude by asking, "Are we treating you as a missionary in our organization with justice and truth?" Or better yet, we might ask, "How have we failed to treat you with justice and truth?" Most will be afraid to answer these questions honestly, unless we can create "safe places" where they will not experience shame or fear rejection or the stigma of failure.

The attrition of missionaries is one of the major issues affecting the worldwide mission movement, and it is a critical factor in Korean missions as well. Sending missionaries to the Muslim world is a particularly difficult and challenging work. The amount of training required for a team is expensive, and the amount of support that must be raised to deploy them for such ministries is high.

One of my Korean Ph.D. students at Fuller Theological Seminary is working specifically on the issue of on-field crises leading to the attrition of highly trained Korean field missionaries. She has found that few Korean mission organizations and churches have evaluated carefully the reasons for missionary attrition. This loss of personnel is often credited to health issues, when in fact the deeper issues are the emotional and ministry conflicts that lead up to the decision not to return to the field.

My observations of Korean missionaries at Fuller suggests that their churches are very strong to articulate a global vision, mobilize their people to go, and prepare them for the specific mission task such as church planting. Yet few of them have seriously considered how to care for the wounded and the organizational casualties of their mission force.

# 10

## Accountability in Mission: Black Rock Congregational Church as a Case Study

### Larry Fullerton

BLACK ROCK CONGREGATIONAL CHURCH is an evangelical church in Fairfield, Connecticut, with more than 1,000 members and a weekly attendance of approximately 1,500 people at its five worship services. Among evangelical churches in New England (though not in the United States as a whole), it is relatively large.

Black Rock Church has a regional and, some would say, a national reputation for its global missions program. This reputation can be attributed to the size and scope of its annual missions budget, currently in excess of $1,130,000, which represents one-fourth of Black Rock's total operating budget.

Through its missions budget, Black Rock supports over seventy-five missionary families or singles, the majority of whom serve overseas, and all of whom serve cross-culturally. Black Rock–supported missionaries serve in over twenty-five countries throughout the world. Several serve in "creative access" countries and therefore are not listed on Black Rock's Web site or in its publications.[1] Through its missionaries, Black Rock is affiliated with forty sending agencies, which include AIM, AWM, Campus Crusade, CrossWorld, and SIM.

Black Rock also supports twelve local ministries serving the poor and those recovering from addictions. These ministries are primarily in Bridgeport, Connecticut's largest city. Additionally, the church is com-

1. For further information, see www.brcc.org/missions/missions.html.

mitted to sending short-term teams to serve locally and abroad; in the decade 2000–2010, more than 500 Black Rock members and attendees have been part of one of these teams.

## REASONS FOR GROWTH

Why is Black Rock's missions program so expansive and well known? I believe there are three factors. First, Black Rock Church, founded in 1849, has supported missionaries throughout its long history. Support of missionaries to Africa began in 1933. By 1958 the church was supporting eight missionary couples. Since then, the missions program has grown consistently to its present size and budget.

Second, Black Rock has embraced the responsibility for taking steps, in both word and action, to fulfill the Great Commission which Jesus gave to the church before his ascension (Matt. 28:18–20). Sharing the Gospel with those who have never had the opportunity to hear it has always been one of the core values of the church. Missions is part of the very DNA of Black Rock Church.

Third, in my years since 1997 at Black Rock Church, the missions program has been guided by two axioms—give recognition and avoid anonymity—which indirectly support a high level of accountability on the part of our missionaries.

1.  The best advertisement for Black Rock Church's missions program rests with its currently supported missionaries. The church is very intentional in celebrating Black Rock missionaries; their work and dedication are privately and publicly applauded. For example, when visiting missionaries are introduced during the annual Missions Conference, they are always welcomed with a standing ovation. Members of the congregation consider it a privilege to host missionaries in their homes and for their children to spend time with missionaries. Missionaries are our heroes!

2.  Conversely, support of "anonymous" missionaries and missionary organizations supported is detrimental to the success of a vibrant missions program in a local church. People in the church will not give to or pray for missionaries or ministries they do not know, which makes an entire missions program suffer.

At Black Rock Church, from the senior pastor to every member of the pastoral staff, Elder Board, and Board of Missions, all are committed to "high exposure" and "high accountability" of Black Rock missionaries. The remainder of this chapter details how the church instills in its missionaries an understanding of the requirements and benefits of accountability.

## APPLICATION PROCESS

Missionary accountability begins with the application process. Because of Black Rock Church's missions reputation, especially in New England, the church annually receives fifty or sixty inquiries from individuals or families seeking support. This has forced the Board of Missions to prioritize its commitments and to refine its application process. The board recognizes two priorities:

1. A commitment to support prospective missionaries who are considered Black Rock "family members." These are persons who have grown up in the church or who have filled an integral role as an active Black Rock member over a period of time.

2. A commitment as to where a prospective Black Rock missionary will serve. The church's current focus is on people groups or countries whose population has fewer than 2 percent evangelical Christians.[2] This means that most new missionaries are sent to unreached people groups or countries where the majority are Muslim, Buddhist, or Hindu. The prayer guide *Operation World* is used to identify such countries or people groups.[3]

Prospective missionaries who meet these two criteria (with rare exceptions) are invited to submit biographical information, along with information about their ministry, where exactly they intend to be serving, their sending agency, and their needed financial support. The missions pastor then schedules a personal interview, and if that interview is favorable, they are asked to complete a formal Black Rock application. Next, they are interviewed by the Executive Committee of the Board of Missions before a formal interview with the entire board is scheduled. After the board interviews the applicants, they are either granted or de-

2. Black Rock is an active member of the National Association of Evangelicals and supports only missionaries of similar doctrine.

3. Patrick Johnstone and Jason Mandryk, *Operation World*, 6th ed. (Waynesboro, Ga.: Authentic Lifestyle, 2001). See now *Operation World*, 7th ed., by Jason Mandryk (Colorado Springs, Colo.: Biblica Publishing, 2010).

nied acceptance. The latter seldom occurs, since the initial screening is so extensive.

What does all this application procedure have to do with missionary accountability? Quite simply it is that, because of the amount of time and interest invested in candidates before their acceptance as Black Rock–supported missionaries, we want them to understand that the church really values them, is committed to them, and expects their full cooperation in the various expectations we outline. Black Rock has indeed found that the "accountability quotient" is extremely high among new missionaries added in this manner.

This accountability quotient is further strengthened by the Mission Covenant (see Appendix A) that each new missionary is asked to sign subsequent to approval by the Board of Missions. You will note that seven expectations are listed.

1. To maintain an active ministry.

2. To correspond with the Board of Missions quarterly.

3. To submit an annual report of ministry progress and financial statistics to the Board of Missions by January of each year.

4. To visit with the Board of Missions and spend time with Black Rock families during home service.

5. To forward all requests for funding to the Board of Missions.

6. To advise the Board of Missions of changes in agency and/or field location, marital status, new family members, or major changes in ministry emphasis.

7. To faithfully contact their Black Rock prayer partners and keep them apprised of current prayer requests.

This covenant states Black Rock's expectations for the newly approved missionary and is key to the accountability structure. Additionally, the covenant establishes the responsibilities of Black Rock Church in relation to the missionary. The church agrees:

1. To uphold the missionary and his family in prayer.

2. To make the missionary's ministry known to Black Rock.

3. To faithfully support the missionary financially each month.

4. To care for personal, emotional, and spiritual needs as Black Rock is able, and to provide field visits by the missions pastor.

5. To offer practical assistance during home service.

The covenant's intention is to clearly establish Black Rock's expectations for both parties. As stated, one way that Black Rock supports and also monitors the missionary's activities is through a visit from the missions pastor. It has been an unofficial policy for the missions pastor to visit, if at all practical and possible, all new missionaries during their first two years of overseas ministry. If a new missionary is going to withdraw from his or her field of service early, before the end of the first term, in most cases this will occur within the first two years. Thus it is extremely beneficial for the missionary to receive a visit from the missions pastor within those first two years, when stress is high from culture shock and from initial exposure to a new and foreign field. (For obvious reasons, a visit is not always possible in limited-access countries, since the visit itself might raise suspicion within the host country.)

The second accountability tool that Black Rock employs is the third item on the covenant's list of missionary responsibilities. Each missionary is required to submit an annual report. (See Appendix F, "Missionary Annual Report.") In November each year we send this form to all missionaries, requesting them to return it to Black Rock by the middle of December. Among other things, missionaries are asked to state their ministry goals for the coming year. The mission pastor reviews the completed form to ensure compliance with Black Rock's understanding of the missionary's long-term goals.

Concurrently, Black Rock asks for a report from each missionary's supervisor. (See Appendix C, "Ministry Evaluation Form.") This form is used to audit the accountability structure in place between the mission agency and the missionary supported by Black Rock. Please note that the supervisor is asked to identify the missionary's three main goals for the past year. Furthermore, the supervisor is asked to rate the effectiveness of the missionary in accomplishing those goals. It is not the job of the missions pastor or of the Black Rock Board of Missions to provide on-site supervision of the Black Rock missionary. That responsibility rests with the mission sending agency. A percentage of the missionaries' financial support package is to be used by the agencies to provide field services to the missionaries, and Black Rock has no desire to control missionaries in their ministry. That responsibility rests with their supervisors on the field.

Note that the final line of the document asks that the supervisor send a copy of the completed supervisor's form to the missionary. We want our missionaries to see their supervisor's evaluation.

Finally, Black Rock Church's commitment to accountability is evident in the Annual Missions Conference policy. Black Rock requires missionaries to attend our mission conference at least once every four years. During this visit, the missionary is given maximum exposure to the congregation through a variety of means, including introductions during all worship services, a time of interaction with small groups, exposure to youth and children's programs, and individual meals in homes.

In summary, from the prospective missionary candidate to the veteran missionary, accountability is stressed and encouraged. The missionary's commitment to accountability to Black Rock Church is one of the missions program's best advertisements. Black Rock expects accountability, even as the missionary expects Black Rock Church to be accountable for providing financial, prayer, and emotional support.

## A STORY OF SUCCESS

Black Rock's missionaries are generally self-starters and, given the expectations laid out carefully in advance, generally also have a high regard for accountability. This attitude has resulted in a missionary force with little turnover. The Black Rock missionary with the longest term of service has been active since 1954.

On numerous occasions, Black Rock has served as the "middle man" when disputes have arisen on the field between a missionary and a supervisor. Black Rock has even intervened to the point of stating our lack of approval when missionaries were to be assigned duties that did not coincide with their career goals.

## NOT-SO-SUCCESSFUL STORIES

As mentioned, it is our policy for the missions pastor to visit first-term missionaries. Early in my career as a missions pastor, I visited a missionary couple who had recently started ministry in Africa. The wife had grown up as a missionary kid, but the husband had never been out of the

United States. I spent almost a week with the couple. I talked and quietly probed them concerning their ministry and potential stresses on their marriage. I also spent about two hours with their immediate supervisor. I concluded that, although they had experienced some culture shock and stress in adapting to a new cross-cultural ministry location, they had adjusted well. The visit with their supervisor seemed to confirm my favorable appraisal.

I proceeded on my trip to a country farther north to visit veteran missionaries supported by Black Rock. This veteran couple happened to work with the same mission agency as the first couple. At one point this older missionary casually mentioned that he hoped that the young husband whom I had previously visited would be able to "get over the other woman."

"What other woman?" I asked with some surprise. He replied, "We don't want to gossip, but a report has been sent through the conference e-mail asking us to pray for this situation. There is another woman who is very close to the husband. Both he and she had gone through similar culture shock, and they intimately bonded with each other. There had been no violation of the marriage covenant, but the husband and the woman had been admonished, and they were asked not to see each other."

In the course of my visit with them, neither the husband involved nor his supervisor had seen this relationship and the action of the missionary as being serious enough to inform me of the issue, even when I had asked both parties if there were any "stresses" in their marriage. I realize that the supervisor may have wanted to protect the missionary family, but the incident was very well known through the agency's missionary community, and I felt that either the supervisor or the husband should have told me, in ministerial confidentiality, of the issue. I was accountable to give a report to the Board of Missions upon my return, and although I would not have broken a pastoral confidence, I would have requested prayer for their marriage.

I also recall the time when a Black Rock missionary changed his missionary sending agency without consulting us. His only way of notifying Black Rock of his change of agency was by requesting that his monthly support check be sent to a new address. Needless to say, he heard from us and was asked to give us his rationale for the change.

A more recent occurrence also illustrates the way accountability between us and a missionary and his or her agency can fall short. Black Rock approved funding of a ministry that provides seminary education in a developing country. It involved a five-year commitment of $20,000 per year, for a total of $100,000. The leader of the seminary was invited to preach at our Missions Conference (which gave him very high exposure), and he agreed that, since Black Rock was committing $100,000 to the ministry, he would diligently send timely reports. Black Rock sent the first check and all subsequent checks. For the next three years, however, we received absolutely nothing from the missionary or from those in the seminary, except the receipts for our financial contributions. Only after threatening to cut funds did we receive communication. Although we subsequently found that the funding was well spent, our inability to tell the congregation how their money was being spent during those three years was detrimental to the ongoing missions ministry at Black Rock. It illustrates the point that anonymous missionaries and ministries tend to deaden a missions program.

## CONCLUSION

The two axioms of our missions program have served us well in regard to missionary accountability. The best advertisement for our missions program is our missionaries. Black Rock has found that the more we give missionaries a sense of worth and the more we convey to them that their conduct on the mission field has a direct relationship to the well-being of their home church in America, the more the missionary will respond to accountability issues. And as we, their supporting church, demonstrate that missionaries, often serving in a far-off country, can count on the members of Black Rock Church to pray for them and to be on their side in the midst of the rigors and spiritual battles of ministry, the more they respond to our on-site supervision and requirements of accountability.

# Appendix A

## BLACK ROCK CONGREGATIONAL CHURCH MISSIONS COVENANT

We believe that we are mutually responsible before God to honor our commitments to one another while obeying the Great Commission. This covenant serves to clarify and unify our work for the Kingdom.

## BLACK ROCK CONGREGATIONAL CHURCH HAS THESE RESPONSIBILITIES TOWARD YOU, OUR MISSIONARY:

- To uphold you and your family in prayer.
- To make your ministry and prayer requests known in our church, through Annual Missions Conferences, *News from the Harvest Field* bulletin features, and the Global Information Center.
- To faithfully support you financially each month and to consider any special financial needs for your ministry, personal needs, or emergencies as we are able by God's provision.
- To care for personal, emotional, and spiritual needs as we are able through correspondence and field visits by the Missions Pastor.
- To offer you practical assistance during home service as we are able.

You, our missionary, have these responsibilities toward Black Rock Congregational Church:

- To maintain an active ministry as represented to and supported by the Board of Missions.
- To correspond with the Board of Missions at least quarterly. We prefer that you send us your monthly prayer letter or communicate at least monthly through e-mail.

- To submit an annual report of ministry progress and financial statistics to the Board of Missions by January for consideration in budget development.

- To visit with the Board of Missions and spend time with Black Rock families during home service. We expect you to visit us at least once every four years, preferably during either our Fall Festival or Annual Missions Conference.

- To forward all requests for funding to the Board of Missions.

- To advise the Board of Missions of agency and/or field location changes, changes in marital status, new family members, or major changes in ministry emphasis.

- To faithfully contact your Black Rock prayer partners and keep them apprised of current prayer requests.

**Please note:** If you return to the U.S. to work in the home office or in a U.S. assignment, Black Rock's Board of Missions may elect not to continue financial support, as we are committed to having a majority of our missionaries serve overseas.

By God's grace and with His help, we covenant to honor these commitments to one another.

Missionary's signature_____Date _____
Spouse's signature_____Date_____
BOM Chairman's signature_____Date_____
Missions Pastor's signature_____Date _____

*"And this gospel of the kingdom will be preached in the whole world as a testimony to all nations, and then the end will come."*

—MATT. 24:14

## Appendix B

### FINANCIAL SUPPORT FORM

November 5, 2010

Dear Friend,

We ask that this form be completed by financial personnel in the home office of each of our missionaries. As is customary, I will also be requesting that the missionary fill out a similar form and return it to me. Occasionally I have found significant discrepancy between the forms returned from your office when compared to the missionary-completed form. If there is a discrepancy, I will contact your financial personnel. Forms may be mailed to our office or faxed to us at 203/259-7791.
Thank you for your prompt attention to this as it assists us in our effort to financially care for our missionaries.

As God's blessings rest upon us, it is a pleasure to work in partnership with you.

In His grip,


Larry Fullerton

Black Rock Congregational Church
3685 Black Rock Turnpike
Fairfield, CT 06825

Missionary's name _____

Form completed by_____

Agency_____

Address_____

Phone_____

Fax_____

E-mail _____

1. What was the support total recommended by your board for the 2010 or previous fiscal year? _____

2. What total was actually received by the missionary for the 2010 or previous fiscal year? _____

3. Total year 2011 support budget recommended for above
    missionary: _____

   Breakdown:

   Salary_____

   Overhead to agency_____

   Administrative or ministry expense costs
       Medical/dental insurance _____

   Ministry expense_____

   Retirement_____

   Other (specify)_____

   **Total**_____

4. List any one-time expenses that you project for this coming year:

5. Any other information that you could provide us regarding the missionary's budget or financial information:

Please e-mail completed form to Dawn Brehm at dbrehm@brcc.org, or fax to 203/259-7791.

Please return this form no later than December 15, 2010.

Agency —Financial

## Appendix C

### MISSIONARY EVALUATION FORM

November 5, 2010

Dear Friend,

It continues to be a pleasure for Black Rock Church to partner with you in sending out and financially supporting missionaries. Additionally, you continue to provide a very important ingredient in our missionary support by screening and equipping them and providing logistical support for them on the field. You provide a supervisory role for the missionaries that I, as a Missions Pastor, cannot. Thus, I rely on you to provide that supervision and missionary care for our far-flung missionary family. Thank you for your diligence and pastoral heart.

We appreciate your help as we annually ask you to complete an evaluation form. Because e-mail addresses change and personnel changes, we are now asking our missionaries to forward these forms to the appropriate individuals. Please return the form to Dawn Brehm at dbrehm@brcc.org by December 15, 2010.

We would also ask that you forward a copy to the missionary for whom you are completing the form.

Thank you for your help. Receiving the completed evaluation forms assists us as we personally care for our missionaries.

As God's blessings rest upon us, it is a pleasure to work in partnership with you.

In His grip,

Pastor Larry Fullerton

Black Rock Congregational Church
3685 Black Rock Turnpike
Fairfield, CT 06825

To be completed by Field Supervisor:

Missionary's name _____
Organization _____
Form completed by_____
Date _____
Position or relationship with missionary _____
Phone_____ _____
Fax_____ _____
E-mail _____

1. What were this missionary's three main goals or tasks this past year?

    A.

    B.

    C.

2. How effective or successful was the missionary in accomplishing the above?

    A. _____Highly Successful

    B. _____Partially Successful

    C. _____Unsuccessful

    Comments:

3. How do you see this missionary utilizing his/her spiritual gifts in this ministry?

4. What concerns or issues does this missionary currently face in terms of ministry effectiveness?

5. What trends/developments do you see as positively or negatively affecting this ministry's success?

6. Please list for us one prayer request for this individual.

Please e-mail completed form to dbrehm@brcc.org. **Please return as an attachment and not as part of the e-mail body.** You may also fax 203/259-7791.

Remember to send a copy to the individual for whom you are completing this form.
Please return no later December 15, 2010.
Agency—Financial

*Appendix D*

## CORRESPONDENCE REPORT

Please return as soon as possible, but no later than December 15, 2010.
Please print.

Name _____

Date _____

Your current e-mail address _____

Your current phone number:

country code ____ number _____

1. Briefly describe your work/responsibilities:

2. What are your goals for the next year?

        A.

        B.

        C.

3. List any items that we should remember that are broad in nature and applicable for the coming year.

        A.

        B.

        C.

4.  Next date you may be visiting BRCC:

   Month(s) _____ Year _____

The dates of our upcoming Annual Family Gatherings are listed below. Please indicate which you may be able to attend.

___ April 2–10, 2011

___ March 4–12, 2012

5.  Tell us one brief story of your work and the people you serve.


6.  Family Information. Please list the names and birthdays of all your family members. (We are trying to keep records updated.)

   Name                    Birthday

# *2010 Fiscal Year Report*

Name _____

Date _____

  I.  Financial support:

    A. Total financial package for upcoming year (2011): $ _____

        Breakdown

| | |
|---|---|
| Salary | $ _____ |
| Medical/Dental | $ _____ |
| Insurance | $ _____ |
| Retirement | $ _____ |
| Schooling | $ _____ |
| Other | $ _____ |

    B. *Actual* received fiscal year 2010: $ _____
      % of total need: _____%

    C. Expected for 2011: $ _____ % of total need: _____%

  II. Do you have a retirement program?  Yes ____ No____

       If yes, how much money annually goes into your retirement
       account?  $ _____

III. List any specific financial needs that we ought to be aware of:

Agency—Financial

*Appendix E*

## PASTORAL FORM

(For Pastor Larry's eyes only)
Please return by December 15, 2010
Name _____
Date _____

1. The mission field can be a place of tension and conflict. Are there things happening on the field that you would be free to mention to me? Please list.

2. If you are married, are there marital or family issues about which I can pray?

3. If you are single, are there single issues about which I can pray?

4. Are there other personal issues about which I can pray?

5. As Christians, we believe in spiritual warfare (Eph. 6:12–19). List any spiritual warfare concerns that I can uphold for you before God's throne of grace.

6. Finally, are there things that I can do that will assist you or your ministry?

7. Would you like for me to give you a phone call so we can talk and pray about an issue?

Yes _____      No _____      Maybe_____

What is the issue? (Optional)

Report—Pastoral

*Appendix F*

## MISSIONARY ANNUAL REPORT

Please return by December 15, 2010

Name _____

Date _____


Your current e-mail address _____

Your current phone number: country code _____ number _____

Birth dates of **you** and **your children**

    (please include the year each child was born).

      Name              Birthday


1. Briefly describe your current ministry:


2. List three specific goals that you have for your ministry this next year.

    A.

    B.

    C.

3. List ongoing prayer requests that we may share with the congregation. (These should be broad in nature so that they will apply for an extended period of time.)

A.

B.

C.

4. Next date you may be visiting BRCC: Month(s) _____ Year ___

5. Will you be present at any of the following missions conferences? (Check any that apply.)

_____ April 2–10, 2011          _____ March 4–12, 2012

6. What specific forms of communication would you appreciate from your prayer partner group? Check which form is best, and cross out those you wish not to or cannot receive:

Cards/notes/letters ___ E-mails _____ Other (describe) _____

Small packages _____ (How is it best to send them?) _____

Please list mailing restrictions and/or sensitive subjects to avoid in letters:

7. One brief story of how God is working in the lives of people through your ministry (use additional sheet if necessary):

**2010 MISSIONARY FINANCIAL REPORT**

Name _____

Date _____

A.  Financial support:

1.  Total annual financial support <u>recommended</u>
        by your sending board for 2011: $ _____

    Breakdown (list dollar amount if possible):

    Salary                              _____
    Housing/Utilities                   _____
    Food                                _____
    Clothing                            _____
    Children's Education                _____
    In-country Transportation           _____
    Health Insurance                    _____
    Foreign/U.S. Taxes                  _____
    Retirement                          _____
    Furlough Expenses                   _____
    Ministry Expenses                   _____
        List                            _____   ___

                                        _____   ___

                                        _____   ___

        Other                           _____
        List                            _____   ___

                                        _____   ___

        Total                           _____

2.  *Actual* support received last fiscal year: _____
        % of total need: _____

3.  Financial support anticipated for 2011 (total amount): _____
        % of total currently committed: _____

B.  Are there any one-time expenses, not included above,
        for which you are raising money (i.e., to purchase
        an automobile, computer, etc.)? List item and cost:

Has this expense been approved by your mission board?

_____ Yes _____ No

C. Does your mission agency have a retirement program?

_____ Yes _____ No

Does your support include contributions to retirement?

_____ Yes _____ No

What is the amount annually contributed by your mission agency?

_____

What is the amount you annually contribute yourself? _____

## 2010 Ministry Evaluation

1. How do you feel about the support and supervision given by your home office this past year?

___ excellent _ adequate _____ poor __needs improvement ____ terrible

Comments:


2. How do you feel about the support and supervision given to you by your mission field supervisor?

_____excellent

_____adequate

_____poor

_____needs improvement

_____non-existent


3. How do you get along with your fellow missionaries?

_____excellently

_____well

_____poorly

_____conflict is present

_____terribly

_____needs improvement

4. Have you received an effectiveness report from your supervisor this past year? _____ Yes ___ No

5. If yes, what was his or her evaluation of your ministry?

6. If you were to evaluate your own ministry this past year, using your own goals and expectations, where would you score yourself?

   Low 1   2   3   4   5   6   7   8   9   10   High

   Comments:

7. If you were to evaluate the effectiveness of your mission in the country where you serve, how would you score it?

   Low 1   2   3   4   5   6   7   8   9   10   High

   Comments:

Report—Annual

# Appendix G

## LETTER TO MISSION SUPERVISOR

November 5, 2010

Dear Friend,

As we have expressed before, it is a pleasure for Black Rock to partner with you in sending out and financially supporting field workers. Additionally, you continue to provide a very important ingredient in our partner support by screening and equipping them and providing logistical support for them on the field. You provide an important supervisory role that I cannot. Thus, I rely on you to provide that supervision and care for our far-flung family members. Thank you for your diligence and shepherd's heart.

We appreciate your help as we annually ask you to complete an evaluation form. Because e-mail addresses change and personnel changes, we are now asking our partners to forward these forms to the appropriate individuals. Please return the form to Dawn Brehm at dbrehm@brcc.org by December 15, 2010.

We would also ask that you forward a copy to the individual missionary for whom you are completing the form.

Thank you for your help. Receiving the completed evaluation forms assists us as we personally care for our overseas friends.

It is a pleasure to work in partnership with you.

In His grip,

Pastor Larry Fullerton

Black Rock Congregational Church
3685 Black Rock Turnpike
Fairfield, CT 06825

*Appendix H*

## PERSONAL FORM 2010

(For Pastor Larry's eyes only)
Please return by December 15, 2010
Name _____
Date _____

1. Living overseas can be a stressful situation. Are there things happening that you would be free to mention to me? Please list.

2. If you are married, are there marital or family issues of which I should be aware?

3. If you are single, are there single issues of which I should be aware?

4. Are there other personal issues that I should know about?

5. Finally, are there things that I can do that will assist you during your time overseas?

Reports—Personal

# 11

## Response to Larry Fullerton, "Accountability in Mission"

### Won Sang Lee

CHRISTIANITY IS BASED ON a covenant relationship between God and man, in which we could say that man is accountable to respond by faith to God's grace. A Christian is accountable first to God and then, because of this relationship, accountable also to other people. Unless we keep in mind these basic principles, we cannot expect to accomplish God's purpose in missions. I am very concerned that we plan to finish the overall mission task and that we give every assistance to those whom God is using to complete this task. Are we pleasing God in this matter? Are we accountable to one another for the part of this mission that has been given to us?

The chapter on the missionary accountability practices of the Black Rock Congregational Church, by Missions Pastor Larry Fullerton, is an excellent case study that explains clearly the practicalities of mission oversight by a local church. Church mission directors will find it a useful model for self-evaluation, a tool for better focusing local church missions and being more accountable in applying biblical mandates.[1] Indeed, we could hope that many churches in the global community will follow the principles and practices of Black Rock Church in regard to accountability in missions.

1. For Black Rock's mission Web page, see www.brcc.org/missions/missions.html.

## BLACK ROCK CONGREGATIONAL CHURCH

Black Rock, founded in 1849, is a model church that has long pursued the biblical mandate for world mission. During the past fifteen years in particular, the church has advanced in its misson involvement by supporting seventy-five missionary family units serving in twenty-five countries. It now has an annual mission budget in excess of $1 million, which is about a quarter of the church's total operating budget. The church also supports twelve local ministries serving the poor and those dealing with addictions. This outward focus involves the unified effort of the senior pastor, the mission pastor, the Elder Board, the Mission Board, and the entire congregation. Together, these various parts of the church motivate missionaries and agencies and hold them accountable, not only to the home church, but also before the Lord. All this is certainly the mark of a healthy church.

Larry Fullerton, Black Rock's mission pastor, has played a key leadership role in the mission program of his church. Over the past fifteen years he has developed the handbook for the Board of Missions, which addresses the range of policies and practices actually needed "on the ground." I highly recommend this handbook for any local church serious about deepening accountability in its mission program. The handbook is particularly important during the application process for missionary candidates, for it spells out clearly the church's guidelines for the missionaries it is prepared to support. And the "Missions Covenant" (see appendix A in Fullerton's chapter) identifies the specific expectations that church and missionary will have of each other, all of which helps ensure that the church's mission goals are well carried out. As Black Rock perseveres in this commitment, and as countless local churches around the world do likewise, we indeed move closer to the actual completion of the Great Commission.

## BIBLICAL PERSPECTIVES

Accountability in mission requires a process of three-way interaction and evaluation involving the home church, the missionary, and the mission agency. Since the Great Commission was given to the church, we could say that, biblically, the home church is like the headquarters, carrying out the task by means of its missionaries and the mission agencies.[2] The

---

2. David J. Bosch, *Transforming Mission* (Maryknoll, N.Y.: Orbis Books, 1999), p. 380.

church thus carries more responsibility than the other two members of this partnership. If the church does its part in missions correctly, problems will be considerably reduced. Fullerton's case study of the Black Rock Church allows us to reach just such a conclusion.[3]

The Board of Missions Handbook (sec. 4.5) provides priority guidelines for supporting Black Rock members who are called into mission service, following the biblical example found in Acts 13:1–3. There the first two missionaries, Paul and Barnabas, were commissioned by and from their church in Antioch. For Black Rock, members of the church for three years or more who are actively involved in the church's ministries are eligible to be considered for support of at least 30 percent, to a maximum of 50 percent, of the total support required. The idea of a homegrown missionary is biblical and beneficial for helping ensure a close tie between missionary and congregation, and for motivating missions in the church. Such a relationship enhances a missionary's commitment to be personally accountable to the whole congregation.[4]

## SPECIFIC OBSERVATIONS

Black Rock practices accountability by receiving annual evaluations of its missionaries from their field supervisors. Would a similar covenant be useful between the church and the mission agency? It could address expectations regarding their respective responsibilities during a missionary's home assignment. Similarly, it could help define steps to follow in the event of a crisis affecting a missionary.

The church has chosen to define mission fields that it supports as geographic locations with 2 percent or less evangelical Christians in the population, as reported in *Operation World*. To make a church's mission operations more focused and efficient, it is wise to select missionaries and mission fields according to the church's own long-term mission goals instead of simply accepting the mission fields and ministries chosen by the various missionary candidates.

---

3. See Patrick Johnstone, *The Church Is Bigger Than You Think* (Pasadena, Calif.: William Carey Library, 1998), pp. 192–96. How can a local church become mission minded? Johnstone answers this question by proposing twelve principles, each of which Black Rock practices.

4. See Mary T. Lederleitner, *Cross-Cultural Partnerships: Navigating the Complexities of Money and Mission* (Downers Grove, Ill.: IVP Books, 2010), pp. 101–9.

Black Rock is wise to require annual financial reports from the missionaries it supports and the mission agencies it works with. This goes far in maintaining the integrity of the relationships and in encouraging ongoing support and loyalty of each party in the relationship.

Spiritual accountability is the most important issue, for spiritual maturity will be the answer to many problems. Maturity cannot be measured by a visible standard, hence the need for continual evaluation of each missionary's spiritual progress.

In conclusion, Black Rock is certainly an exemplary model for local church missions in its vision, commitment, management, organization, leadership, and accountability in carrying out the Great Commission of the Lord. May God richly bless the ministry of Black Rock for his kingdom!

# 12

## Accountability Issues
## Among Korean Missions Organizations

*Bahn Seok (Peter) Lee*

T HE KOREAN CHURCH IS actively participating in global mission, and
its influence in international missions is increasing. Yet only limited
records are available that would help us determine the health of mission
organizations in terms of their financial accountability. In fact, a string
of recent embezzlement cases involving mission organizations in Korea
clearly indicates the need for stronger financial accountability within
our cultural matrix.

On May 12, 2007, Korean newspapers reported the arrest of Rev.
Gi-hong Jin (also known as Young-shik Kim, or Gajo), founder and
chief executive officer of Yerang Mission (Yerang Seongyo-Hwe).[1]
Suspecting Jin of embezzlement, mission supporters and Yerang office staff requested that police investigate a possible misuse of mission
funds. Previously, office staff and missionary trainees had asked their
leaders for an internal accountability audit, for there seemed to be much
questionable expenditure. Their requests were flatly denied. After investigation, the authorities charged Jin with using more than 2 billion won
(approximately US$2 million) for personal gain rather than for its des-
ignated mission purposes. From March 2002 to November 2006, over
ten thousand people had made donations to Yerang Mission to support

---

1. Seungkyu Lee, "Yerang Seongyohoe Daepyo Hoengnyeong mit Chakbok
Hyeomuiro Gusok" (Arrest of representative of Yerang Mission for accusation of embezzlement), *NewsNjoy*, December 20, 2007, www.newsnjoy.co.kr/news/quickViewAr
ticleView.html?idxno=20979.

its work in China for North Korean refugees. Prosecutors found that the donations in fact were not sent to China but instead were used in South Korea. On October 18, 2008, Jin was sentenced to two years in jail.

In April 2010 the Washington D.C. edition of the *Korea Times* quoted an article appearing in the *Washington Post* regarding a case of embezzlement by Eun-tae Lee, the administrative manager of Seed International, a U.S. based Korean-American Christian ministry.[2] Lee was arrested for having misappropriated over $700,000 of ministry funds for his personal use. The ministry's chairman of the board told reporters that he was unaware of any suspicious activity in the financial reports presented to the board at previous board meetings. The ministry had never had its books audited by a certified public accountant.

In May 2008 Rev. Paul Yong-gi Cho of the Full Gospel Yoido Church resigned from his position as senior pastor. This was three months earlier than his planned retirement date.[3] The world-renowned Cho was pressured to take his hands off church business early because he was operating the church as a family business. Pastor Cho's sons and relatives were in key managerial positions of the various church-sponsored organizations. Though he was forced to resign from his pastoral position, Cho was allowed to assume the chairmanship of the Full Gospel Mission, which controls the transferred assets of the church. People were comforted by the fact that the Full Gospel Mission is a foundation that is subject to audit by the Korean Tax Department and because some family members were removed from managerial positions.

Recently the Seoul District Court issued a lien on the bank accounts of members of the Korea Council of Christian Mission Organizations (KCCMO) to recover a large sum of money. The Executive Board of KCCMO, a not-for-profit organization formed in 1977, had gotten involved in profit-making activities and had failed to operate them profitably. As a result, their creditors asked the court for an injunction to freeze the bank accounts of KCCMO and to collect their debts from all the member organizations. In 1983 the Korean government had made special provision for it to serve as an umbrella organization for smaller mission organizations, making it possible for all of them to use the same

---

2. Byunghan Lee, "Jisang Gonggaehae Uihok Jegi" (Opened the facts to eliminate suspicion), *Korea Times*, April 20, 2010, www.koreatimes.com/articles/589231.

3. Seok Lee, "After Yoinggi-Cho, Door Has Opened, but . . . ," *Sisa Journal*, September 30, 2010, www.sisapress.com/news/articleView.html?idxno=53278.

tax identification number. Small mission organizations joined and operated their ministries under this tax umbrella. From the government's perspective, this eliminated the burden of having to verify the nonprofit status of every newly formed mission organization. By 2004 there were sixty-four members of KCCMO. Under the existing regulations, when one member of the council is liable, all the other members are jointly liable. As the result of the injunction to freeze KCCMO-related bank accounts, many completely innocent members could not access their own funds. In some cases, funds of legitimate mission organizations were remitted to the court to cover the insufficient funds of nonprofits that were operating illegitimately.

These are just a few of the scandals that have surfaced recently in Korea. They are symptomatic of the deeper issue that many organizations are not accountable for their ministry's financial activities. Very few organizations submit audited financial statements to the public or even to their own board of directors. It seems either that leaders of Korean mission organizations misunderstand their responsibility for accountability or that the organizations themselves follow a culturally bound administrative structure that does not support this type of transparency.

Donors certainly have the right to know how their contributions are being spent, yet either these donors have been ignored by management or have no means to demand their rights of accountability. Based on the recent cases mentioned above, it seems that donors desired accountability from the organizations they contributed to but were unable to obtain it.

## ISSUES

Five of the world's ten largest churches are in Korea, and Korea ranks second in the world in terms of the number of missionaries serving in other countries. As of January 2010 the Korean World Mission Association (KWMA) reported 20,840 missionaries working in 169 nations. Of this total, 12,915 missionaries were sent by 229 mission organizations, with the remainder sent directly by churches.[4] Informal figures suggest that the total amount of missionary support required may be as much as US$10 million per month (assuming even a minimum monthly income of $500).

4. Insook Jeong, "Statistics of Missionaries in Various Nations as of 2009" (electronic version), *KWMA Newsletter*, March 19, 2010, vol. 17–58, p. 4.

With the increase in the number of missionaries and mission organizations, attempts have been made to educate mission administrators regarding financial accountability.[5] Many Korean mission organizations, however, are not required to be accountable for their ministry activities, either by their constituents or by any government authority.

The issues of transparency and accountability in Korean missions require that attention be given to historical, cultural, and systemic perspectives. The core issue I wish to consider is, Why do Korean mission organizations have such a difficult time being accountable for their ministry and in being transparent about their decisions? This chapter will attempt to identify Korean cultural elements that relate to these issues and to offer a solution that takes into account legal and systemic perspectives. This chapter does not address accountability issues for churches or nongovernmental charitable organizations but is limited strictly to the matter of financial accountability of mission organizations in South Korea. Further studies could address accountability in other contexts—political, social, ethical, managerial, market, and indeed in all areas of our human life.[6]

## HISTORICAL PERSPECTIVE

Even though missionaries first arrived in Korea over a century ago, active Korean engagement in foreign mission endeavors is very recent: slightly over twenty years old. We are still in the learning stage of sending out missionaries and at a very immature stage in terms of operating mission organizations. Because of our rapid change over the past three decades from being a missionary-receiving nation to becoming a missionary-sending nation, we are coming under external pressure to adapt to globally accepted rules and operating procedures for nonprofit organizations. One of the areas of greatest stress for us is in the overall concept of accountability.

In 1832 Karl Gützlaff, pioneer Protestant missionary to China, tried to set foot in mainland Korea but was not allowed to do so. In

5. Since its inception, KWMA has presented numerous seminars and offered training to raise awareness of financial accountability and to prepare its member organizations for it.

6. Kevin P. Kerns, *Managing for Accountability: Preserving the Public Trust in Public and Nonprofit Organizations* (San Francisco: Jossey-Bass Publishers, 1996), p. 7. See also "Accountability," http://en.wikipedia.org/wiki/accountability.

1866 Robert Thomas, a Welsh missionary carrying a Chinese Bible, actually entered Korea—but soon afterward was martyred. The Scotsman John Ross was prevented from entering Korea, but from his base in Manchuria, China, he hired Korean-language assistants to translate the Bible into Korean. One of Ross's translators, Sang-ryun Seo, brought portions of the Korean Bible with him as he returned to his hometown, where he planted the first Korean church in 1883. In June 1883 a Mr. Nakasaka, a Japanese Bible colporteur working for the National Bible Society of Scotland, became the first foreign missionary in Korea, entering Busan. Two American missionaries, Henry Appenzeller and Horace Underwood, arrived at Chemulpo on April 5, 1885, and began a variety of missionary activities, including planting churches, translating the Bible, and building schools, hospitals, and seminaries. In the early twentieth century, the Korean church sent missionaries to Chejoo, Japan, China, and other countries. Because of Japanese colonial rule, however, no additional Korean missionaries were allowed to leave the country, and by 1942 all foreign missionaries then in Korea had been expelled. Although Koreans were gaining some experience administering churches in the democratic manner of the foreign missionaries, we still had not begun to learn how to administer international missionary ventures.

During the Korean War in the 1950s, sixteen nations came to rescue South Korea from the invasion by North Korean Communists. Korea received donations and humanitarian assistance from many nations after the war. Many Western nations sent missionaries to propagate the Gospel, plant and rebuild the churches, and raise up leaders. The church expanded, but the Korean church was turned in on itself and did not yet participate in foreign missions. During Expo 74 in Seoul, over 100,000 students stood up in answer to a call to be foreign missionaries, but at that time Koreans were restricted from overseas travel, and there was at that point no infrastructure that might support them in putting their commitment into practice.

Only when Korea hosted the Seoul Olympic Games in 1988 was the Korean church able to open its eyes to foreign nations. Koreans were finally allowed to travel overseas more freely, and now the church awoke to the Great Commission. Mission work increased at a rapid rate. In 1988 there were fewer than 200 Korean missionaries working outside of Korea. A mere twenty-two years later, that number had increased over a hundredfold. The number of mission organizations has also increased—

from fewer than 20 to 229 sizable organizations today, plus at least 200 additional small mission agencies.

Until recently, mission has been an individual endeavor rather than being carried out through formal mission organizations. Most missionaries raised their own support and then simply left home to begin their missionary work. Individual missionaries appealed to their circles of relationships and received support. Now, rather than setting a common vision or strategy or providing encouragement, training, and support, the role of mission organizations has tended to be simply that of a conduit for the collection and remittance of funds to the missionaries. The donors give because they personally know and trust their missionary; they are not supporting the mission organization, and thus they do not ask the mission organization to be responsible for the manner in which their funds are used.

As the number of people in mission organizations has increased, the volume of mission work has increased proportionally. Mission executives have been busy finding and sending missionaries to the field. These leaders tend to be charismatic personalities, pastors who have little or no administrative experience. They tend to seize opportunities and enter into their role without having adequate time to prepare in terms of understanding global mission or in receiving managerial training. Few mission executives have had the privilege of studying missiology in the West. Fewer still have had exposure to formal training in the administration of mission organizations.

Some Korean leaders, while they were in the West, may have joined overseas mission organizations. Others may have been exposed in their training to the concept of accountability as it applies to mission organizations. On their return to Korea, however, they have had a difficult time implementing this concept. Korean culture is relational, and people are judged based on the quality of their ongoing relationships rather than on their performance or efficiency. The concept of accountability as separate from relationships is still foreign to many Korean organizations and their leaders. There is strong cultural resistance to reducing the value of relationships by enforcing some external standard of accountability. Administrative patterns also favor relationship over effectiveness. For this reason, accountability is a concept that mostly has been given only lip service until the recent scandals that have rocked mission organizations.

## CULTURAL PERSPECTIVE

Korean culture has no historical connection with Roman law, Greek philosophy, Catholic morality, European ideas of government, or French and American ideals of democracy. These concepts in their totality are foreign to Korean thinking and application. Instead, as a long-term, semi-independent but vassal state of China, Korea overlaid its deep shamanic roots with inherited Confucian hierarchical structures, a Taoist sense of fortune and fate, Buddhist piety, and a deeply ingrained pragmatism. Behind a protective screen of social politeness and conformity, whatever power and resources Koreans have been able to grasp within their social structure was and is unashamedly used for the furthering of one's own family fortune. Christian morality, with a short history of less than 130 years in our nation, finds it difficult to compete with the cultural imperatives laid down and imbibed for over 6,000 years. The result has been that the church finds itself shaped, if not compromised, by social pressure from the native Korean culture. One of these compromises is that, in order to be able to lead in ways the culture expects, pastors have to embrace the nearly absolute power demanded of Korean cultural leaders. The same absolute power is expected of those directing mission organizations. In this context, questions of any type regarding the leader or his use of resources are seen, at best, as impolite; at worst, they are viewed as expressions of disloyalty.

It should come as no surprise that Korean culture has little place for the logical and rational worldview that serves as the foundation of Western decision making. Rather, as part of the broader Asian culture, the Korean worldview has relationships as its core reality. Everything happens based on the strength or weakness of relationships; there is little room for rational behavior when dealing in values wholly bound to the realm of human relationships. Pragmatism is most important: how will this or that decision affect my existing or potential relationships, and how will the response of those above me affect my prospects in the future?

Generalizing from these comments, I note that administration of an organization in Korean culture is viewed as the appropriate management of existing relationships and the development of more influential relationships that will support you in accomplishing your will within society. Short-term issues such as efficiency or effectiveness are thus not as important as the potential benefits or costs of putting pressure on existing relationships. A primary element in Confucian thinking is loyalty to those who are over you. Thus, the level of personal loyalty to the mission organization administrator and tightening the strings of obligation (*budam*) that decrease potential for disloyalty are key considerations for Korean administrators. A great majority of working relationships in Korea today, including those in mission organizations, are still based on loyalty to the leader. Culturally, this loyalty is absolute and is an unconsciously accepted norm in all hierarchical relationships—and, for Koreans, all relationships are hierarchical.

In return for being allowed to be in relationship and associated with the leader, dependents or subordinates are expected to show the appropriate respect and unconditional obedience that is their cultural duty. The will of the leader is the driving force of any organization, which is effectively implemented without comment or disagreement by those in relationship with the leader. Any questions raised or differences of opinion are culturally perceived as disrespectful of the leader's position and bring distancing from, or even severing of, the relationship, effectively ending the person's possibilities for advancement within the organization. With the cultural assumption that leadership should take action in accordance with the relationships that sustain and support it, a demand for accountability in itself can be perceived as disrespectful, and any attempt to make the organization more accountable may easily be considered disloyal, as it implies questions about the person and integrity of the leader himself.

Because Korean culture retains its foundation of Confucian roots, which call for absolute loyalty to king, teacher, and father, it subconsciously shapes every relationship in accord with these non-Western principles.[7] In most Korean organizations, "all decisions are made and things are done by order of the senior. They are done without comment by the lower level person for fear of being considered disloyal."[8]

---

7. Charles O. Hucker, *China's Imperial Past: An Introduction to Chinese History and Culture* (Stanford, Calif.: Stanford Univ. Press, 1975), pp. 75–76. Confucianism was established to bring order to the disordered shamanistic populations during the Han Dynasty (202 b.c.e.–220 c.e.). The ruling classes implemented a Confucian social order to control a people who, for the most part, followed a shamanistic culture. They ensured the absolute power of the emperor by designing an interlinked social structure that shared its absolute downward power with the most significant linkages in society; for example, even the poorest father enjoyed absolute power over his family. But in order to exercise this power, the father had to accept the unequal power relationships of the entire system.

8. Robert Vergara, "What's the Difference? A Comparison of Cultural Traits: Korean

This automatic social loyalty is also applied to elders within the society: the elder males in a relational network have the greatest authority; the grandfather, father, or eldest brother has the last word in any family decision. Contemporary Korean culture still requires that, out of respect, lower-level persons should not participate in the decision-making process, nor should they speak in discussions when elders are speaking and making a decision. Though lower-rank persons are expected to be present in the meeting and learn the heart and will of their leader, any suggestions they make will be viewed as objections to the leader's capability of leadership. The cultural framework allows no room for expression of the democratic principles common in the Western world. It strongly discourages sharing opinions or alternative perspectives. Though the firm hold of Confucianism is slowly eroding because of the influence of Western media and contact with Western organizations, the culture itself offers multi-layered resistance to change.

To make matters worse, most mission organizations are headed by an ordained minister. In the Korean cultural system, ordained ministers are ascribed absolute spiritual authority over their congregation or organization. Members of the board of directors merely reaffirm the relationship they have with the leader. Rather than scrutinizing the leader's plans or inquiring about his use of funds in the interests of accountability, which would imply his incapacity to provide appropriate direction, board members simply affirm their positive relationship with the leader by approving and standing in agreement with his decisions. In many cases, the members of the board are hand-picked by the president of the organization or are members of the church of which the leader is pastor. The board's cultural role is to approve and support all the decisions of the executive. Most board members simply fulfill their culturally appropriate duty and resist any attempts at calling for accountability, not perceiving that they might have a higher responsibility than to conform to the expectations of their culture. Accordingly, boards offer little accountability to missionaries, staff, members, or donors involved and merely participate in fulfillment of their formal relational obligations.

The Korean donor public is culturally conditioned to make decisions based on emotion rather than logic. When a missionary comes to speak at their church, they give based on their emotional response to the

and American" (paper prepared for Cornerstone Ministries International, Seoul, Korea, 2008), p. 3.

speaker. If they respect the speaker, then they ask no questions about how the funds will be spent. Furthermore, because of their Confucian cultural roots, they view the missionary as a pastor and teacher, so it would be disrespectful to ask for details about what he really does and how he spends the funds he receives. The financial supporters may not have total confidence in the person because their relationship may not be strong, but the risks of making this financial investment are acceptable within the culture. Their motivation for giving is to strengthen their relationship and ties of obligation with the speaker rather than to accomplish a particular task. All this is to say that the problem of lack of accountability is systemic.

## SYSTEMIC PERSPECTIVE

After reviewing ways that Korean culture tends to work against organizational financial accountability, we focus more widely in this section on aspects of the overall society that make it difficult for Korean mission organizations to practice meaningful financial accountability.

### Lack of Financial Management and Financial Statements

In his book *Managing a Nonprofit Organization in the Twenty-first Century*, Thomas Wolf observes that "financial management is, for many, one of the most forbidding aspects of the administration of nonprofit organizations. This is because they come into nonprofit organizations with no financial background and, in some cases, a numbers phobia. Often they have chosen to work as staff members or serve on boards because of a knowledge and commitment to education, conservation, child abuse, or some other activity. For them, the financial area—budgets, reports, and procedures—seems unrelated and dull, something for the 'financial' people to deal with."[9]

The situation in Korea is even more severe than what Wolf here describes. Because of the short history of Korean missions, we are dealing with first-generation management issues; not many people in mission have a financial background. Not many organizations are able to support well-trained professionals; the salaries offered mission staff are very low, and most mission organizations have yet to recognize their serious need

9. Thomas Wolf, *Managing a Nonprofit Organization in the Twenty-first Century* (New York: Simon & Schuster, 1999), p. 175.

for accountability. Not only are there few proficient people, but because of the limited career paths in mission organizations, the turnover rate for office staff is high in comparison with that of other industries.

Because they lack experience and staff in financial management, mission organizations at best keep only the most basic accounting records. According to Jung-nam Kim, "Accounting in nonprofit favors single-entry bookkeeping for recording cash receipts and disbursements or cash-based accounting principles. Therefore, many still are tied to the most primitive methods of bookkeeping."[10] The financial system for most Korean nonprofit organizations is not set up on an accrual basis, where expenses are recognized not only when payments have been made but also when expenses are incurred and income is committed.

In the United States, GAAP (Generally Accepted Accounting Principles) requires that financial statements be presented using the accrual basis of accounting.[11] If a small organization is set up and keeps records on a cash basis, it can convert to acceptable accrual basis at the end of the year and present its annual financial statements using the accrual basis of accounting.[12] This is an acceptable approach, provided it does not result in financial statements that are materially different from those prepared solely on an accrual basis. In addition, when the annual financial statement is prepared for a nonprofit organization, it should include:

- A statement of financial position as of the end of the reporting period (also referred to as a balance sheet).

- A statement of activities for the reporting period (also referred to as a statement of revenues and expenses).

10. Jung-nam Kim, *Jonggyo Beobin-ui Seomu-wa Gyohoe Jaejeong Gwanli* (Tax accounting for religious organizations and for church financial management) (Seoul: Doseo Choolpan Youngmoon, 2004), p. 78.

11. Glenn A. Welsch, Charles T. Zlatkovich, and John Arch White, *Intermediate Accounting*, 3rd ed. (Homewood, Ill.: Richard Irwin, 1972), pp. 15–16. Generally accepted accounting principles (GAAP) refers to the rules of accounting developed and accepted by the accounting profession in conformity with the objectives of accounting, the fundamental underlying assumptions, and the basic theoretical concepts. Generally accepted accounting principles also must have the substantial authoritative support of the profession.

12. Evangelical Joint Accounting Committee, *Accounting and Financial Reporting Guide for Christian Ministries*, rev. ed. (S.L. EJAC, 2001), p. 6.

- A statement of functional expenses required for Voluntary Health and Welfare Organizations and encouraged for all others as a separate statement, schedule or note.

- A statement of cash flows for the reporting period.

- Accompanying notes to the financial statements.[13]

This is generally acceptable accounting practice in the United States. Currently in Korea very few mission organizations submit audited financial statements to their boards, to their donors, or to governmental bodies.[14] Most Korean boards appoint auditors from among the board members as part of their by-laws and have these auditors provide oversight in working with management only in reviewing the financial matters of the organization. The auditor/board member then submits an internal financial report to the board. Often this financial statement is deemed audited simply because it was presented by the auditor appointed by the board. Members of boards serving as auditors, however, are often not professionally trained and seldom spend the amount of time required to understand and monitor all aspects of the organization's financial matters. Though such auditors may inspect every transaction, their reports cannot be considered credible financial audited reports, since they lack the professional training to ensure the validity of the data presented.

If Korean auditors were preparing reports to U.S. standards, the financial statement would have to meet the criteria of the GAAP, as the U.S. Financial Accounting Standards Board states in paragraph 4 of its standard no. 117:

> The primary purpose of financial statements is to provide relevant information to meet the common interest of donors, members, creditors, and others who provide resources to not-for-profit organizations. Those external users of financial statements have common interests in assessing (a) the services an organization provides and its ability to continue to provide those services and (b) how managers discharge their stewardship responsibilities and other aspects of their performance.

13. Evangelical Council for Financial Accountability, "ECFA Standard 3—Financial Oversight" (www.ecfa.org/Content/Comment3). This standard is based on Financial Accounting Standards Board, "Statement of Financial Accounting Standards No. 117: Financial Statements of Not-for-Profit Organizations" (June 1993), available at www .ecfa.org/Content/Comment3.

14. Gi-Yul Kim and Byun Youngseon, *Biyeongli-beobin Hoegye-wa Seomu Silmu* (Accounting for nonprofit organizations and practical tax accounting), rev. ed. (Seoul: Samil Infomine, 2010), p. 34.

To fulfill this criteria, most boards of directors for Western organizations hire an outside auditor to perform the financial audit and report the result of their independent audit to the board. The process of an independent audit by a CPA may provide financial accountability in Korea, but there is a greater need: improvements of internal control of financial procedures to ensure accountability.

### Lack of Accounting Principles

Currently, there is nothing like GAAP for Korean mission or other non-profit organizations to use as a standard.

> Accounting principles for nonprofit organizations do not exist, as opposed to the generally acceptable accounting principles in place for profit-making businesses. Public organizations, hospitals, schools, social service organizations, religious organizations, and other similar legal entities must conform to the laws pertaining to them under the regulations of the relevant government ministry. Some regulatory bodies have provided certain accounting principles. The reality, however, is that different organizations have applied accounting principles differently, though they fall under the same government ministry. Recognizing such discrepancies, the Korean Accounting Standards Board prepared and announced in 2003 a set of accounting principles for nonprofit organizations. Since it was not made mandatory to follow these principles, however, it is rare to see nonprofit organizations applying the principles and auditing their financial statements based on them.[15]

In 2004 Chang-nam Sohn, a Korean CPA, prepared guidelines for Korean Christian mission organizations on how to present financial statements. He presented these guidelines after KWMA surveyed its membership in 2003 in relation to the proposed Korean accounting principles for nonprofit organizations announced the year before.[16] Sohn's guidelines were specifically designed for mission organizations. There is no inducement, however, for their implementation. Jung-nam Kim has stated, "Accounting practices in our country do not have a fixed logical structure; each nonprofit organization utilizes whatever type of ac-

15. Ibid.

16. Chang-nam Sohn, "Seongyeo Danche-eui Jaemoo Jepyo-e Gwanhan Yeongoo" (Study of financial statements for mission organizations) (paper prepared for KWMA, Seoul, Korea, 2004).

counting they find best serves the tax-accounting rules pertinent to their organization and meets their own business accounting requirements."[17] Because there is no obligation or incentive to implement them, neither the accounting principles of the Korean Accounting Standards Board nor Sohn's suggested accounting principles for nonprofit organizations have so far been accepted as GAAP for Korean mission organizations.

### Lack of Korean Governing Laws

Under existing Korean law, there is no specific law that covers definition of a religious organization as a legal person, and there are no basic or special laws pertaining to religious entities other than Civil Law Article 32.[18] Civil Law serves only as a set of general guiding principles, not as specific, enforceable laws. Civil Law allows for the existence of a nonprofit organization or a foundation. Permission can be obtained to become a legal entity of these two types by applying to the relevant ministry that oversees education, religion, charities, arts, social, and other nonprofit groups. On December 31, 2008, Article 32 of the Civil Law was modified to change the approval process and administrative responsibility for religious entities from the Ministry of Culture and Tourism to local government bodies.

Because of the lack of specificity of Civil Law, forming a nonprofit organization is difficult. The vagueness of Civil Law allows the various local governments to exert whatever level of authority they deem necessary to determine their approval of nonprofit legal status. Obtaining legal status for a small mission organization, while not impossible, is so complicated and the requirements so vague that most small organizations hesitate to pursue legal status. Many small mission organizations exist only informally, without formal legal status. Because they thus have no need to provide financial reports to the government, these informal organizations have little concern for financial accountability.

To help small organizations meet government requirements, the government has allowed the existence of umbrella associations such as KCCMO and KWMA. These membership associations allow small organizations to pay a small annual fee to become a formal and legal part of the association. Each member organization can operate as a quasi-independent nonprofit organization and offer its donors tax

---

17. Jung-nam Kim, *Jonggyo*, p. 89.

18. Gi-Yul Kim and Byun Youngseon, *Biyeongli-beobin*, p. 1341.

benefits. The downside is that all of these organizations share the same organization tax number. They are seen by government as one macro entity, each fully liable for the activity of the whole. We have already discussed the danger of this shared exposure in the freezing of bank accounts of all members of KCCMO for the misdeeds of a few.

The government has not imposed strict procedures to ensure the accountability of each organization under the umbrella associations. Likewise, the association does not require detailed financial reports of its members. That is, given the current informal state of nonprofit organizations, professional financial management is not essential. In short, organizational accountability is neither understood nor required.

## SUGGESTED SOLUTIONS

There are many possible solutions to the problems reviewed above, but they all hinge on being adopted by our highly pragmatic mission leaders, who, at this time, have no driving motivation to focus on the accounting aspect of their ministries. Regardless of the cultural issues that seem to block change and progress in areas of financial accountability, I would suggest the following practical and adoptable steps toward increasing the accountability of Korean mission organizations.

### Educate for Awareness

Commenting on accountability in Christian partnership, William D. Taylor, former executive secretary of the WEA Mission Commission, has urged us to "overcome a popular misconception that accountability is geographically and culturally bound. In fact, we often imply, with great inaccuracy, that accountability is a Western concept—that somehow Korean churches grow without accountability, that Brazilians train and send cross-cultural missionaries without it, that the Evangelical Missionary Society of Nigeria can train and deploy over 800 missionaries without any concept of accountability. . . . The concept of accountability is a universal concept. . . . In fact, accountability seems to be essential to any meaningful relationship between persons in all cultures. It may be called different things and described in different ways by different cultures, but the concept is there all the same."[19] I grant that the concept of

19. William D. Taylor, *Kingdom Partnerships for Synergy in Missions* (Pasadena, Calif.: William Carey Library, 1994), pp. 119–20.

accountability is universal. We cannot forget, however, that the practice of accountability is inevitably shaped by one's cultural worldview.

In his *Geography of Thought*, Richard Nisbett acknowledged the subtle role of culture when he commented, "Confucius praised the desire of the gentleman to harmonize and distinguished it from the petty person's need for conformity."[20] In Korea we focus on accountability in terms of our relational economy. The elements of accountability have to do with harmony, loyalty, respect, and knowing one's place. As long as these indicators are adequately conserved, in our culture, accountability is deemed to have been observed. Fiscal accountability, the type of accountability described by Taylor and Western agencies, is always subordinate in importance to what we are looking for in terms of our relational economy. Fiscal irregularities in order to meet relational obligations or duty are understood, even expected, within our cultural parameters. This is not to justify them, only to say that Korean culture does not stress the importance of the fiscal process when compared to the relational reality. I do not expect that it will be easy for many non-Koreans to understand the paradigmatic differences between a relational economy and a fiscal economy.

Many Korean mission organizations are feeling pressure to adopt Western methods and principles of accountability. Many are claiming to follow the templates offered by the Western GAAP. Culturally, however, the motivation for compliance is paradigmatically opposed to that of Western organizations. The same motivations do not drive our behaviors. With the Korean focus on face, relationships, and harmony, the reports may easily tend to reflect an idealized reality that effectively meets the expectations of those demanding them, usually Western partners. This would not only be culturally acceptable, but culturally expected. The value of long-term relational harmony is culturally understood to overrule the need to recognize relationship-weakening temporal reversals. It would not be surprising that the only report provided as a result of a fiscal accountability audit would be sent to foreign partners, the only party that would require it in within our culture's relational context.

While I am not justifying our cultural focus, I am trying to explain that, within our relational paradigm, few situations would call for or encourage the level of transparency involved in fiscal accountability.

20. Richard E. Nisbett, *The Geography of Thought: How Asians and Westerners Think Differently . . . and Why* (New York: Free Press, 2003), p. 7.

So how do we begin to encourage the adoption of a concept that is not available or considered relevant within our worldview?

Changes in Korean culture will not take place without drastic causes and reasons; time will be required to erode the interlocking attitudes that sustain our cultural integrity. Thus, it will demand intentional efforts to educate the leaders and staff of mission organizations, board members, and donors. Voluntary breaking with cultural precedents will demand long-term determination and a few brave organizations to model this level of transparency for the rest.

On May 15, 1995, public supporters and many nonprofit organizations were shocked when the U.S. Foundation for New Era Philanthropy asked the court for protection under Chapter 11 of the U.S. bankruptcy code. "Several hundred nonprofit organizations and highly respected philanthropists had invested millions of dollars in New Era's fund based on promises by its founder and chief executive, John G. Bennett."[21] As the result of this case, the nonprofit world woke up and began to scrutinize its organizations. Much stronger accountability standards have been imposed and implemented since then.

Korea seems to be in a similar situation. With the recent scandals suffered by mission organizations in Korea, some groups have begun asking questions of financial accountability of those with whom they have only a weak relationship. But as we have also seen in the case of Yong-gi Cho, even when there are fiscal grounds for token disciplinary action, the relational economy provides an entirely alternate basis for judgment, allowing Cho to retain his controlling position over the global assets and activities of the Full Gospel Mission. The chairman of the Samsung group recently convicted of financial malpractice went through a similar lateral shift allowing him to retain his position and privilege.

As scandals continue to be uncovered, the Korean Christian donor public is beginning to take a closer look at those they subconsciously trust implicitly. Obvious misappropriation of funds is beginning to be reported by staff or disillusioned donors, as happened in the case of Yerang in 2008. On November 29, 2010, the Cheeup Portal (Job Portal) in Seoul surveyed 773 office workers on their end-of-year giving. The result was that 39.6 percent stopped donating altogether because of the nonprofit organization scandal, and 24.7 percent of respondents said they would first review the trustworthiness of an organization before

21. Kerns, *Managing for Accountability*, p. 4.

198 ACCOUNTABILITY IN MISSIONS

donating to it.[22] As time continues uncovering the fiscal irresponsibility allowed and even encouraged by Korean culture, a time will come when only those organizations that meet and provide financial accountability will survive.

For the kingdom of God to be furthered, we must begin voluntary efforts to educate our donors, staff, management, and boards on the importance of program and fiscal accountability, and we must offer transparency in our financial reporting. With this understanding, various mission organizations have come together to study the accountability issue and in recent years have begun teaching practical solutions to mission officers. An excellent example is the efforts of KWMA in this regard. It has provided accounting and bookkeeping classes to its member organizations and offers them individualized assistance in setting up basic accounting systems and reporting.[23] A few years ago KWMA performed an evaluation of its membership in the areas of organization and financial accountability. The results of their evaluation were made public and served as a source of comfort to donors.[24]

### Enact More Specific Laws

Because of its fundamental cultural focus on a relational economy, Korea's legal system is based on law written in broad generalities, allowing for diverse application depending on various relational factors. This same paradigm controls board and management meetings, where the give-and-take in decision making is relational rather than rational. Unless a more specific law is enacted, the boards and management of nonprofit organizations will not voluntarily pursue the improvement of their financial accountability systems or see the need to protect the rights of their donors.

The Korean government, which holds quite strictly to the separation of church and state, has taken a noninterventionist approach to the operation of nonprofit organizations. They have not focused on these groups because they are not a source of tax revenue. With the growth of the Korean economy, however, the government is beginning to change

22. Hee Ahn, "Jikjangin Gibudanche Biriro Gibu-uihyang Eopseojyeo" (Forty percent stopped giving because of scandals in public nonprofit organizations), *Chosun Newspaper*, November 29, 2010.

23. See www.kwma.org.

24. Chang-nam Sohn, "Seongyeo."

its practices. It is in the process of looking more closely at nongovernmental organizations, since people are claiming tax deductions for their contributions to such organizations, whether or not they are fully qualified as nonprofits.

I strongly urge mission associations to prepare themselves to provide input to the government as it begins to consider regulating or enacting laws to ensure the proper use of donations so as to protect the charitable giving of its citizens. More important, nonprofit organizations must band together and lobby the government to increase the specificity of the law regarding nonprofit organizational status, making it easier for legitimate nonprofit organizations to be registered as such. Alternatively, a law limiting the financial liability of association members to just the offending parties would make association membership more attractive to the majority of mission organizations.

*Develop an Organizational Supervisory Body*

Because of the highly informal situation of nonprofit mission organizations, there are no generally acceptable standards regarding their management, operation, or financial accounting practices. Many mission organizations are unable to provide financial accountability simply because they have no formalized decision-making systems; many have only names on paper as their board of directors. Before focusing on fiscal accountability per se, we must encourage our mission organizations to understand the role of a working board of directors. Even though our culture and our government do not demand it, we should voluntarily move toward a countercultural valuing of transparency and accountability. It starts with transparency and accountability to a board of directors that exists as more than just a formality. If the board of directors of Seed International had implemented appropriate checks and balances, conducted regular financial audits, and encouraged a proficient staff, they might have avoided the embezzlement of their funds.

Ideally, it would help our various mission organizations to have some form of organization dedicated to help us understand, develop, and maintain voluntary fiscal accountability, to underscore the view of accountability as involving "answering to a higher authority in the bureaucratic or interorganizational chain of command."[25] While un-

25. Kerns, *Managing for Accountability*, p. 7.

derstanding our cultural imperative that supervisory bodies base their policies and actions on relational factors, it is time for Korean mission organizations to come together and establish an organization like the Evangelical Council for Financial Accountability (ECFA) in the United States to provide motivation and guidance as we continue moving voluntarily toward financial accountability.

## CONCLUSION

As we have seen, Korean culture supports a relational economy that does not naturally encourage accountability, financial or otherwise. Thus, any solutions that will fit our situation will have to be voluntary divergences from what are considered acceptable cultural norms. It is important that we discover the road to these solutions for ourselves rather than relying on solutions offered (or demanded!) by our Western partners, which may come across as prepackaged or culturally unimplementable. Any real progress will require an initial building of awareness, education, and assistance in implementing financial systems among multiple publics: board, leaders, staff, and donors.

The process of developing awareness of the need for, gaining an understanding of, and implementing financial accountability is a subset of a much deeper issue we must face in Korea, namely, finding a Christian alternative to the fundamentally Confucian model of leadership and social dynamics that defines our entire culture.

There is no easy solution. However, as we struggle with the cultural implications surrounding financial accountability, we will become aware of the greater issues that may help us clarify our thinking and actions as Christians and further clarify our role in global mission.

# 13

## Response to Bahn Seok (Peter) Lee, "Accountability Issues Among Korean Missions Organizations"

### *Marvin J. Newell*

B AHN SEOK LEE HAS done the world of missions an immense service by providing this insightful study pertaining to accountability issues related specifically to the Korean mission context. In this day of ever-increasing international partnerships, such in-depth studies are imperative if global mission organizations are to develop relationships of true understanding and trust. The overriding issues of accountability internal to Korean missions that emerge from its historical and cultural background are relevant the world over. Though local expressions may differ in practice, in many respects the root issues are the same. Lee has provided a masterful study that details core Korean issues that lead to undesirable outcomes. In response, I would first like to make some general observations about accountability and the necessity of standards.

Consider for a moment what our world would be like without standards of accountability—without some measure of comparison for quantitative or qualitative value. Baseball batting averages and times for running a marathon would be meaningless. Drug prescriptions would be dangerous. Professionals, products, organizations, and businesses would not merit our confidence. We would be lost in a sea of confusion and mistrust. Only by adherence to exact and acknowledged standards can performance, products, people, and even our best plans be measured.

In his book *Dare to Discipline*, American child psychologist James Dobson relates a study in which social psychologists observed elementary school children in a playground protected by a high fence. The children ran with abandon, playing joyfully within the confines of the fence, unaware of and unconcerned about the busy street just a few feet from the play area. Some theorists decided that the fence was too restrictive, that it inhibited the children, who should have more freedom. So the fence came down.

When the children entered the playground the next day, instead of running with their previous abandon, they huddled together at the center of the play area. Unsure of their limits, they appeared insecure and fearful. The conclusion was and is clear: we need normative parameters in life. We need fences and standards. We need to know where the limits are. In missions, we can live with transparency within those limits and standards and can have the freedom to develop global partnerships with confidence and trust.

## SCRIPTURE

If anything could be said to be lacking in Lee's well-researched and well-documented paper, it would be a minimal scriptural perspective that would help inform believers, no matter what their cultural heritage, on universal principles of accountability. One biblical account that readily comes to mind in this regard is the well-known sin of Ananias and Sapphira recorded in Acts 5. This story of blatant deception is also an instance of people clearly acting without accountability. And if God had not supernaturally intervened, their deception most likely would have gone undetected. It is interesting to note that the very first public sin mentioned within the early church was exactly that with which we are dealing here—fiscal accountability. It seems the church of every age must deal with this issue!

From this early-church incident involving the handling of property (of which finances are a part), four overriding principles are readily apparent:

- property is valuable and, as such, is a significant resource for the promotion of God's purposes;

- property is vulnerable to manipulation and misrepresentation by dishonest believers;

- property is visible, the handling of which represents a public test of one's heart condition before God and man;

- property owners are stewards of what God has entrusted to them, the misuse of which may "put the Spirit of the Lord to the test" (Acts 5:9 NRSV).

These fundamental principles are transcultural and transtemporal. As such, Koreans, Americans, Europeans, Africans, and all others are responsible to deal with them.

## KOREAN REALITIES

From the start, Lee makes three realities clear from the instances of financial indiscretion that he cites. The first is that the mishandling of funds is manifold and multifaceted. Though fiscal abuse is a failure that should not be named among believers, especially those involved in the work of missions, the unfortunate reality is that it does occur. Some lapses involve a single mission agency (Yerang Mission), some a mission-charitable organization (Seed International), some an association of mission agencies (KCCMO), while others are church based (Full Gospel Yoido Church). The mishandling of funds and property is not limited to any one genus or entity in Korean Christianity. Although mission agencies were predominately singled out by Lee, he appropriately detailed the issue in the wider Christian context in Korea.

A second reality that Lee describes in detail is the deep-seated cultural mix of the Confucian, Taoist, and Buddhist heritage that lies at the very core of interpersonal relationships. Lee describes clearly the Korean relational and hierarchical worldview of personal loyalty tied to obligation. Any environment in which leaders wield absolute power and demand absolute loyalty of subordinates makes a perfect setting for nonaccountability. Lee goes on to show that a mission executive (who in many cases is also a pastor) typically goes unchecked; a subservient board may be in place, but culturally it does not have the right to press for accountability. These cultural observations are of great help to us in the West in understanding the root issue behind what Jim Plueddemann identifies as "high-power distance cultures."[1]

The third reality cited is the general lack of mechanics for accountability in Korea itself. Lee notes that, by contrast, U.S. organizations follow the recognized Generally Accepted Accounting Principles (GAAP) upon which regular audits are based. CrossGlobal Link has long required

---

1. James E. Plueddemann, *Leading Across Cultures: Effective Ministry and Mission in the Global Church* (Downers Grove, Ill.: IVP Academic, 2009), p. 93.

of its members the submission of an annual GAAP audit. To date, thankfully, none of our members has been censored by either the government or a watchdog group for financial impropriety. I believe this has been the case mainly because this standard of accountability is adhered to.

Lee describes a fundamental tension that is very difficult for us in the West not only to understand but also to accept. This tension arises from the competing demands made by the "relational economy" of Korean culture and by the "fiscal economy" of the West, in terms of which we are seeking together to understand biblical accountability. Lee states, "Fiscal irregularities in order to meet relational obligations or duty are understood, even expected, within our cultural parameters. This is not to justify them, only to say that Korean culture does not stress the importance of the fiscal process when compared to the relational reality. I do not expect that it will be easy for many non-Koreans to understand the paradigmatic differences between a relational economy and a fiscal economy" (p. 196).

This observation would be worth discussing and debating in more detail than is possible here. The crux of the matter seems to be that, insofar as this statement is true, we must ask whether longterm international partnerships with Korean mission entities are realistic and sustainable.

## CONSEQUENCES

The misappropriation of funds and misuse of property in any country or context has its consequences, which Lee identifies throughout the final sections of his paper. It is instructive to cluster them together for clearer awareness:

- Disillusioned donors—who are becoming increasingly reactive in Korea toward questionable fiscal practices and/or nonaccountability in mission organizations.

- Organizational survival—only those mission organizations that provide financial accountability will survive long-term.

- Propagation of the Gospel—God's kingdom work cannot be reputably furthered if it lacks fiscal responsibility. The mission movement will have long-lasting positive impact only insofar as it is known for being reputable and responsible. A basic leadership principle states, "If you don't believe in the messenger, you won't believe the message."[2]

2. James M. Kouzes and Barry Z. Posner, *The Leadership Challenge* (San Francisco: Jossey-Bass, 2002), p. 33.

- Increased government regulations—there will be increased intervention on the part of the Korean government to regulate nonprofit organizations. Missions will increasingly come under the heavy hand of government scrutiny.

- United voice—the increased need for nonprofits to band together as a united voice to be represented to the government. This representation would function, as Lee has suggested, in lobbying for direction-giving standards and regulations. I would suggest, however, that they will also need to lobby for noninterference in the other internal affairs of mission organizations.

- Need for a supervisory body—Lee has made a valid case for the establishment of a recognized supervisory body that can give oversight and set standards for mission groups that encompass the fuller realm of accountability, such as board functions. I urge that other institutional standards be included as well. These would consist of guidelines for membership, organization, operations, and personnel, as well as defining conflicts of interest. Only when the full scope of corporate structures is monitored can loopholes and mismanagement be avoided. Due diligence demands that accountability be applied holistically across the organizational structure. Indeed, that is one of the primary functions of CrossGlobal Link for North American missions. Credentialing is granted to missions that meet and maintain standards in each of these areas.

## CONCLUSION

The concluding plea from Lee for an understanding of Korean "relational economy" and how it takes precedence over normative Western accountability standards is worth heeding. Herein lies the fundamental tension: how can we in the West not demand "prepackaged or culturally unimplementable" accountability (p. 200), while at the same time being confident that there is an adequate foundation of trust on which to build partnerships? Mutual respect demands mutual trust. At the very least, a mutually agreed upon process should be engaged in that will point the way toward mutually agreeable solutions.

# 14

## Broken Trust: Sexual Abuse in the Mission Community; A Case Study in Mission Accountability

### B. Hunter Farrell

THE CALL TO ACCOUNTABILITY in mission is understood by the Presbyterian Church (U.S.A.) to be rooted in humanity's redemption from sin by Jesus Christ and in believers' shared calling to "present [our] bodies as a living sacrifice" (Rom. 12:1 NRSV) and give all that we are to Christ's mission. God, through Christ, has freed us from the power of sin and calls us to live as agents of God's reconciling mission in the world: "All this is from God, who reconciled us to himself through Christ and gave us the ministry of reconciliation: that God was reconciling the world to himself in Christ, not counting people's sins against them. And he has committed to us the message of reconciliation. We are therefore Christ's ambassadors, as though God were making his appeal through us. We implore you on Christ's behalf: Be reconciled to God" (2 Cor. 5:18–20 TNIV).

This call to accountability to God in mission in all areas of our life—financial, theological, missiological, behavioral, and even sexual—pushes against the constraints of our North American cultures, challenging our ecclesiastical structures and cultural taboos with Christ's proclamation of a kingdom where "the last shall be first" (Matt. 19:30 KJV) and where children are lifted up as examples of the emerging realm, "for the kingdom of heaven belongs to such as these" (Matt. 19:14 NIV; see also 18:1–5). While it is difficult and sometimes extremely awkward to speak publicly of any General Assembly Mission Council (GAMC) shortcomings, it is particularly difficult in the area of sexual misconduct, but the integrity of the commitment of GAMC to Christ's mission requires it.

Since its founding in 1770, the Presbyterian Church (U.S.A.) has understood itself to be a missionary society, engaged in the mission of Jesus Christ in the world. Initially through active participation in the American Board of Commissioners for Foreign Mission (1812–70) and through women's regional missionary associations, Presbyterians sought ways to respond to God's call to spread the Gospel of Jesus Christ throughout the world.[1] Beginning in the 1830s, missionaries were sent by the national denomination to Native American populations in North America and to dozens of countries on five continents: the Gospel was preached, churches were established, primary and secondary schools and universities were founded, clinics and hospitals were built and equipped, literacy programs were established, and national Christian leaders were trained.

## ANTECEDENTS TO THE PRESENT CASE

One of the countries to which the Presbyterian Church sent missionaries was the Congo (former Belgian Congo and Zaire; today, the Democratic Republic of the Congo). Presbyterian work there began in 1890 and has resulted in the planting and growth of two Presbyterian denominations,[2] which together number nearly two million Christians today.

In 1998 the GAMC's World Mission office received a report of sexual abuse by a retired Presbyterian missionary who had served in the Congo. An Independent Committee of Inquiry (ICI) was established "to investigate allegations of abuse of children in the Democratic Republic of the Congo (formerly Zaire) for the period 1945–78. The Independent Committee of Inquiry functioned independently and made its report (including any recommendations for additional action) to the Executive Committee of the General Assembly Council" (GAC). The specific mandate of the ICI was not disciplinary or for the purpose of establishing

1. For the purposes of this paper, "Presbyterian Church" refers to the General Assembly Mission Council (GAMC) and its predecessor bodies of the Presbyterian Church (U.S.A.). The GAMC is the mission agency for the denomination and is accountable to the General Assembly. It functions as the major mission-sending agency for this denomination of over 2 million Presbyterians.

2. Communauté Presbytérienne au Congo (located in West and East Kasaï, Shaba, and Kinshasa administrative regions) and Communauté Presbytérienne de Kinshasa (located in the capital city of Kinshasa and the Bas Congo and Bandundu regions).

civil legal liability but was to be "essentially pastoral in nature, to help survivors, the well-being of the larger Christian community, the General Assembly level offices, and the integrity of the Presbyterian Church (U.S.A.)."[3]

In its final report in 2002, the ICI found that an ordained Presbyterian minister who served as a missionary for thirty-three years had in fact committed at least twenty-five acts of sexual abuse against missionary children at the Central School, located in Lubondai, Congo. The commission's thirty recommendations were received by the GAC, and it acted favorably upon all the recommendations except one (#29, which was not feasible in a Presbyterian system of governance) and one subrecommendation (#14–B) that raised legal issues beyond the mandate of the General Assembly Council.[4] The GAC distributed the report publicly and took additional measures beyond those recommended by the ICI in an effort to increase awareness of the problem of child sexual abuse and to prevent future acts of abuse.[5] During the ICI's investigation, allegations were received from former Presbyterian missionary children of incidences of abuse in other countries and time periods, especially Egypt and Cameroon. On June 27, 2003, the GAC Executive Committee chartered the Independent Abuse Review Panel to investigate these and other allegations of abuse "in other mission fields, including Cameroon and Egypt."[6]

## THE INDEPENDENT ABUSE REVIEW PANEL

The Independent Abuse Review Panel (IARP) was given a mandate "to pursue the truth, encourage healing, and promote justice on behalf of those making allegations and those accused" and "to further the integrity of the mission and witness of the Presbyterian Church (U.S.A.)."[7] The GAMC perceived the allegations of sexual abuse as inconsistent with Christ's valuing of children and as a threat to the integrity of the

3. *Final Report of the Independent Commission of Inquiry* (Louisville, Ky.: Presbyterian Church (U.S.A.), 2002), p. 33.

4. Ibid., p. 394.

5. The list of the ICI's recommendations and subsequent actions taken by the GAC appear in ibid., Appendix B, pp. 393–410.

6. James Evinger, Carolyn Whitfield, and Judith Wiley, *Final Report of the Independent Abuse Review Panel, Presbyterian Church (U.S.A.)* (Louisville, Ky.: PC[USA], 2010), p. 396.

7. Ibid., p. 4.

church's witness. For seven years the IARP pursued its mandate and sought out witnesses;[8] in all, it received and investigated 131 reports involving 81 possible victims and 47 alleged offenders at mission schools in Cameroon, Congo, Egypt, Ethiopia, India, Kenya, Mexico, Pakistan, Thailand, and Zambia. It interviewed more than 200 victims, witnesses, and alleged offenders. In October 2010 the panel issued a 546-page report detailing its findings.

The panel stressed that the report was not intended as an indictment of the missionary enterprise or of GAMC's mission; to the contrary, the overwhelming majority of GAMC missionaries served faithfully, and many of their children reported highly positive memories associated with their experience as missionary children. Even so, the panel concluded that thirty incidents of abuse had occurred in eight countries (eleven instances of sexual abuse by adults, eighteen instances of sexual abuse by minors, and one instance of physical abuse).[9] In addition, the panel also concluded that there had been one instance of a "failure to protect," that is, a situation in which a board established by the church had failed to protect children in its care and had failed to report instances of abuse to the mission agency. The report detailed each instance of abuse in the eight countries. The panel publicly named nine offenders, using a naming protocol it created, since there were no existing models to use. Seventeen other offenders were not named because they were minors at the time abuse occurred. None of the offenders is currently working as a missionary.

The IARP concluded that the situation facing many missionary children has several layers: for one thing missionary children are "third culture kids" (TCKs), that is, children raised in a cultural context decidedly different from that of their parents.[10] This creates a special environ-

---

8. The IARP conducted intentional outreach to former mission workers and their adult children. It also developed an outreach video that was distributed and posted online.

9. In numerous instances, the panel did not have enough information to reach a conclusion.

10. TCKs are children who grow up in a country different from their "passport country," that is, were raised outside their parents' culture. In a profound sense, an American child raised in Ethiopia is culturally neither American nor Ethiopian, thus the designation of belonging to a "third culture." There is a growing body of literature on the "third culture kid phenomenon"; see, for example, David C. Pollock and Ruth E. Van Reken, *Third Culture Kids: The Experience of Growing Up Among Worlds*, 2nd ed. (Boston: Nicholas Brealey Publishing, 2001).

ment, different from the one facing most U.S. children, an environment that has both advantages and challenges. TCKs describe themselves as "constantly coming and going," assimilating elements from each culture, yet their sense of belonging was their relationship to other missionary children, rather than to a specific community or place. A second layer noted was that a relatively high percentage of the missionary children in the period studied (1950–90) attended boarding schools, sometimes from a very early age, and sometimes at a location quite distant from their parents. This separation, while tolerated by some, was felt by other missionary children to be unnatural and painful: "Boarding school pulled us away from our parents. There is a common sense of brokenness." Of the five major areas of investigation, four (Cameroon, Congo, Ethiopia, and Pakistan) had Presbyterian-affiliated boarding schools for missionary children. The IARP report noted the correlation between boarding school settings and instances of abuse (p. 320).[11]

The impact of abuse on children documented by the report includes feelings of guilt, worthlessness, isolation, confusion, and fear, as well as struggles with faith in God. In some instances, missionary children felt their parents had chosen "God's work" over their own children's welfare. These feelings of worthlessness and guilt inhibited some missionary children from reporting acts of abuse (pp. 319–31).

The report documents a number of factors that may have rendered more difficult the denominational office's task of supervising missionary work and missionary family life overseas. The panel noted a high degree of correlation between the denominational mergers during the periods identified in the report and the high numbers of allegations of abuse, suggesting that the organizational changes brought about by the mergers introduced uncertainty and discontinuity in reporting structures. Through this time period the role of mission workers shifted from that of pioneer to that of manager and, finally, to that of specialist. This fundamental change in roles introduced significant uncertainty into the life and work of Presbyterian mission workers, which increased stress. During the period studied, the GAMC provided for missionaries' housing, salary, pension, children's education, travel costs, and furlough arrangements in a policy the report describes as "benevolent paternalism" (pp. 82–87, 89); missionaries thus often believed that the mission board

---

11. IARP *Final Report*, pp. 309–15, 320. Subsequent references to this report appear in the text in parentheses.

would provide for their and their children's needs. Yet the panel found that "children were virtually invisible. The Panel's conclusion was that children were viewed as solely the responsibility of the parents, because the Church collected no information on them in a systematic way. At the same time, missionary parents were trusting the Church to provide what they needed in order to focus on mission work" (p. 93).

Other factors compounded the situation: the stress of missionary life because of differences in climate, health conditions, and culture; the "irksome problem" of the education of missionary children (p. 101); and the GAMC's dependence on boarding schools to solve the problem. The report notes that "most of the allegations the IARP received centered on schools and boarding facilities as the settings for alleged abuse. Children are at greater risk of abuse in settings where they are separated from parents, and where the number of children, relative to the number of adults, provides challenging monitoring and supervision" (p. 103).

In the boarding schools of Cameroon, Congo, Ethiopia, and Pakistan referenced in the report, the physical plant of the schools and boarding facilities was often characterized by numerous small rooms and hiding places and extensive grounds, which made adequate supervision extremely difficult, given limited staff. In addition, the social topography of the mission community, characterized as a hierarchical system in which adults were more powerful than children, older children were more powerful than younger children, and adults were perceived to be wholly dedicated to God's work, may have increased the possibility of acts of abuse and the flourishing of a culture of silence and impunity surrounding those acts.

Sexual abuse silences the voices of its victims by using the power of the secret to damage the victims' psychological and spiritual well-being. The offender's behavior has already devalued the victim and enlisted his or her tacit support by surprising the victim with unanticipated illicit behavior that turns normal human relationships upside down. Many victims are so surprised and baffled by the first sexual advance by the offender, usually a trusted parent-figure or a peer/friend, that they "freeze," unable to respond normally. "Offenders use this frozenness, this silence, to their advantage and often continue or push their abuse further at these times. The lack of resistance allows them to consolidate their advantage in physical size, experience, or chosen circumstances to exert even more control over the incident" (p. 322). If it were simply a case of an illicit sexual advance against a child that was acknowledged and addressed effectively in a public way, the damage to the victim, while significant, would be less profound. "If, however, the offender's behavior is tolerated, excused, minimized, dismissed, or accepted, then there often follows a whole set of reactions for the child. Now they feel the community's negative judgments about them and their worth, as well as the offender's negative judgment about them and their worth. *Many victims reported to the Panel that the hurt and harm done by the community judgment of worthlessness was worse than the hurt and harm they felt from the act of abuse itself*" (p. 324, my emphasis).

As one witness stated, "The greater community remained silent as well. It is hard to imagine that among all the missionaries—men and women who have devoted their life to 'God's work'—not one stepped forward to be our advocate" (p. 324). Judith Herman describes the community's response to a traumatic act as critical: "The damage to the survivor's faith and sense of community is particularly severe when the traumatic events themselves involve the betrayal of important relationships. . . . [The survivors'] sense of self has been shattered. That sense can be rebuilt only as it was built initially, in connection with others." Even more important, the community response to the revelation of instances of sexual abuse, which by its very nature is traumatic, becomes a critical factor in opening up a way for healing and recovery: "Restoration of the breach between the traumatized person and the community depends, first, upon public acknowledgment of the traumatic event and, second, upon some form of community action. Once it is publicly recognized that a person has been harmed, the community must take action to assign responsibility for the harm and to repair the injury. *These two responses—recognition and restitution—are necessary to rebuild the survivor's sense of order and justice*" (my emphasis).[12]

The high number of allegations of abuse the IARP concluded had been committed by minors (forty cases were reported) surprised the panel and caused it to study the phenomenon. It noted that behaviors of sexual "acting out" may have been related to the stress generated by parents moving to a new or more distant mission station or to their increased in-coun-

---

12. Judith Herman, *Trauma and Recovery: The Aftermath of Violence—from Domestic Abuse to Political Terror* (New York: Basic Books, 1997), pp. 55, 61, 70. See also Raul Silva, *Post-traumatic Stress Disorders in Children and Adolescents* (New York: Norton, 2004).

try travel. In addition, "at least two offenders in the Panel's inquiries cited sexual abuse on the mission field as playing a role in their own subsequent behavior" (p. 106). More than half of the sixty allegations of sexual abuse in the Cameroon were said to have been committed by minors in the context of an overcrowded boarding school and dormitory located in a remote part of the country supervised by overworked houseparents (pp. 158–66). In this context, the panel documented a disturbing pattern of abuse over the years, links between several perpetrators, and an inappropriately sophisticated knowledge of sexual activity by a large number of children in the school and dormitory. Based on the fact that a disproportionately large number of abused children go on to abuse others, these patterns led the panel to conclude that "there was a pattern of transmission of [sexual] information between older male students that led to the victimization of a significant number of younger, smaller, and more emotionally vulnerable students. . . . It is possible that the pattern began with an adult sexually abusing a child, with the child then potentially passing on the behavior to other children" (p. 175).

## THE GAMC EXECUTIVE COMMITTEE'S RESPONSE TO THE REPORT

One of the key messages of the IARP members to the GAMC staff was the critical importance of the GAMC's response to the report. The GAMC had invested significant resources and effort to seek out victims and witnesses, to investigate the allegations, to guarantee the independence of the panel so that the panel could work with integrity and without undue pressure, and to distribute widely the published *Final Report*. (The printed report was mailed to all persons who had come forward as witnesses, victims, or offenders.)

In closed session on October 8, 2010, the IARP presented the 546-page report to the body that had commissioned it, the General Assembly Mission Council Executive Committee. The committee received the report and directed the chair to send a letter of apology to the persons who had been abused, acknowledging the reality of the suffering that had been inflicted upon them. The Executive Committee then presented the report to the full General Assembly Mission Council, and the council voted to offer a public apology to the victims. A press conference was held that afternoon, and church and secular media carried the story. The full text of the *Final Report* was put online to permit easy and anonymous access to the report's findings.[13] Partner church leaders in the countries investigated and ecumenical partners who collaborated with the PC(USA) in the various "mission fields" during the period investigated were all informed of the findings and sent a link to the Web version of the report. All of these churches and missions were assured of the PC(USA)'s willingness to collaborate with their own investigative processes, should they decide to initiate them.

A working group was named to consider appropriate action on the eleven pages of recommendations formulated by the panel members, victims, and witnesses. The panel also organized a retreat for victims approximately six weeks after the publication of the report, during which the victims who attended were able to receive information about the effects of sexual abuse on mental and spiritual health, to share their individual experiences of abuse and participate in a ritual of prayer and healing, and to speak with GAMC leadership about their experience of abuse and of the GAMC's silence.

It is too early to assess how helpful the GAMC's response will be in the healing process of victims and also of offenders. The publication of the *Final Report* has both generated controversy[14] and motivated other victims to come forward to share their stories. The report has been publicly acclaimed as a model of organizational integrity but faulted as exposing the GAMC's mission to unnecessary criticism. However, it is clear that, according to the *Final Report*'s assessment of the necessary conditions for personal, social, and spiritual healing, the GAMC took some critically needed steps. Its response to the IARP' recommendations can potentially make a significant contribution to continued healing for many.

Because of a noteworthy increase in educational options for the children of missionaries sent by the GAMC's World Mission, fewer than 2 percent of Presbyterian missionary children attend boarding schools today. Greater attention is given to issues of work/life balance,[15] and

13. See the full text at www.pcusa.org/resource/final-report-independent-abuse-review-panel-presby.

14. The fact of controversy was noted in an article published by the Presbyterian Outlook, an independent news agency that covers news of the Presbyterian Church. See Leslie Scanlon, "Six Persons Named by Abuse Review Panel in Physical, Sexual Abuse Investigation," www.pres-outlook.com/news-and-analysis/1-news-a-analysis/10520-six-persons-named-by-abuse-review-panel-in-physical-sexual-abuse-investigation-.html.

15. "Presbyterian World Mission Strategic Direction" (Presbyterian World Mission, 2010), p. 2, www.pcusa.org/media/uploads/global/pdf/wm_strategic_direction.pdf.

children receive more attention today than they did in previous decades. Even so, there are still asymmetries of power that may contribute to increase the risk of missionary children to abuse. Likewise, the struggle of missionaries to balance their twin callings to honor God through their families and through their work is very much alive today. The GAMC continues its review of its policies and practices that can help reduce the possibility of child abuse in mission settings.

Central to the self-understanding of Presbyterians as part of the people of God is the Reformation era's dictum *ecclesia reformata, semper reformanda* (the reformed church, always being reformed). Although we are redeemed from sin by Christ's sacrifice, we live in daily need of God's grace and forgiveness. The need for self-examination, confession, and correction in order to walk faithfully as disciples of Jesus Christ motivates us to take risks. The courage of the victims and witnesses to come forward and share their story, despite their perception of the mission community's and the church's historic unwillingness to hear them, was noted repeatedly by the panel in its final report and was acknowledged in the GAMC Executive Committee's letter of apology.

In "A Brief Statement of Faith," the last of the eleven historic confessions that guide U.S. Presbyterians,[16] the church declares:

> In a broken and fearful world
> the Spirit gives us courage . . .
> to hear the voices of peoples long silenced.[17]

In the work of the Independent Abuse Review Panel and the response it made to the panel's *Final Report*, the GAMC has attempted to keep listening to the voices of victims, offenders, and witnesses. Other churches and believers can help us see more clearly how our church might keep faith with our shared commitment to mission accountability.

---

16. For Presbyterians, confessions are the church's public declarations about what it believes about God and the world. The confessions adopted by the Presbyterian Church (U.S.A.) include the Nicene and Apostles Creeds from the Patristic era, Reformation era confessions such as the Scots Confession and the Westminster Confession of Faith, and more contemporary statements such as the Barmen Declaration and the 1991 Brief Statement of Faith.

17. "A Brief Statement of Faith," in *The Constitution of the Presbyterian Church (U.S.A.)*, part 1: *The Book of Confessions* (Louisville: Office of the General Assembly, 2004), pp. 263–66.

# 15

## Response to B. Hunter Farrell, "Broken Trust"

### Yong Joong Cho

HUNTER FARRELL'S CASE STUDY summarizes well for us an extensive and unprecedented investigation into incidences of sexual abuse among missionary kids (MKs). The thoroughness of this investigation, the resources allocated to it, and the attention it has received are revealing on many levels. As a Korean, I come at this with an outsider's perspective, and I would ask your forgiveness in advance if at any point my response seems insensitive. That is certainly not my intention. As a Presbyterian and as an international mission leader, I am also looking at this through another set of lenses, which also color how I understand this issue. It is obviously beyond the scope of this brief response to evaluate in detail the methodologies, findings, and conclusions of the investigation itself. Rather, I offer a broader review of some of the relevant biblical, administrative, and cultural issues.

### BIBLICAL PERSPECTIVE

A fundamental premise of this investigation is that we have a biblical responsibility to examine historical abuses in order to "pursue truth, encourage healing, [and] promote justice on behalf of those making allegations and those accused."[1] There is certainly biblical warrant for this pursuit. The apostle Paul instructed Timothy, "Do not entertain an accusation against an elder unless it is brought by two or three witnesses. Those who sin are to be rebuked publicly, so that the others may take

---

1. James Evinger, Carolyn Whitfield, and Judith Wiley, *Final Report of the Independent Abuse Review Panel, Presbyterian Church (U.S.A.)* (Louisville, Ky.: PC[USA], 2010), p. 429.

warning" (1 Tim. 5:19–20 NIV). Thus the Bible is interested in protecting both the accused and the accuser. In a few of the alleged cases investigated by the panel, the accused are no longer living. This raises the question of whether we have biblical justification to pronounce people guilty of a crime without their ability to defend themselves. What is especially sensitive is the issue of releasing the names of the accused who are now deceased. Should names in these cases have been withheld? Perhaps this concern comes from my Korean cultural perspective, in which shame is carried over to the entire family and community. Given the public humiliation that will no doubt ensue from this report, is there any concern about what effect these accusations might have on the children and grandchildren of the accused? This reality should not be lightly dismissed. In ten New Testament epistles the church is warned against the dangers of slander. Paul went so far as to tell the Corinthians that slanderers will not inherit the kingdom of God (1 Cor. 6:10)! Thus from the perspective of the accused we are obligated to give all due diligence to their defense. In U.S. courts of law the accused are presumed innocent until proven guilty. However, in the court of public opinion when someone is accused of sexual abuse, he or she is generally deemed guilty until proven innocent. In such cases this puts the accuser in a very powerful position in the American cultural context.

## ADMINISTRATIVE PERSPECTIVE

The investigation itself into the alleged sexual misconduct of PC(USA) missionaries demonstrates great integrity and diligence on the part of the mission society. It is unclear what liability issues came into play in relation to this investigation, but it would appear that, in such a thorough investigation, for an organization to openly admit "failure to protect" is to make it much easier for alleged victims to file suit against it. Though there may be statute-of-limitations laws that would prevent this, the mission society does not appear to have concerned itself with this matter either way, and from the perspective of pursuing truth, justice, and healing, such an attitude is entirely commendable.

Farrell mentions that the report has been "faulted as exposing the GMAC's mission to unnecessary criticism" (p. 214). However, given the widespread prevalence of child sexual abuse that has been revealed in the Catholic Church scandals, as well as in many other institutions, it is probably safe to assume that this is not the scandal it might have been twenty or thirty years ago. Having said that, there does seem to be a plethora of investigations taking place in the last several years of a variety of mission boarding schools, including those affiliated with New Tribes Mission, SIM, and C&MA, as well as interdenominational mission schools. The scandal-hungry secular press seems only too happy to report each case. The long-term effect of this negative attention on the mission enterprise is as yet unclear.[2]

Two administrative issues this report touches upon hold particular relevance, especially for us in the Korean mission context. The first is that much of this abuse took place during a time of major transition in the mission society. This is very revealing. It tells us that abuse looks for opportunity, and when it is denied that opportunity, it is minimized. Second, this report leads me to wonder what we might be missing today in our oversight. As future generations look back upon us, what might they see that would cause them to shake their heads in disbelief at our "failure to protect"? What opportunities for abuse are we not recognizing? For example, what measures are being taken today to look into the possibility of parental abuse of children on the mission field? Could it be that in the mission field context, parental abuse could go more unreported and unnoticed than back at home?

Admittedly, Korean mission agencies have not even begun to discuss these important topics, and we have much to learn from our Western counterparts. According to a survey conducted by MK Safety Net, almost all major Western agencies, such as Wycliffe, NTM, and MAF, have policies and procedures in place to deal with allegations of child sexual abuse.[3] I am not aware, however, of a single Korean agency that has such a policy. Sadly, preventative and contingency policies are often put into place in mission societies only after tragedy has already occurred. In any case, it will be important for Korean and other non-Western agencies to stay informed of the latest developments, both within the church and in the secular arena, especially where we can learn from the mistakes made so that we do not repeat them.

For example, even among psychologists there is a continual learning process with regard to child sexual-abuse cases. In a recent study a

2. This trend may have been encouraged by the recent film *All God's Children* (2008), which details the horrific accounts of children who were abused in C&MA's West African boarding school Mamou Alliance Academy.

3. See www.mksafetynet.net for the results of the survey.

panel of experts in the United States was asked to evaluate reports of abuse to see whether they could distinguish between real and false reports. Only 46 percent of the false reports were correctly identified as such.[4] Ongoing studies into why children misreport cases of abuse, or why they imagine that such events took place and begin to increasingly believe they did as time progresses, obviously need to be further examined. Thus from an administrative perspective, if experts can be wrong half the time in distinguishing between real and imagined cases of abuse reported by children, how much more could we expect nonexperts to have difficulty?

The PC(USA) report states that "the Panel was confronted with no instances of recovered memory."[5] This is surprising, given the extensiveness of the investigation. Could it be that the controversy over "repressed memory recovery" has discouraged victims from being forthright about how "continuous" their memory of the event actually is, for fear of not being believed? The fact that this issue did not seem to come up at all with the panel raises a red flag that this might be happening.

## CULTURAL PERSPECTIVE

Finally, a word must be said from the perspective of cultural critique. It is valuable for cultures to critique one another because they bring a perspective that may be unique, and perhaps more objective. Thus I welcome your critique of my culture, as I hope you will welcome mine. Frankly, and honestly, my initial reaction to all this is that we again have a case of the church being unduly influenced by its host culture. I am not suggesting that the PC(USA) did anything wrong in pursuing this matter with such diligence and reporting everything to the press. But I do believe it was caught in a kind of catch-22 situation, which may be part of a cycle of decay and decline that is symptomatic of the dying process. That is, Western culture is increasingly turning against the church and organized religion, with the media seizing upon scandal with great enthusiasm, thus supporting a cultural trend. The PC(USA) investigation is obviously part of this cultural trend. Has it then unwittingly participated in an exercise that will contribute to an overall decline? Now the

---

4. Megan Smith, ed., *Child Sexual Abuse: Issues and Challenges* (Hauppauge, N.Y.: Nova Publishers, 2008), p. 34.

5. Evinger, Whitfield, and Wiley, *Final Report*, p. 496.

problem is that the PC(USA) really had no choice in the matter. But in what other areas might we have a choice that could keep us from being subverted by self-destructive cultural trends?

One area in which we obviously do have a choice is how we respond to the homosexual agenda and lobby within the church today. Again, without denying that this is an issue requiring great sensitivity, could it be that we have lost all ability to see homosexuality clearly from both a biblical and a psychological perspective? It is now not even possible for a psychiatrist in the United States to treat homosexuality as a disorder under the rules of the American Psychiatric Association.[6] But given that a high percentage of homosexuals were sexually abused as children, do we not have an obligation to bring healing in this area, and promote recovery?[7] Furthermore when science is being silenced by culture, does not the church have a responsibility to be a prophetic voice?

## CONCLUSION AND RECOMMENDATIONS

The efforts being made by the PC(USA)'s global mission department, along with other missions, to address a dark chapter in recent mission history is overall commendable. The fact that the pain inflicted upon victims was increased by the lack of community response in the past makes this redress, however belated, all the more essential to help bring healing.

I have just two recommendations for moving forward from here. First, given that this issue has affected almost every major mission, and that there are numerous reports of abuse coming forth from various boarding schools, most of which relate to incidents twenty to thirty years ago, perhaps a wider study should be commissioned to examine what can be learned comprehensively. Second, it would seem prudent that mission societies consider offering annual psychological examinations for missionary children, and perhaps provide other forums for them to express themselves without fear of condemnation from their parents or the mission community. The evidence suggests that MKs tend to be afraid to express their true feelings because of the stigma attached to any

6. See Ariel Shidlo, Michael Schroeder, and Jack Drescher, eds., *Sexual Conversion Therapy: Ethical, Clinical, and Research Perspectives* (New York: Haworth Medical Press, 2001), p. 118.

7. See Richard Cohen, *Coming Out Straight: Understanding and Healing Homosexuality* (Cleveland, Ohio: Oakhill Press, 2000), p. 43.

possible jeopardizing of the work of their parents. Given this dynamic, it will be important for such psychological evaluations to be done in such a way that the entire family views them positively, and not as a test for "mission field worthiness." Maintaining this balance will not be easy, but for the health both of our mission endeavors and of those we send in its name, it may prove absolutely essential.

# 16

## Accountability in Mission:
## A Case Study of Korea Presbyterian Mission
## (Kosin)

### Shin Chul Lee

THE MAJORITY OF MISSIONARY sponsorship in Korea comes through the local church rather than through mission organizations. Therefore, because of the extreme importance of accountability in missions, it is a privilege to present this case study which focuses on the administration of the Korea Presbyterian Church (Kosin). I do this on behalf of our denomination (hereafter abbreviated KPC), trusting that this kind of transparency and openness will improve Korea Presbyterian Mission's accountability and foster further growth within our denomination.

In 1952 KPC was the first group to break away from the Korea Presbyterian Church. It preserves the same name, Korea Presbyterian Church, but is also known as Kosin. In brief, it is Calvinistic, Reformed, conservative, and evangelical. It has about 1,700 churches, with over 400,000 adherents. In 1956, at its first General Assembly (GA), the delegates voted unanimously to establish a world missions committee—the Korea Presbyterian Mission (KPM). To commemorate the birth of the GA, it was further decided that a missionary would be sent overseas. In 1958 KPM sent Rev. Young-jin Kim to Formosa. Since then, KPM has become a fairly well-organized church mission in Korea. As of 2011, it had 328 missionaries working in forty-seven different countries. It recently completed construction of a new mission center in Dae-jeon on land that the Presbyterian Church in America had left for KPM to use as it wished.

## AIM AND TERMINOLOGY OF THIS CASE STUDY

I would like to point out some areas within KPM that need further attention relating to financial transparency and accountability. In this discussion I consider the supporting churches and the headquarters and mission fields of KPM. I do not deal with the ministerial accountability of KPM, which seeks to establish self-supporting Reformed churches in the mission fields. So far it has not developed specific strategies for doing so, and thus it is difficult to evaluate its work in this area.

Although the terms "transparency" and "accountability" are often used as synonyms, I wish to distinguish them. I take the word "transparency" to apply more to the procedural aspects and accuracy of financial management and administration. This includes areas such as budgeting, receipt confirmation, deposits and withdrawals, exchange and transfer, account and property management, debt and interest management, settlement of accounts, and auditing. The issue of transparency is critical in matters of finance. The banking industry, for example, stands or falls based on its transparency and trustworthiness in managing its organizations. The field of missions, like banking, requires excellence in transparency and integrity.

I see the term "accountability" as more concerned with the purpose behind the use of finances and the overall responsibilities and trustworthiness of the organization's financial operations. These areas include ethical and effective fund-raising, efficiency and relevance in cash disbursement, fair budgeting, legitimate and purposeful expenditures, and similar matters. In Jesus' parable of the talents, the man with one talent was transparent, but he failed to act accountably; the other two men in the parable, in contrast, were transparent and did act accountably.

## THE ORGANIZATIONAL SYSTEM OF KPM

In order to discuss meaningfully the present financial practices of KPM, it is necessary to summarize its organizational structure. The KPM Committee is responsible ultimately to the GA for carrying out the world missions of KPC. The KPM Committee consists of nine GA delegates, each of whom serves a three-year term. At each GA, three new delegates/members are appointed to the committee, and three old members leave the committee. In order to strengthen their task efficiency, six other persons are invited to join with the nine GA delegates to form the larger KPM Executive Committee. Those six persons are:

- the general director of KPM

- the principal of the KPM Missionary Training Center (KMTC)

- the head of KPM Mission Policy Committee

- three representatives from the KPM Supporting Churches Association

All important matters are discussed and decided in the fifteen-member Executive Committee.[1]

With input from the extended KPM Executive Committee, the KPM Committee governs all matters of KPM's world mission work. To oversee its administration the committee, with the approval of the GA, appoints a general director of KPM Headquarters (HQ), who serves a three-year term. Under the supervision of the KPM Committee, the general director is in charge of HQ administration and the supervision and coordination of all KPM ministries. These ministries include KMTC, Research and Development, Administration, Missionary Affairs, Finance, and Information and IT. Recently, Member Care Coordinator was added as a staff position at HQ. (See chart 16.1.)

The KPM HQ has organized each designated mission field so that it includes at least two missionary units (i.e., missionary families or singles). The members of most of KPM's mission fields have some connection in personal fellowship but lack specific strategies or goals in terms of an actual team ministry. They meet at field conferences, but for the most part there is no serious agenda or issues to discuss and implement. The focusing of mission fields on concrete ministry goals and the consolidation of mission fields are two of the most urgent tasks that KPM faces. At the moment, KPM HQ is striving to reorganize each mission field to have at least five missionary families or singles by merging the smaller mission fields.

---

1. Recently one of the board members of the KPM Missionary Fellowship was invited as a temporary observer. In the future, however, he will become a full member of the Executive Committee.

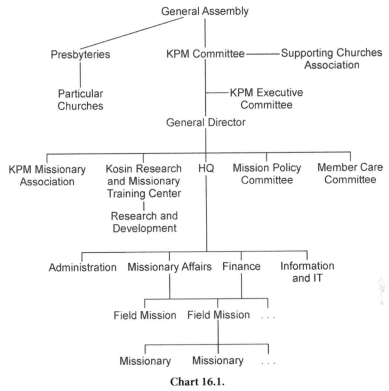

**Chart 16.1.**

Organizational chart of Korea Presbyterian Mission (Kosin)

## SUGGESTIONS FOR IMPROVING FINANCIAL TRANSPARENCY AND ACCOUNTABILITY

In the following pages I have grouped steps that KPM can take to improve transparency and accountability under three headings. The suggestions all involve handling and reporting of finances, fund-raising, and property. The first heading covers relations between the KPM committee, KPC churches that support KPM missionaries, and the ways missionaries receive that support. The second addresses relations between the KPM committee and KPM headquarters and expectations of oversight and accountability for handing of disbursements. The third brings together a number of suggestions for improving supervision and financial accountability between KPM headquarters and missionaries in the field.

## KPM Committee and Supporting Churches

In the six months from June to November 2010, an average of 644 KPC churches (out of a total of approximately 1,700) financially supported one or more KPM missionaries.[2] According to KPM guidelines, this support should be sent to KPM HQ, which in turn forwards it to the missionaries. If churches or individuals send funds directly to KPM missionaries, without going through KPM HQ, then missionaries are required to report this information to headquarters, giving full details of the amount and source of each contribution. Internal regulations of KPM require this information specifically to maintain transparency in managing and reporting the support that missionaries receive.[3] KPM HQ, however, has no means of stopping local churches from sending their money directly to missionaries, although it has repeatedly encouraged them not to do so, as has the KPM's Supporting Churches Association.

KPM officially sends out missionaries to their respective mission fields, but it is the churches that provide them with the much-needed financial support. Mission support from local churches is not equal for all KPM missionaries; some missionaries receive more, and others get less.[4] KPM HQ makes public the amount of support given to each missionary, partly in the hope of decreasing discrepancies in support levels between missionaries. Individual local churches, however, can choose whomever they want to support. In fact, only 20 percent of KPM's supporting churches follow KPM guidelines when selecting which missionaries to support; in most cases they decide whom to support based on their previous connections with individual missionaries.

In order to have KPM missionaries receive financial support more equally, I suggest that KPM HQ establish a general fund for missionary support. By not specifically designating which missionaries are to be supported, supporting churches can allow KPM HQ to distribute funds equally to each missionary. The more monies that churches contribute to this general fund, the more equal can be the support that each missionary or missionary family will receive. This general fund does not

2. Throughout this chapter, all information about KPM finances comes from the KPM Finance Office.

3. *KPM Internal Regulations*, chap. 8, 1 (2), p. 26.

4. In the 2008–9 fiscal year, the highest amount of support to a single missionary family was ₩137.6 million (a little over $100,000); the lowest to a single family, by a factor of 8, was only ₩17.0 million (approx. $12,500).

need to entirely replace the present method of support; for the time being, we could work with both systems. Up until now, KPM HQ has not been actively involved in raising financial support for missionaries, for it has been aware that not all missionaries would benefit equally. A general fund such as I am describing, however, would benefit all KPM missionaries equally. It would encourage more churches, both large and small, to take part in supporting KPM missionaries and would help to bring the focus back to supporting all missionaries, setting the stage for the development of a more comprehensive and organized system.

During the decade 2001–10, the money given annually by KPC to KPM missionaries increased, though the last two fiscal years have seen a decrease, as the accompanying table indicates. Reasons for this decline in giving may include the building of the KPM Mission Center in Dae-jeon and, certainly, the 2008 global financial crisis. Some churches stopped supporting KPM missionaries altogether during those years.

Increase/decrease of KPC's annual support for KPM missionaries, 2001–10

| | Income and expenditures, in millions of won | | | | | |
|---|---|---|---|---|---|---|
| Fiscal year | Income | Annual incr./decr. | % incr./ decr. | Expenditures | Annual incr./decr. | % incr. decr. |
| 8/01–7/02 | 4,808.7 | 622.0 | 14.9 | 4,714.3 | 256.7 | 5.8 |
| 8/02–7/03 | 5,093.3 | 284.7 | 5.9 | 5,084.4 | 370.1 | 7.9 |
| 8/03–7/04 | 5,125.6 | 32.3 | 0.6 | 5,489.0 | 404.7 | 7.9 |
| 8/04–7/05 | 5,740.6 | 615.0 | 12.0 | 5,683.0 | 194.0 | 3.5 |
| 8/05–7/06 | 6,839.1 | 1,098.5 | 19.1 | 6,365.5 | 682.5 | 12.0 |
| 8/06–7/07 | 7,283.8 | 444.8 | 6.5 | 6,942.1 | 576.6 | 9.1 |
| 8/07–8/08 | 7,916.5 | 632.6 | 8.6 | 8,235.9 | 1,293.8 | 18.6 |
| 9/08–8/09 | 7,318.1 | -598.4 | -7.6 | 7,620.3 | -615.6 | -7.5 |
| 9/09–7/10 | 6,951.0 | -367.1 | -5.0 | 7,176.1 | -444.3 | -5.8 |

*Source:* KPM Finance Office.

**Table 16.1.**

KPC support for KPM missionaries, 2001–10

The KPM Training Center prepared a questionnaire that included questions about financial support for KPM missionaries. In October 2009 the center sent it to 700 pastors and elders of seven presbyteries and received 308 responses. They sent the same questionnaire to pastors at the Pastor's National Conference on May 25, 2010. Of the various respondents, 18 percent represented churches that had been supporting more than one KPM missionary for longer than twenty years, and 20 percent were from churches that had stopped their sponsorship of some KPM missionaries within the past five years.[5] We do not know precisely why they canceled financial support to their KPM missionaries. Whatever the reason—perhaps a result of a change in the senior pastor, or a negative view of the missionaries they were supporting, or a reduction in church offerings—cutting support certainly has a damaging impact on the missionaries and their work. I would like to suggest that supporting churches and KPM HQ make a contract with each missionary that support during the current term on the field (usually for four years) not be cut unexpectedly. If for some reason the church feels it needs to reduce or cancel its support, it should first seek counsel from KPM HQ. Headquarters would then grant a reviewing period before reaching a final decision.

According to the KMTC survey, only 20 percent of the respondents stated that their church supported only KPM missionaries. The rest reported that their churches also support missionaries affiliated with other missions, or send and support their own missionaries, or support no KPM missionaries at all. Ways must be found to encourage more KPC churches to support their KPM missions and missionaries. I believe that a local church has the authority to send or support missionaries as it chooses, but as a Presbyterian church under the Kosin denomination, it is natural to expect KPC churches to join KPM in its work of establishing Reformed churches around the world.

KPC churches have their own task of improving financial transparency and accountability regarding mission funding, but here I have been addressing mission funding given by KPC churches in support of KPM missionaries. The main points I would wish to make include church responsibility in joining KPM and, second, in supporting KPM missionaries faithfully and with a willing heart. KPM cannot pressure churches to do this, but it can encourage them by explaining clearly their accountability and by candidly sharing about the ministries and financial situations of KPM missionaries. Finally, I strongly suggest that KPM introduce the idea of having a general fund system that could be used for the purpose of funding missionaries equally.

5. This figure is provided by the principal of KMTC.

## KPM Committee and KPM HQ

All support for KPM mission work goes through KPM Headquarters. It is therefore crucial that KPM HQ be transparent in its financial administration and that it follow the highest standards of accountability. Members of the KPM Committee, as well as the KPM Executive Committee—with the exception of the general director of HQ and the principal of KMTC—have their regular duties as pastors or elders. The administrative work of the mission is carried out by members of KPM HQ.

The KPM Committee elects the general director of Headquarters and gives him the authority to direct and coordinate all administrative management. KPM General Regulations contain the following guidelines for financial dealings:

- KPM must disburse cash according to the budget approved by the KPC General Assembly.

- Any expenditure for items not included in the budget must be approved by the KPM Executive Committee.

- Cash disbursement must be confirmed by the final authority in KPM, namely, the chairman and treasurer of the KPM Committee.

- The general director of KPM HQ is authorized to disburse cash in advance, but only if it is within the budget and in accordance with General Regulations.[6]

In actuality, however, confirmation by the chairman and treasurer of the KPM Committee of cash disbursements (point 3 above) has been neither regular nor detailed. That is, the financial transparency and accountability of the KPM HQ depend almost solely on the word and trustworthiness of the general director. The HQ staff of course has some knowledge of how the general director distributes funds. The present general director, Rev. Han-jung Kim, has made some effort to regularize finance dealings. For example, he has urged the treasurer of the KPM Committee to review and confirm all cash disbursements as often as he can. Kim has also occasionally invited three accounting professionals to review and audit all the accounts. These commendable efforts, however, do not remove the weakness of having financial authorization rest essentially in the hands of one person. A point of concern is that, while Kim was rearranging the administrative system after his appointment

---

6. *KPM General Regulations*, chap. 7, art. 19, 3 (2), p. 6.

in September 2009, financial authorization for expenditures in all departments of HQ was often delayed simply because he was absent from the office. The office manager, who is involved in handling day-to-day financial matters and transactions, also failed to check things frequently. Now that the reshuffling of HQ's administrative system is complete, the general director should discuss with his staff the full details of the financial matters he authorizes. I would also suggest that the director share the details of all cash disbursements that he authorizes with the head of the department involved, including KMTC, R & D, Administration, Missionary Affairs, Finance, and Information and IT. I also suggest that the Internal Regulations be rewritten to include practical guidelines for cash disbursements that the general director authorizes.

Supporting churches send their monetary support to KPM HQ in won (₩), but headquarters sends monthly allowances to missionaries in dollars. In 1997, when the IMF crisis in Korea occurred, the exchange rate jumped from ₩840/$1 to a peak of ₩1,962/$1, later settling to around ₩1,300/$1. During the 2008 global financial crisis, the exchange rate again shot up: from ₩900/$1 to almost ₩1,600/$1. During these times, if KPM HQ had sent the missionary allowances at the market exchange rate, the mission account would have been overdrawn and gone bankrupt. During the first crisis, KPM HQ set its own exchange rate in order to avoid bankruptcy of its missionary account, which meant that the missionaries were receiving fewer dollars than their regular allowance called for. KPM HQ continues to apply its own exchange rate (now ₩1,100/$1), which has allowed KPM HQ to keep its mission account solvent. However, since the market rate has gone down nearly to ₩1,100, not as much money is being saved in the mission account.

I suggest that KPM HQ eliminate its artificial exchange rate. This method is no longer relevant for today and does not benefit the missionaries. Neither does it allow for financial transparency. Missionaries should receive aid according to the current exchange rate, even if this means that they receive less whenever the exchange rate goes up. In such times, it should be up to the churches to come to the aid of the missionaries by sending more funds to compensate. This prolonged manipulation by KPM HQ of the exchange rate has distorted the real situation regarding mission support and funding. It was thought that the Mission Account was in good shape and had a surplus of funds from supporting churches. Now that the actual situation of missionary support has been brought fully to light, it is clear that the churches' overall financial support for missionaries has not increased much at all and, in recent years, has actually decreased.

## KPM HQ and Missionaries

### MONTHLY ALLOWANCE FOR LIVING

KPM requires that, before leaving for the field for the first term, or before returning to the field after any sabbatical year, all missionary units (families or single persons) raise their financial support to the amount of 110 percent of the standard monthly cost of living set by KPM HQ for their country of service.[7] (See the accompanying table.) For example, a missionary couple with two children between the ages of seven and twelve serving in Bangladesh must raise $1,441 of monthly support (i.e., 110 percent of $1,310). If a similar couple serves in Australia, their required monthly support would be $1,947.

KPM standard monthly cost of living, by person and by country group

| Person | Country groups (all figures in dollars) | | | |
| --- | --- | --- | --- | --- |
| | Group 1[a] | Group 2[b] | Group 3[c] | Group 4[d] |
| Single | 550 | 550 | 550 | 600 |
| Couple | 700 | 760 | 900 | 900 |
| Child (0–6 yrs.) | 70 | 70 | 80 | 90 |
| Child (7–12 yrs.) | 105 | 110 | 120 | 135 |
| Child (over 12 yrs.) | 140 | 150 | 150 | 180 |
| Housing—single | 270 | 330 | 330 | 380 |
| Housing—couple | 400 | 450 | 500 | 600 |

[a] Group 1: Bangladesh, Cambodia, India, Indonesia, Kazakhstan, Laos, Myanmar, Nepal, Nigeria, Philippines, Romania, Somalia, Sri Lanka, Thailand, Uzbekistan, Vietnam.
[b] Group 2: Angola, China, Côte d'Ivoire, Egypt, Ghana, Jordan, Kosovo, Mongolia, Morocco, Sierra Leone, Tunisia, Turkey.
[c] Group 3: Argentina, Brazil, Lesotho, Paraguay, Puerto Rico, Russia, South Africa.
[d] Group 4: Australia, Fiji, France, Guam, Hong Kong, Japan, Mexico, New Zealand, Portugal, Singapore, Spain, Taiwan.

**Table 16.2.**

KPM standard monthly cost of living

7. *Internal Regulations*, chap. 8, art. 19, 3 (4), p. 27.

The monthly allowance system, however, is impractical and unrealistic; it does not include costs for initial arrival and settling in the field, education, travel, vacation, cost of visas, insurance, retirement savings, or ministry expenses. KPM HQ actually recommends ₩3.5 million (approx. $3,250) as, on average, a reasonable monthly support level for a family. This huge gap between recommended amount and the required cost of living figures arose from the unstable dollar/won exchange rates of 1997 and 2008. It is not sound to leave this wide gap unaddressed. Such lack of support can cause critical problems in missionaries' living and work in their mission fields. I would suggest that KPM HQ include ministry expenses in the monthly allowance and make the budget more comprehensive. I would also suggest that KPM HQ calculate the required monthly support amount actually needed for a missionary family or single according to their country of service and make sure that their supporting churches have this information.

## Designated support

In recent years, the amount of ministry allowance requested by missionaries has gone down, but designated support from supporting churches has sharply increased. The category "ministry allowance" is for items related directly to the Christian work of the missionaries on the field. At the end of the year, missionaries submit their ministry budget to HQ, which then grants, denies, or adjusts their requests, depending on the balance of their "virtual" account.

The category "designated support" refers to funds sent to missionaries as special gifts from their supporting churches, designated for some particular expense. This support is usually raised at the initiative of the missionaries, who must get permission to raise these funds from the mission field and from the general director. The designated amount is usually sent through HQ, but there is subsequently little or no means of checking how the funds were actually spent. During the fiscal year September 2008–August 2009 the total amount of money sent for ministry allowance was ₩593.1 million (= $505,000, given the present mission exchange rate of ₩1,175/$1), which was 7.8 percent of the amount of all support money transferred to missionaries. In the following fiscal year the ministry allowance declined to ₩478.5 million ($407,000), or 6.1 percent of the total amount forwarded to missionaries. The amount of church designated support in the 2008–9 fiscal year was ₩515.6 million ($439,000), or 6.8 percent of the total; in 2009–10 the figure jumped by 64 percent to ₩847.9 million ($722,000), which was 10.8 percent of the total monies forwarded to missionaries.

Ministry allowance and designated support, in millions of won

|  | Sept. 2008–Aug. 2009 | % of total ₩ sent | Sept. 2009–Aug. 2010 | % of total ₩ sent |
|---|---|---|---|---|
| Ministry allowance | 593.1 | 7.8 | 478.5 | 6.1 |
| Designated support | 515.5 | 6.8 | 847.9[a] | 10.8 |

*Source:* KPM Finance Office.
[a] By percentage, these funds were used for building projects (42.5), miscellaneous ministry expenses (27.1), children's education (13.6), and vehicle purchases (13.0). The remainder of the funds were used for medical treatment, housing, initial settlement expenses, gifts, and further education.

**Table 16.3.**
Ministry allowance and designated support

It is urgent to analyze the reasons why the amount of designated support money is increasing. I do not want to doubt or be skeptical of any missionaries, but we also need to be careful not to leave any room for temptation. These temptations could include missionaries asking their supporting churches to have their support funds specifically designated to them in order to avoid KPM administrative charges (i.e., 6 percent of the undesignated amount to missionaries), or using the designated support money for expenses other than the ones for which the funds were originally requested. For the sake of greater transparency and accountability, it is essential to monitor closely the actual use of designated support from churches to missionaries.

CHURCH BUILDINGS

Consider one of the main reasons why missionaries request designated support. KPM missionaries do not apply to their building policies the so-called Nevius Methods, which have been so effective in Korean church history. These methods include the principle that Christians should be self-supporting when it comes to their church buildings. Yet KPM HQ tends to allow missionaries to raise special funds for their building needs from Korea, not from the mission fields themselves. In general, HQ does not feel so free to allow transfer of money when missionaries request funds for their own needs or needs that are less related to their mission goals. Furthermore, supporting churches are often highly motivated to take on building projects as if it were their own goal to accomplish, so KPM HQ finds it difficult to prevent these churches from funding missionary building projects that the missionaries have requested from the field. An important factor is that Korean coworkers or leaders in the mission fields hesitate to estimate objectively the funds such projects might require, for fear of losing face. In the effort to improve the transparency and accountability of KPM, it is critical that these people evaluate honestly whether fund-raising for these projects should be allowed. Furthermore, only if the mission field itself agrees with the relevance of the building projects should a building project ever proceed. These kinds of issues require the full and honest input of the native coworkers in the mission fields.

### Personal vehicles

Another common request from missionaries for special monetary support involves the purchase of a vehicle. It is an item that almost every missionary anticipates buying sooner or later. However, a car should not automatically be provided just because a missionary announces that he or she needs one. It takes time for any of us to save up until we can afford any big purchase. I suggest that missionaries who wish to acquire a car either save money themselves or get special financial help from a church back home. It is not appropriate for missionaries to expect the full amount of money to purchase a vehicle solely from the designated support funds of their church. Having regular financial support should not automatically qualify a missionary to be given the amount needed to purchase a car. There is a delicate balance, of course, between how much missionaries should save in their personal account and how much they should raise in funds for an item. I suggest that KPM encourage missionaries to save a certain amount of money for a vehicle before submitting a request or applying for vehicle purchasing through KPM. If a vehicle is so urgently needed that saving a certain amount of money in their own mission account is not feasible, then perhaps they could get an advance loan from the general Mission Account, and later repay the loan.

### Education

If an MK ("missionary kid") is being educated in an international school or abroad, the cost may become prohibitive for the parents, given their fixed allowance. Moreover, expensive needs such as children's education in international schools or abroad are often not fully understood by average members of the supporting churches in Korea. Most Christians in Korea cannot afford to send their children to those kinds of schools. Therefore, this subject is a highly delicate matter for KPM. For the problematic matter of education of MKs, KPM needs to be more active and to provide more options. These options could include recruiting teacher-missionaries to supervise home schooling in the mission fields, funding and granting scholarships for MKs, erecting or connecting MK schools to KPM MKs in nearby countries, or providing home stay options in Korea for MKs.

## MISSIONARY ACCOUNTS WITH NEGATIVE BALANCES

It is unusual for missionaries to request additional designated support or funds for their ministry expenses. In most cases, the balance in their overall mission account is low, and in many cases they have a negative balance, which means that requests for additional ministry expenses would probably not be granted. Even if more support were to be transferred into their account, they do not expect to be able to get everything they need from the normal ministry allowance until their minus balance is recovered. In that case, they typically prefer getting what they need through the channel of designated support rather than through ministry allowance. When money comes in as designated support, KPM does not withhold it but sends the full amount that is received.

In order to improve transparency and accountability in designated support from churches, I suggest that KPM needs to regulate the categories of designated support that it will allow and must evaluate the proper procedure for approving fund-raising requests. It would be preferable to list what to designate and what not to designate. I do not think that legitimate ministry expenses should be handled through designated giving. KPM needs to upgrade the field missions so that they can handle applications for designated support without having to send everything to KPM HQ for evaluation. I would recommend that KPM set a maximum limit to the amount that can be designated for a given item. The most realistic solution is to increase the general support amount for ministries. We also need to find ways to restore the accounts of individual missionaries that are overdrawn.

KPM HQ remits the monthly allowance twice a month, regardless of the balance situation of their individual mission account, doing so until the end of each term (usually four years). If support funds for a certain missionary have been reduced during his or her term, or if there have been unexpected additional expenses beyond the normal allowance, that missionary's account could go in the red—which in fact has happened in roughly half of all accounts!

Missionary accounts, by positive or negative balance

| | Dates (with exchange rate) | | |
|---|---|---|---|
| Accounts | Oct. 8, 2008 (₩1,347/1$) | Oct. 8, 2009 (₩1,182/1$) | Oct. 8, 2010 (₩1,128/1$) |
| With a positive balance | | | |
| missionary units | 90 | 74 | 82 |
| value (in million ₩) | ₩1,453.7 | ₩1,280 (approx.) | ₩1,170 (approx.) |
| value (in thousand $) | $1,079.2 | $1,082.9 | $1,037.2 |
| With a negative balance | | | |
| missionary units | 69 | 76 | 83 |
| value (in million ₩) | ₩1039.7 | ₩1,180 (approx.) | ₩1,400 (approx.) |
| value (in thousand $) | $771.9 | $998.3 | $1,241.1 |

*Source:* KPM Finance Office.

**Table 16.4.**

Missionary accounts

However, there are other alarming situations; some missionaries who are being supported quite well overall (as much as ₩3.5 million per month) still have a chronically overdrawn account. This kind of situation should not occur indefinitely, for it is a serious matter of accountability (see table 16.4). If missionaries do not restore their account to a positive balance while on their sabbatical year, it should become the problem and responsibility also of KPM HQ and the KPM Executive Committee to verify their financial situation before they are allowed to return to the field.

## PROPERTY OWNED BY KPM

On the subject of the ownership of property on a mission field, the General Regulations of the KPM states:

1. Domestic property purchased from church offerings, gifts, or donations must be registered under the ownership of the General Assembly Juridical Foundation.

2. If it is not possible for mission fields to register the property under the ownership of the GA Juridical Foundation, then alternatively, the property should be registered under the name of the Field Mission or under joint ownership of the missionaries. Lastly, the owners should submit a memorandum or a written pledge to the KPM Committee.

3. Foundations that own mission property in the mission field must be unified under the supervision of the mission field.

Even if it is possible, I question whether it is ever acceptable for the GA Juridical Foundation to own properties in a mission field. Supporting churches that wish to fund properties should consider that they have no clear commission of God to use or manage such properties. Properties that are obtained or built with the purpose of aiding mission work in a mission field most naturally should be given to the corresponding field mission, which will be the party actually utilizing the building for mission work. Until that mission organization leaves the field, it is entitled to use that property. After the KPM organization departs the field, ownership can be transferred to a self-supporting institution in the field. The details of such arrangements will differ in the various mission fields. Some countries may not allow foreigners or foreign foundations to own any property without joint native ownership. In such cases I think that it might be wise not to purchase any property but rather to wait until the church is functioning and able to take responsibility as the owner of the property. Some mission fields may lease rather than buy the land, which means that they have only temporary ownership. In this case, it should not be a problem to acquire a plot of land to erect a building. Some missions fall under one set of property laws for urban areas, and another for rural areas. Therefore, mission policies on purchasing property need to be written and adjusted specifically for the particular field in which they apply.

## PROPERTY OWNED BY MISSIONARIES

Another property-related issue is whether missionaries themselves should be allowed personal ownership of property in the mission fields, so long as the financing does not come from church offerings or donations but from separate personal funds. Some missionaries buy private homes using money from their previous jobs or money they have saved from their housing allowance. Or they buy a house using loans, with the intention of combining this with their housing allowance. A KPM missionary once stated that the previous KPM general director allowed the ownership of private houses as long as missionaries borrowed no money at all from the mission fund.

The issue of property funds for missionaries is not a straightforward one; there are many factors to take into account. If a missionary purchases his own property by taking out a loan, the responsibility of repaying the loan can cause significant long-term stress. Unforeseen circumstances may force the missionary to leave the mission field unexpectedly, and then what should he do? Since KPM provides a housing allowance for its missionaries, we could say that it implicitly discourages missionaries from being involved in or distracted by owning their own property.

Mission fields must be part of any decision regarding the details and procedures of purchasing property. If any property is purchased with designated or undesignated support for mission work, the mission field should claim ownership of that property and appoint a missionary as manager to oversee all matters regarding the property. If the property is registered in the name of (that is, as being owned by) a local church, it is necessary to get a memorandum that can certify missionary use of the property until the mission leaves the country. Overall, KPM needs to improve its regulations governing the ownership and use of mission properties.

### TENTMAKERS AND ASSOCIATE MISSIONARIES

Many of the missionaries that KPM sends out are pastors—but not all. As of July 2010, KPM's 328 missionaries included 21 lay or bi-vocational missionaries who receive monthly allowances from KPM. The mission categorizes tentmakers separately; currently, there are six persons so designated. KPM has also begun to accept some missionaries who are being supported by Kosin churches and who want to work with the KPM missionaries in the field as "associate missionaries." We now have eight such associate missionaries within KPM. The mission also accepts pastors of Korean churches who are working among Korean Christians in the larger cities of foreign countries as full members. As the various types of missionaries become ever more specific and varied, issues involving the transparency and accountability of their finances will increasingly demand our attention.

The most important point I would like to make is that, if missionaries earn a salary or make a profit from their professions in the mission field, they should report the amount of this income and indicate how much support they still need from the KPM mission account. Currently, some missionaries' wives have side jobs in the mission field, yet KPM often has little knowledge of this or of their income from these jobs. Some KPM missionaries are also involved in ministries in Korean churches overseas for which they receive income but which they have not reported to KPM. I believe that KPM needs to take strong action to learn of such situations and include accurate calculations of all additional income. If the income from these jobs or the allowance received from the additional church work is greater than the KPM mission allowance, it would be appropriate to classify such missionaries as tentmakers or associate missionaries.

# 17

## Response to Shin Chul Lee, "Accountability in Mission"

### Dick McClain

IT IS A SPECIAL honor for me to respond to Shin Chul Lee's excellent case study. I say this because of a family connection I have with Korea that goes back many, many years. In 1925 my maternal grandparents, the Reverend Orville and Eileen French, arrived in Korea with their first child to begin their missionary career. That child was my mother, who was one year old at the time. The calling to cross-cultural ministry that began with my grandparents extended to my parents, to my wife and me, and now to one of my children. By God's grace we now have eighty-six years of continuous missionary service in my family. My grandparents were transferred to China the following year, resulting in my mother's being raised there rather than in Korea. Nevertheless, our family's missionary history began in Korea.

Responding to Lee is also an honor because his reflections are a product of the unprecedented growth of the church in Korea during the twentieth century and the remarkable missionary movement that has emerged out of the Korean churches in recent decades. The fact that the Korean missionary enterprise has progressed to the point where its leaders are wrestling with serious issues of mission agency and missionary accountability suggests that it is a movement that has come of age. Its leaders are to be commended for being willing to reflect on such challenges, not just within their own community, but also in conversation with the wider global missionary community and, specifically, mission leaders from the West. Such transparency and vulnerability bode well for the future of the Korean church's global involvement.

Lee's personal cross-cultural experience (he served among the Dagomba people of Ghana), coupled with the track record of a denomination that established a missionary sending structure at its first General Assembly, suggests considerable substance to the case study that he presents and the solutions he proposes. In this chapter he describes a constellation of challenges currently facing the Korea Presbyterian Mission (KPM), its constituents in the Korea Presbyterian Church (Kosin), and its missionaries, including but not limited to the following points.

One is the tendency of missionaries in a field to function independently of one another. What is currently defined by KPM as a "field" might in actual practice be more accurately described as an association of independent missionaries.

In my judgment the most significant of the challenges facing KPM is the apparent disconnect between KPC congregations and KPM. Many KPC congregations elect to send their support directly to their KPM missionary partners rather than through KPM's headquarters, which gives rise to several potential difficulties. At the very least it complicates KPM's work in effectively leading and managing its missionaries. Beyond that, the practice seems to have spawned widely varying levels of support among KPM's missionaries. Additionally, the potential for resources not to be properly used or accounted for is magnified when the leadership and oversight of the sponsoring agency is circumvented.

The relationship between churches of KPC and the KPM does not seem to reflect the level of collaboration and partnership needed to sustain a growing international missionary movement. One wonders whether the KPC churches really embrace KPM as their mission arm. This is a critical issue that must be thoughtfully and prayerfully addressed if KPM is to be an effective agent of mission for the denomination.

In a similar vein, a pattern of designated giving has emerged that provides supporting churches a means of bypassing both administrative fees and the normal budgetary processes. Even if these funds were fully reported to KPM, as policy dictates (though it appears this is not being done on a consistent basis), it still leaves the mission powerless to give effective leadership to or oversight of its missionaries' work.

Establishing a reasonable and accurate missionary support quota that adequately encompasses not only personal allowances but also costs such as travel, establishing a home on the field, educating children, paying for ministry expenses, acquiring vehicles and property, and a host of other factors has proven to be difficult. Unrealistically low missionary budgets result in missionaries having to raise funds well in excess of their stated needs. As a result, communicating support needs becomes embarrassing for missionaries, and detailing one's needs becomes difficult, if not impossible.

Among several other challenges is the difficult issue of property ownership, both mission property (whether KPM is legally able to hold title or not) and missionaries' personal property.

To these challenges, Lee proposes a number of creative and thoughtful responses, only a few of which I will enumerate.

- Consolidation of mission "fields" into groupings of at least five families or singles.

- The establishment and promotion of a general fund to support missionaries that would allow KPM to distribute available support more equitably among its workers.

- A series of policies and procedures designed to enhance both transparency and accountability within KPM's financial management.

- Revising missionary budgets to accurately reflect projected ministry costs, and carefully studying the use of designated funds in order to more adequately anticipate these needs and reflect them in missionary budgets.

- Transparency in KPM's communication of the real costs of ministry among KPC churches, so that missionaries do not have to fear losing face when they discuss financial realities with their supporters.

- The establishment of policies regarding missionary vehicles, MK education, property ownership, and outside employment on the field, to name just a few. In the past, such things have been left up to the missionaries to sort out. Today, however, the magnitude of KPM's global enterprise and of the funds involved suggests that a more deliberate, policy-driven approach to these issues is needed.

Having summarized the main points of Lee's paper, let me offer several observations and recommendations of my own. These grow out of my own experience of twenty-five years with The Mission Society, as well as my observations of many mission agencies and congregations with which I have worked over the years.

In Lee's paper I noted allusions to the kind of independence and rugged individualism that in my mind are more characteristic of us Americans. Left unchecked, such traits have at times hindered our efforts to proclaim Christ and model his kingdom globally. To the extent that these tendencies are also reflected within KPC and KPM, and perhaps also the larger Korean missionary community, they stand in need of God's redeeming and transforming work, as surely as they do within the Western church.

Let me suggest a few additional responses to the challenges Lee has outlined. I offer them in the hope that these suggestions might provide fertile ground for KPM's future planning.

- KPM should consider establishing policies that would limit missionaries' authority to receive designated funds directly from their supporters. As long as the current practice is allowed to continue, it is difficult to see how KPM can address the challenges that grow out of inadequate financial supervision and control.

- In order to strengthen the bonds between KPM and KPC congregations, KPM should consider how it can enhance the services it provides to local churches and to its missionaries. KPM should be actively engaged in missions mobilization within the churches, approaching the task with the conviction that missions is first and foremost the mission of the church. As KPM becomes an ally with church leaders in stimulating a mission vision and providing mission resources across the KPC, congregations in turn will be inclined to cooperate more fully with KPM. Similarly, every effort should be made to enhance KPM's services to its missionaries in areas of training, member care, and effective leadership and administration. That in turn will encourage missionaries and their supporting congregations alike to recognize the value of a strong denominational sending agency and will generate greater trust in and support of KPM. The goal should be a new spirit of collaboration between supporting congregations, KPM, and the missionaries, allowing the three to "close the triangle" and function as a dynamic missional community.

- While the proposal to move toward funding missionaries out of a general support account appears sound on paper, in actual practice it may not provide the hoped-for remedy. In the United States, such an approach typically lacks the personalization required to generate sustained and sacrificial giving. Though I admittedly am not familiar with the Korean culture and mind-set, it seems doubtful to me that that this approach will be effective in Korea because of what appears to be the strongly independent spirit of its people and churches. I would suggest an approach that keeps the personal touch of supporting individual missionaries while using the organizational structure to administer and lead in mission endeavors.

- Lee's excellent proposals regarding enhanced financial management within KPM could be strengthened even more with the addition of a required annual independent audit of the agency's finances. This audit would be made available to any individual or congregation requesting it.

- I recommend segmenting missionary budgets into "launch," "missionary support," and "ministry/project support," providing a more adequate means of projecting actual costs and of managing donor support. Additionally, ministry funds (including designated gifts) should be released only after proper documentation of expenses has been provided by missionaries. This would enhance KPM's ability both to monitor and to manage expenditures.

While a range of policies is needed and should indeed be implemented, the larger issue is the need to establish a covenant relationship and mutual trust between KPM and its missionaries, between KPM and KPC churches, and between KPC churches and the missionaries. Living out such covenants reminds the community that the issue is not one of control, but of mutually agreed-upon guidance regarding how its members are to live and minister together in a way that reflects the spirit of Jesus to the watching world. The result could be ministry relationships that reflect a high level of trust and commitment, that demonstrate love and honor for one another, that yield personal prerogatives for the sake of Christ and the community, and that allow the missionary enterprise to be conducted in a way that is fully approved by the Lord of the Harvest.

# 18

## Administrative Accountability in Mission: An American Case Study

### *Jerry A. Rankin*

IT IS INTIMIDATING FOR an American mission administrator to address the issue of administrative accountability knowing that the implications are to be applied to Korean missions experience. Cross-cultural sensitivities require us to understand that there may not be a wrong way and a right way to practice accountability in mission structures and practices, but I trust we can profit from case studies and experiences that highlight principles applicable to the common mission of God, to which we are all committed.

One of the most thrilling experiences in my seventeen-year tenure as president of the Southern Baptist International Mission Board (IMB) was speaking at a gathering of Korean denominations and mission agencies in Seoul in 2008. Sponsored and hosted by the Global Mission Society, this gathering brought together leaders representing churches and organizations that altogether sent and supported more than 17,000 missionaries serving outside Korea. This speaking opportunity did not come about simply because of my status as an American mission leader; the invitation evolved from several years' investment in building relationships, first with Korean-American churches, then in an expanded form with Korean Baptist churches, and finally, through those networks with the larger Great Commission Korean community. Of special significance was the twofold topic I was assigned: how to move Korean mission strategies to focus on unreached people groups instead of the

Korean diaspora and areas of open harvest, and how to facilitate field strategies that would result in indigenous church-planting movements.

That meeting in 2008 has borne fruit. At the same time as the Korean Global Mission Leadership Forum met at the Overseas Ministries Study Center in New Haven, Connecticut, in February 2011, Korean missionaries serving with the Southern Baptist IMB, the Korean Baptist Foreign Mission Board, and various South Korean churches gathered from all over the world in Chiang Mai, Thailand, for an unprecedented working conference of consultation, inspiration, and ministry. The conference was also attended by leaders of sponsoring entities.

## KOREAN-AMERICANS AND THE IMB

Although a few ethnic Koreans had served with the IMB in former years, language barriers, restrictive requirements for appointment, and the difficulties of serving in the context of American teams inhibited the growth of this segment of IMB personnel. When I was president of the IMB, my initial encounters with Korean-American Southern Baptists were confusing and challenging. My background was in a denomination that regarded the IMB as the default channel for doing missions. Churches were expected to provide generic support for the sending and support of missionaries, relinquishing the administration of mission work and the formation of strategies to the mission board. Although the Council of Korean Southern Baptist Churches (CKSBC) consists of churches affiliated with the Southern Baptist Convention, this group of more than 600 Korean-American churches continues to function rather autonomously. In the past these churches sent out and supported their own missionaries through their own CKSBC Department of Foreign Missions, usually without a great deal of oversight or administrative accountability. When we met, our encounters were always cordial and the conversation was gracious, but there was an obvious tension when the IMB could not agree to lend financial support to CKSBC missionaries. A more serious impasse came with the IMB's refusal to allow the CKSBC to infringe on IMB's processing of missionary candidates by granting the CKSBC authority over selection and approval.

Consultations did result in IMB field teams' being encouraged to relate to independent Korean missionaries in fellowship, family ministry, and strategy insofar as possible. Though the need for such relationships was obvious, divergent strategies made its achievement difficult.

Anglo-American missionaries tended to work in communities formed of expatriates with common backgrounds, values, and interests, to which it was difficult for Koreans to relate. I am grateful that this situation has changed significantly, for most IMB teams have become multicultural. Yet while it is commendable that American missionary teams now work in partnership with international missionaries from Latin America, Asia, and Europe, and with local national partners, these partnerships have posed significant challenges for administrative accountability.

## THE IMB'S APPROACH TO ACCOUNTABILITY

The IMB has a strong accountability structure. Missionary candidates are thoroughly screened to establish their integrity, divine call, doctrinal soundness, and moral purity. These attributes, along with issues of stewardship and lifestyle (which should be frugal), are monitored and periodically assessed by team leaders and through peer evaluations. Failure in any of these areas can result in corrective actions and, potentially, in termination.

Once a candidate is approved for missionary service, pre-field orientation and initial training on the field focus on seven areas of competency. The core competency is to be, and to be growing as, a disciple of Jesus Christ, to which is linked competency as a cross-cultural witness, servant-leader, family member, team player, mobilizer, and facilitator of church-planting movements. Contrary to common misconceptions, missionaries are not accountable for reporting a certain number of baptisms or churches planted. Baptisms and churches planted are viewed as spiritual results and are attributed to the work of the Holy Spirit. Missionaries, however, are accountable for doing things that would lead to spiritual results. For example, an annual performance review might ask questions such as, Are you consistently finding opportunities to share an evangelistic witness with lost people? or, How many new believers are you meeting with regularly to nurture and disciple?

Every missionary is expected to be a part of a team in which a body-life of fellowship and transparent accountability is practiced. Team membership has proven to be a more effective form of accountability than is reporting periodically to an authoritative supervisor who lacks a day-to-day relationship with the missionary. While accountability to peers is vulnerable to judgmentalism, in practice it creates a healthy environment of mutual edification that is encouraging and supportive.

With the incorporation of ethnic Korean members into IMB teams, a unique aspect of team accountability has become apparent. Korean commitment to excellence means that Korean missionaries will suffer a loss of face if they fail to measure up to expectations. A tendency to want to succeed and to be perfect in every regard supplants the more balanced recognition that everyone has strengths and deficiencies and that accountability is a tool that enables one to grow.

## MISSION RALLIES FOR KOREAN-AMERICAN SOUTHERN BAPTISTS

In 2003 pastors from several of the largest Korean-American Southern Baptist churches invited the IMB to conduct mission rallies and training conferences in areas of the United States where Korean churches were concentrated. It was a time of unprecedented enlargement in the IMB's missionary force; the remarkable rates of church growth on the mission field and engagement of unreached people groups were well-known. The Korean-American pastors expressed confidence in the IMB's strategy and accountability and indicated they would like to undertake the major shift of sending out missionaries under the auspices of the IMB. Four rallies were scheduled: in Northern California, Los Angeles, Seattle, and on the East Coast. The pastors announced a vision for 100 new Korean-American missionaries to be called by God through these rallies to serve overseas with the IMB. At the first rally more than 200 individuals made a commitment to missionary service. In the attitude and understanding of those making these decisions, I detected a significant contrast with my previous experience. If an individual in an Anglo-American church responded to such a public invitation, it usually indicated an openness to considering missionary service and to continuing to seek God's will concerning the possibility of going overseas in the future. In contrast, I sensed that the Korean-Americans responded to the same appeal fully expecting to receive a passport and airline ticket and perhaps be shipped off to the frontiers of the world the next day. My depiction may be an exaggeration, but an obvious passion and sacrificial surrender charac-terized the Korean-American commitment to missionary service.

In a debriefing after this first mission rally, when the pastors assessed the response and prepared plans for subsequent rallies, they announced that God had led them to enlarge their vision—they were trusting God to call not 100, but 1,000 Korean-American missionaries to serve through the IMB. Each year since then, three or four mission rallies have been held in key Korean-American churches; currently almost 400 Korean-Americans have been appointed and are serving around the world, and more than 600 additional candidates are in the appointment process. Many churches are calling home their missionaries who went out independently and are requiring them to apply for service through the IMB. These churches have begun to recognize the difficulties of sustaining support for members who go overseas and of providing adequately for the administration of their work and their member care.

## KOREAN MISSIONARIES AND ADMINISTRATIVE CHALLENGES

The passionate witness, fervent prayer life, and dynamic faith of Koreans have infused new spiritual vitality into our mission teams. Outstanding Korean professionals who have left prominent careers to serve as missionaries have enabled the IMB to penetrate unreached people groups in restricted locations through creative-access strategies that are beyond what would have been possible with Anglo-Americans. But with the benefits of this influx have come challenges of administration, especially at the field level. Other chapters in this volume deal with the issues of strategic and financial accountability, highlighting the uniqueness of Korean and American approaches. Mission administration, however, encompasses both strategic and financial concerns, for the purpose of organizational structure and leadership is to fulfill certain strategic objectives through the use of personnel and financial resources.

Mission today has inherited a legacy of Korean missionaries who were dispersed around the world, working primarily among communities of expatriate Koreans, to establish and pastor Korean churches. With the economic growth of South Korea during the latter third of the twentieth century, multinational companies such as Samsung, LG, and Hyundai dispersed Koreans into the markets of the world. Korean missionaries, lacking extensive cross-cultural training and administrative oversight, tended to replicate the forms and structures of the Korean church, even among indigenous populations. Even as missionaries learned that replication was not the most effective approach to witnessing and extending the kingdom of God, the sending churches to which missionaries were accountable wanted results. Support funding was given with the expectation that reports of baptisms and pictures of church buildings would be received in return. This desire for results contributed to a pattern of deployment to accessible and responsive mission fields where Korean missionaries could preach in public campaigns and witness openly. Sponsoring churches at home generally lacked an understanding of cross-cultural issues and were unaware of factors related to witness in the context of indigenous worldviews.

## CHANGES IN IMB GLOBAL STRATEGY

Just before establishing the relationship between the IMB and the CKSBC, the IMB had implemented a radical change in global strategy that involved a focus on unreached people groups, indigenous church-planting strategies, and a decentralized field structure in which primary missionary accountability was to a team of fellow missionaries working with a local people group. These new directions and the strategic focus of field administration contrasted significantly with existing forms of Korean mission. When support for ethnic Korean missionaries began to be provided by the IMB, accountability through cooperation with team members and field leaders in the designated field strategy was expected; training, field preparation, and the development of cross-cultural communication skills were not optional. It even became necessary for the IMB to develop Korean-language tracks in its field orientation training. The narrow focus of missionary assignments, however, and accountability to the IMB and the field structure often conflicted with the accountability the missionaries felt toward their sending churches, as well as with the expectations of those churches.

Most mission agencies and organizations see themselves as existing to serve churches in the sending and supervision of missionaries overseas. Parachurch agencies have a clearly defined strategy and purpose; missionaries choose the organization that is compatible with their calling and values. The fact that missionaries have to bring guaranteed personal support to the sending organization creates an unavoidable tension between accountability to supporting churches and accountability to the sending agency. This tension is exacerbated by certain characteristics of Korean culture.

## KOREAN CULTURE AND ADMINISTRATIVE ACCOUNTABILITY

Korean culture, like most Eastern cultures, values submissiveness to elders and to those in authority and senior positions of leadership. This acquiescence is reflected not only in the family structure but in churches as well. Pastors exercise an authoritative role and hold a position of unquestionable respect. They, along with elders, determine church programs, manage budgets, and presume to design mission strategies. The missionary is seldom in a position to question those to whom he or she is accountable, even after initial adjustments and acculturation in a foreign assignment might have brought him or her to an understanding of more culturally appropriate approaches. In numerous instances the zeal to witness in ways one would in Korea or the United States has proven disastrous, causing mission work to be carried out without sensitivity to local worldviews and social restrictions. Even where the missionary's endeavors are well received, churches are often planted around forms and functions common in the missionary's place of origin but alien to indigenous principles of group relationship and decision making.

As mentioned above, Korean culture also values "face" highly. Shaming is therefore to be avoided, often by avoiding straightforward communication and by sidestepping necessary confrontation in the area of accountability. A Korean missionary accountable to a sending church or agency would find it difficult, if not impossible, to contradict instructions from his or her pastor at home or supervisor from the sponsoring agency, even though the missionary may be clearly in disagreement with them. This fact creates a dilemma for the missionary: whether to work in a way that fulfills expectations but is contrary to the missionary's preferences and gifts, or to ignore the responsibility to be accountable to those in authority and, while voicing compliance, to proceed to do what he or she feels led to do. On this point I have found that the profound spirituality and prayer life of Korean missionaries can create a challenge for mission administration. Korean missionaries testify to communion with God in which God clearly reveals direction for their ministry and work. They obviously feel a conviction that God's will should supersede the opinions and instructions of human supervisors.

To present a pretense of compliance with authority accompanied by noncompliance in practice is acceptable in Eastern culture. No one loses face because of confrontation, disagreement, or lack of stated submissiveness. But when it becomes necessary to confront ineffective or misguided work, how can those in authority avoid loss of face? As a result, two levels emerge: a communication level, in which agreement and respect are expressed, and a practical level, in which deviations from instructions are ignored, all under a pretense of compliance and accountability.

## THE TWO DIRECTIONS OF ADMINISTRATIVE ACCOUNTABILITY

Administrative accountability flows in two directions. The missionary is accountable to the sending church, sponsoring agency, and national church with which he or she works, and also to the government and local authorities that have granted permission for living and working in their country. But the church and sponsoring agency also have an administrative accountability to the missionary. While those in leadership may hold a position of authority from which they supervise and direct strategies, they are also responsible for providing support and ministry resources for the assignment, adequate training and guidance, and an administrative structure that provides for the needs of the missionary and missionary's family.

What I have observed suggests that, while both forms of administrative accountability are deficient in many Western agencies, they are even more wanting in the Korean missions context. In practice, Korean missionaries, having responded to the call of God, receive the endorsement of a church and/or a sponsoring agency. After raising support, they depart with their families to the field, often without adequate administrative backing. The cost of living allowance is usually calculated from an idealistic perspective and presumes willingness to adopt a sacrificial lifestyle. Resources fall short of what it takes to provide travel, housing, and adequate ministry expenses. Allowances for contingencies and needs such as medical costs and the education of children are insufficient. In other cases, some missionaries go into the field well-endowed with benefactors who respond to every appeal or need of the missionary and who assume, without real oversight or accountability, that the funds are being used appropriately.

Of central importance is an administrative structure that provides appropriate orientation and training for the missionary before departure to the field so that the missionary family is prepared for the cultural adjustments it will need to make. While sponsoring churches may not be equipped to serve missionaries in this way, partnership with other agencies that provide such training should be a component of churches' accountability in sending missionaries. Also, sending churches would do well to seek advice from various mission agencies regarding their policies on the relationship between missionary and agency and the type of accountability expected. In addition to such policies, a covenant can be drafted to delineate the mutual expectations and commitments of the two parties.

## PRACTICAL ISSUES

An administrative accountability structure that does not sustain adequate financial support for missionaries is negligent, but the same is true if the administrative structure leaves missionaries in the stressful position of having to bear the burden of decisions that should be governed by administrative policies. How much time should be spent on the field relative to home assignments? What guidelines are appropriate for travel, housing, lifestyle, and language learning? What expectations apply to coordination of work with other missionary teams? These are all areas in which the missionary should be served by administrative provisions. Without the support of such administrative structures and accountability, missionaries can spend an inordinate amount of time handling these affairs and caring for the needs of their families, time that could be spent instead engaging in the witness and ministry to which they were called. Just the hours consumed in acquiring a visa and renewing work permits, leasing and renovating housing, registering an automobile, and communicating with the home constituency can be exorbitant unless accountability structures in the sending country and on the field exist to assist the missionary. Such additional "side" responsibilities result in frustration, burnout, and a high rate of attrition; collectively, they work to negate the long-term tenure needed for planting the Gospel effectively on the mission field.

Appropriate administrative accountability will provide guidance, consultation, and periodic evaluation on the field. Such oversight and support are difficult to achieve when a missionary is deployed to a frontier assignment where there are no other missionaries. In such situations, the missionary should understand that he or she is expected to relate in a mutually respectful way with local national believers, be submissive to government authorities, and identify with society as a servant and learner. Wherever possible, the missionary should be required to relate to missionary peers in an ad hoc, if not official, accountability structure. If no personnel of the missionary's church or agency are available, the missionary should be held accountable for establishing relationships with other missionaries working in proximity to his or her assignment for the sake of fellowship, inspiration, encouragement, and strategic planning so as to develop synergy through coordination of work undertaken and to avoid conflicts, competitiveness, and duplication of effort.

Missionaries can be more effective, focus more on the ministry assignment, and contribute to a larger strategic impact by being part of a local group that provides grassroots mutual accountability. But we must recognize that diverse cultural values and language barriers can make such relationships challenging. Many Korean-American missionaries working under the IMB have not felt included as true partners on local teams that are dominated by Anglo-Americans. This sense of exclusion is often the result not of discrimination but of an inability to communicate adequately in English for ideas to be freely expressed or the discussion fully understood. I have been present at gatherings of local missionary teams in which the dominant Anglo-Americans and the Korean team members have resorted to communicating in the local language rather than in English.

A word needs to be added regarding a current and growing tendency whereby more and more Koreans are being dispersed throughout the world as tentmaker missionaries, rather than as full-time missionaries supported by churches and/or mission agencies. This shift diminishes the need for administrative accountability, for the missionary is deployed by the employer, often a corporation, with full provision of financial support. The tentmaker missionary, however, should willingly bring himself or herself into a relationship of accountability with his or her church and should seek to work in partnership with local believers and missionaries. While the accountability of a tentmaker will be more informal and strategic than administrative, it will also ensure that the missionary is more effective.

The typical administrative deficiencies identified in this chapter are, it should be recognized, not unique to Korean missionaries or Korean mission organizations. The growing number of Korean-Americans serving with the IMB and the increasing number of partnerships with other Korean missionaries have been an asset in recent advancements in global evangelization. Interpersonal relationships among missionaries of different ethnicities are vulnerable to misunderstandings and conflict. The lack of administrative accountability structures is a disservice to missionaries who go to pour out their lives for the sake of Christ in sacrificial commitment. Yet in spite of the inherent problems, the grace of God is able to more than compensate for these failures. God continues to raise up and call out Koreans to reach a lost world. South Korea ranks second on the list of missionary sending countries, and ethnic Koreans make up the second largest ethnic group among missionaries serving abroad. The devotion to God and passionate witness of Korean and Korean-American missionaries is being used to penetrate lostness around the world, both with and without humanly devised structures of administration and accountability.

# 19

## Response to Jerry A. Rankin, "Administrative Accountability in Mission"

### Young Choon Lee and Elaine Lee

THE CHAPTER BY JERRY Rankin presents a case study of the steps taken and lessons learned as an American denominational mission, the International Mission Board (IMB) of the Southern Baptist Convention, opened up to incorporate missionaries from Korean-American churches affiliated with the same denomination. It is amazing to read that, just eight years after this step was taken, almost 400 Korean-American missionaries now serve with the IMB around the world, and more than 600 additional candidates are in the appointment process. It is also notable that the initiative for this new step came from pastors of key churches of the Council of Korean Southern Baptist Churches (CKSBC) who made a commitment to send their missionaries through the IMB. Their decision came after some years in which the Korean-American churches had sent missionaries directly, rather than through the IMB. Rankin attributes the shift in the churches' practice to recognition by these pastors that the IMB could provide better strategic and administrative support.

Rankin provides a brief description of how the IMB deals with administrative accountability, but the bulk of his chapter describes some of the blessings as well as some of the administrative challenges, especially at the field level, that have resulted from this rather sudden influx of Korean-American workers. The chapter also addresses cultural factors that may be contributing to these challenges. Rankin uses the term "administration" in an overarching way to encompass both strategic and financial aspects, as he believes that "the purpose of organizational structure and leadership is to fulfill certain strategic objectives through the use of personnel and financial resources" (p. 249). Our response will also consider administrative accountability in this overarching sense. We will compare the experience of the IMB with the experience of WEC International (WEC) with the hope of gaining further insight into the issue of administrative accountability, especially as it relates to Korean workers.

## WEC INTERNATIONAL: ORGANIZATIONAL STRUCTURE AND PRACTICES

We, the authors of this chapter, both Korean-Americans, joined WEC through its U.S. sending base in 1993 to work in Mongolia and have served in the WEC International Office as deputy international directors since 2005.[1] WEC is an interdenominational faith mission that began in Great Britain in 1913 but quickly became international with sending bases established in the United States, Australia, Germany, Switzerland, Brazil, Singapore, and Korea. As of 2011, the organization has sending bases in sixteen countries. Since the establishment of a WEC sending base in Korea in 1997, there has been a rapid increase in the number of Korean workers in WEC; in 2011 about 350 Koreans work in WEC, with about 90 Koreans in the process of joining.

An organization's structure and basic practices provide a point of access for considering its conception of administrative accountability. Since fairly early on in its nearly 100-year history, WEC has functioned in a decentralized manner, emphasizing self-governance by fields and sending bases, which elect their own leaders, make their own decisions about vision and strategy within the overall objectives of WEC, and are financially self-supporting. For issues that affect the whole mission, the final decision-making authority is the Leaders' Council, which comprises the international director, deputy international directors, regional directors, and all elected field and sending-base leaders. The international director, together with the deputy international directors, provides visionary leadership for the whole mission to ensure that members of the organization remain true to WEC objectives and basic principles and practices. (A booklet entitled *Principles and Practices* outlines the orga-

1. Note that "sending base" for WEC has a quite different meaning from "sending churches" as used by Jerry Rankin in his discussion of the IMB. Sending bases for WEC are part of the mission structure.

nization's main objectives, core values, and practices.) The Coordinating Council, composed of all regional directors and other invited members, has some decision-making functions, but its primary role is to assist the international director in planning future advances, in policy making, and in other matters of strategic importance.

### *Self-Governance and Participatory Decision-Making Principles*

The principles of self-governance and participatory decision making are at the base of WEC structure and at the heart of WEC practice. Most decisions are made at the field level, with the final authority on each field (usually defined as a country or people group) or sending base being the "field/sending-base conference," which comprises all full-status members of the field. Major decisions affecting the whole field, such as field vision and strategy, leadership election, recognition of workers as full-status workers, personnel placements, field finance, and new ministry locations, are made at the annual field conference, and it is the responsibility of the field leadership to ensure that these decisions are implemented. If the field is large, some areas of decision making may be delegated to a field committee or local teams within the field. The basic principle is that all members of a local team or field will seek the mind of the Lord together on major decisions that affect them.

In terms of finance, fields and sending bases are completely self-supporting, with no allocation from any central fund. Accordingly, accountability for field/sending-base finance is to the field conference rather than to the international office. Any land or property bought by an individual worker for ministry on a field is considered WEC field property unless there was a clear understanding between the worker and the field at the time of the original transaction that the purchase was made with personal funds and for personal use, rather than for ministry. This policy, we believe, has prevented many potential disputes.

### *Selection and Support of Workers*

Mobilization, screening, acceptance, and orientation of new workers are handled at each sending base. Applicants are screened thoroughly by sending base staff, and those who are eligible are invited to attend a candidate orientation program during which they live at the sending base for a minimum of eight weeks (each sending base can determine the length) to find out more about WEC and give the WEC staff an opportunity to get to know them. At the end of this candidate-orientation program, final decisions about acceptance into WEC are made by the sending base staff, based upon a recommendation from the Candidate Department. Approval by the relevant field is also necessary before the worker can proceed to that field. Upon acceptance into WEC, all workers either sign or verbally agree to the material contained in *Principles and Practices*. Even after workers have gone to the field, they are asked to reread the booklet and reaffirm their commitment to its contents every three years.

In their first two years new workers are evaluated every six months: the worker fills out a self-evaluation form that he or she then reviews with the team or field leader in order to establish how the worker is doing; on the basis of this discussion the leader fills out an evaluation form, a copy of which is sent to the worker's sending base. At the end of the first two years, a recommendation is made by the field leadership, in light of which the field conference decides whether the worker should be granted full status. Recognition as a full-status member may be postponed if there are areas that need to be worked on; in extreme cases a worker may be asked to leave the field.

Whenever the size of the field allows, workers are placed in local teams; factors taken into account in this process may include field vision and strategy, local context and needs, number of workers, personal calling, and gifts. Workers on the field are accountable to their field leader and team leader (if they are part of a team), who in turn are responsible for receiving workers, giving field orientation, providing member care, and supplying guidance that enables workers to stay on track with the team and field vision. The members of teams within a locality meet regularly (often weekly) for fellowship, prayer, and ministry discussions. These meetings provide a natural mechanism for team members to support one another, and they afford a level of accountability as members share about their personal lives as well as about ministry. The degree of team collaboration in ministry depends on team strategy, composition of workers, local context, and type of ministry in which members are involved. In addition, field leaders usually visit each local team once or twice a year. In recent years WEC has encouraged each worker to write up a job or ministry description in consultation with the team or field leader and has urged the leader to review this material periodically with the worker.

Before going home on leave at the end of a term, workers are usually debriefed by field leaders by means of an end-of-term debriefing form. A copy of this form is sent to the worker's sending-base leader, who will also meet (or arrange for someone to meet) the worker for a debriefing when the worker returns to his or her home country. A worker who returns to the home country for furlough or for other reasons is accountable to the sending-base leader until returning to the field.

Another layer of accountability and support is provided by the regional directors, who represent the International Office to the fields and sending bases. The regional directors visit each of the fields/sending bases in their regions at least once a year, usually during annual field conferences. While the regional directors try to connect with all workers during their visit, one of their primary roles is to encourage, support, and coach or mentor the field leader. The role of the regional directors is largely advisory, with no direct authority over matters of self-governing fields. The regional directors, however, play an important role in coaching and mentoring the field leaders, influencing and monitoring field developments, and intervening in crisis situations. They regularly report to and consult with the International Office on any significant developments within their regions.

As this account of the selection, review, and support of workers demonstrates, formal and informal accountability is built into WEC's organizational structure and practices. The importance of accountability for our life and ministry before God and to one another was emphasized again at the Leader's Council conference held in 2006. While WEC's main objectives and core values may draw Koreans into WEC, many Koreans also seem to appreciate the stability of the WEC organizational structure and basic practices, which are built on principles of fellowship and accountability. The attractiveness of WEC principles to Korean workers may be indicative of their desire to live and work together, rather than independently.

## WEC'S EXPERIENCE WITH WORKERS FROM KOREA

Like the IMB, which experienced a large number of Korean workers joining the mission within a relatively short period of time, WEC has enjoyed the blessings of a Korean influx, as well as facing some of the concomitant challenges. For WEC leadership, this situation has highlighted the need to explore the whole issue of multicultural teams and to help all workers and teams deepen their understanding of different cultural values and of how such values affect the way they relate and how they work together. As an international mission, WEC has established resources and has always provided some orientation and training in this area. With the rapid increase in the number of non-Western workers joining WEC in recent years, however, the organization has had to intensify its efforts by offering on-field training and more pre-field training for new workers on the issue of working in multicultural teams. WEC has also incorporated this topic into its in-house leadership training. Furthermore, since 2007 a working group has been assigned to explore this whole area and to bring its insights and recommendations to the Coordinating Council. While the rapid increase in the number of non-Western missionaries has brought new stresses and challenges to WEC fields, it has also caused the organization to reflect upon its customary way of doing things and to determine whether any adjustments are necessary in order, not merely to accommodate workers from Korea or other non-Western countries, but ultimately to become more effective in fulfilling the task of reaching the unreached.

Jerry Rankin writes that the relationship between Korean missionaries and their sending churches becomes a major factor in difficulties the missionaries face in practicing administrative accountability, especially at the field level. Sending churches' high expectations of fruit in the form of churches planted coupled with the challenge of saying "no" to sending-church pastors who might request their missionaries to work in ways that are not consistent with team strategy or practices can lead the missionary to operate on two levels—verbal compliance with team strategy on one level, but noncompliance in actual practice on another level.

To a certain extent similar tensions may also be present in WEC, but they do not appear to be the main factors in the problems Korean workers have faced with administrative accountability in WEC. Discussions at the leadership level and in the working group mentioned above have established that the biggest challenges in WEC have been with the workers themselves, in areas such as communication, the concept of a team, leadership, and decision making. At the root of many of the struggles have been major cultural differences concerning individualism, collectivism, and the characteristics of high- and low-context cultures.

As have many other international mission organizations, WEC has been "international" for many years, with workers from many nations. Until recently, however, most workers have been from Western cultures, which are mostly individualistic and which highly treasure values such as equality, privacy, independence, and freedom of expression. The influx of non-Western workers—Brazilians, Singaporeans, and Koreans, for example—who come from collective cultures, where relationships and the group are primary, was bound to generate tension and raise the need for adjustments.

## COMMUNICATION—A MAJOR AREA OF CHALLENGE

An essential element in administrative accountability is communication, but communication difficulties have caused much misunderstanding and frustration for WEC's multicultural teams and fields. Different levels of fluency in English are one obvious cause of miscommunication, but subtle differences in style of communication have caused even more confusion, miscommunication, and hurt. Koreans come from a high-context culture, in which the assumption is that things do not necessarily have to be spoken out in words, so nonverbal communication or indirect communication using what may be seen as ambiguous statements is quite common, and the listener is responsible for figuring out the meaning from the speaker's few words or the context. This situation is quite unlike that in most Western, low-context cultures, where words—whether written or oral—are important and to be taken seriously, and the speaker is responsible for articulating exactly what he or she means, giving as much detail as is needed to eliminate ambiguity; in such cultures direct verbal communication is the norm.

This disparity has led to situations in which Korean workers believed they had communicated what they needed to share with the team or leader, but other team members or the leaders felt that the Korean workers had not communicated with them or had failed to share openly. For the non-Koreans the Korean communication had been either too indirect or ambiguous, or too general and lacking in the expected level of detail. As a result the perception arose that some Korean workers were not practicing openness or accountability. At the same time, Korean workers felt hurt that their messages were not picked up by the leader or team members, or they held that others were too direct or confrontational and overly concerned with details.

Expectations about the time when things should be shared or discussed also differed. Korean workers who shared a proposal for a ministry or project with the leader after they had been developing the idea for a while might have been deemed to be "not consulting" because the team or leader had expected to be informed during the idea's initial stages, before it was fully developed. From the Korean workers' perspective, it may have seemed better to avoid "bothering" the team or its leader until the idea had been developed to the point that it was worth sharing.

At times during team meetings or at field conferences, decisions would be made without any objections being raised by a Korean worker, who kept silent. For the leader, silence meant agreement. Only later would the leader find out that the Korean worker had not really been in agreement. A number of reasons might account for the failure of Koreans to voice disagreement: they may have felt that they would not be understood by the others or that they had not been given the opportunity to speak or that they did not want to go against the group. Workers from individualistic, low-context cultures are encouraged from an early age to express their thoughts and opinions, but high-context communicators from collective cultures, such as Koreans, are taught to be more reticent about speaking out, especially if their views would go against another's opinion, particularly that of a leader. A specific invitation to share thoughts during the meeting, or a private meeting with the leader before the team meeting or field conference, might help such workers to express their opinions.

While Korean workers have been attracted to the participatory decision-making principle of WEC, communication patterns that have been instilled from childhood often hinder them from participating fully in decision making. With the passage of time and more awareness of these differences, however, most Korean workers are able to adjust and to participate in discussions more freely. At the same time, leaders and workers from low-context cultures can learn to pick up more indirect, subtle messages and to find appropriate ways to draw out the thoughts and feelings of fellow workers from Korea and other high-context cultures.

## VISION AND STRATEGY

Other areas of contrast between high- and low-context cultures are vision and strategy. In his book *Leading Across Cultures*, James Plueddemann describes the difference between high-context and low-context cultures along three axes: vision, strategy, and situation (see accompanying table).[2]

| High-Context Culture | Low-Context Culture |
| --- | --- |
| *Vision* is intuitive with a general sense of direction. | *Vision* is precise with predictable and quantifiable objectives. |
| *Strategy* often arises from unexpected opportunities and spontaneously changes when the situation changes. | *Strategy* is planned far in advance and tightly evaluated in light of measurable objectives. |
| *Situation* comes from an instinctive reading of the environment. | *Situation* is analytically and logically analyzed. |

**Table 19.1.**

Comparison of High-Context and Low-Context Cultures

Although the terms "vision" and "strategy" are used by both cultures, the ways in which these terms are perceived differ markedly. Confusion and frustration have been expressed by members of both cultures: workers from low-context cultures feel that workers from high-context cultures such as Korea act as if they are not accountable to the agreed-upon field vision or strategy, and they are frustrated when Korean workers suddenly want to start new ministries and projects. For their part, Korean workers are frustrated at the seeming inflexibility of team members from low-context cultures and by their slow speed in responding to new situations or opportunities. Workers from low-context cultures would think it worthwhile to have lengthy discussions about just the right words for vision statements or to work out details of strategy before embarking on any ministry; workers from high-context cultures might settle for a broader understanding, preferring to spend more time and energy on actually doing something while working out the details along the way as needed. We need to recognize that there are strengths and weaknesses in both attitudes.

## CONCLUSION

Both the IMB and WEC have experienced the blessing of having a large number of Koreans or Korean-Americans join them in recent years in obeying the Great Commission. This development has given new impetus to the mission of these organizations. In the case of the IMB, it

2. James E. Plueddemann, *Leading Across Cultures: Effective Ministry and Mission in the Global Church* (Downers Grove, Ill.: IVP Academic, 2009), p. 201.

was pastors of Korean-American Southern Baptist churches who made the commitment to send their workers through the IMB; for WEC, it was mostly individual Koreans who took the step of joining WEC, with the support of individuals and churches. Many Koreans and Korean-Americans have expressed their appreciation of the structures and practices of the IMB or WEC that have been developed over many years in order to provide direction and healthy accountability. The response of these Korean workers and churches reflects a genuine desire and commitment to serve with accountability.

At the same time, both the IMB and WEC have experienced challenges in the practical outworking of this commitment, especially at the field level. In his description of the IMB experience, Rankin points to the particular dilemma that Korean workers face when they are caught between the sending church and the mission, being accountable to their sending churches in a way that may not be consistent with the strategy and policies of the mission. WEC's experience suggests that the cultural values of the workers themselves are of more significance in creating complications than is the relationship with the sending church. This discussion has considered two major areas of administrative accountability in which cultural differences have been at the root of much misunderstanding and frustration: (1) communication and (2) vision and strategy. To say that cultural factors are behind many of the struggles in WEC multicultural teams is not to deny the reality of sinful attitudes and other factors such as personality, gender, and age, which can also be the cause of friction.

The constraints of this response have not allowed an exploration of other challenges, such as differences in the concept of team, of leadership, and of decision making, which stem largely from strongly held values of individualism and collectivism. Many of these issues are not a matter of right or wrong, or of biblical versus unbiblical, but of different values and preferences. A deeper understanding of these cultural differences can prevent hasty judgments and motivate the search for ways to live and work together in unity and with synergy.

Those who attended WEC's 2010 Leaders' Council meeting were reminded afresh that organizational structure and policies are not what ultimately hold us together. More fundamental to accountability in WEC are love and passion for Jesus, commitment to the main objective of reaching the lost, and ownership of WEC's four core values, or "Four

Pillars"—faith, holiness, sacrifice, and fellowship. Major global trends and increasing cultural diversity in WEC have brought the realization that ways of living out our fundamental values and working toward our objectives may not be the same today as they were in the past. This recognition does not downplay the importance of structure and policies that provide the framework for accountability, but it acknowledges the need to be flexible and open on nonessentials, without compromising on core values and objectives. While increased cultural diversity within the mission has brought some challenges, WEC believes that, as an organization, it can learn from and grow through this new situation of multiculturalism. WEC believes that the present situation should be seen, not as a problem of just one group of workers, but as an opportunity for all members to be sharpened and enriched by being stretched and by learning from one another.

# 20

## Strategic Accountability:
## God's Mission in God's Way

### *Min Young Jung*

T HIS CHAPTER OFFERS A personal reflection on strategic accountability. It is based heavily on experience I have gained through my
journey of participation in God's mission. As I look back over more than
thirty years of engagement with, on the one hand, Bible translation ministries and, on the other, Korean mission movements, I can recognize a
steep learning curve in the area of accountability.[1] Even though personal
experiences within limited contexts are inevitably subjective, careful reflection on and evaluation of such involvement can be valuable.

### DEFINITION

What is "strategic accountability"? One proposed definition is a "statement of personal promise to achieve specific results within the shared
vision and overall strategic outcomes and targets set in the Balanced
Scorecard."[2] Accountability in mission, however, means much more
than the integrity of balance sheets; it concerns, rather, the strategic use
of God's resources, and is ultimately about doing God's mission in God's
way. Two interconnected criteria, among others, are evident when we
think about accountability in this latter sense: strategic accountability

---

1. I have served with Wycliffe Global Alliance (www.wycliffe.net) and SIL
International (www.sil.org).

2. Susan Kwolek and Karyn Popovich, "Strategic Accountability Agreements,"
www.healthcareleadershipconference.ca/assets/Popovich_-_Strategic_Accountability
_Agreements%5B1%5D.pdf, p. 6.

is about stewardship for achieving optimal (not necessarily maximum) kingdom values and results for God's kingdom; and it is about quality more than quantity, even though both are significant.

## HOW STRATEGIC SHOULD A STRATEGY BE?

As I wrote this chapter for the Korean Global Mission Leadership Forum, one sticky question kept coming into my mind: How strategic should a strategy be? I raise this question as the result of a number of concerns that emerge whenever there is talk about "strategy," especially within the evangelical camp.

- While the concept of strategy is broader and more encompassing than that of tactics, myopic details—functions, items, lists, procedures, tasks—often dominate at the expense of the whole picture.

- In a similar vein, people quickly jump to measurable goals with quantitative scorecards. In some areas quantitative measurement is applicable and even necessary for strategic accountability, but most biblical mandates, especially mission, seem to require qualitative evaluation of a sort that cannot be readily quantified. As a Gallup researcher recently commented, one of the worst mistakes many Christian institutions have made, and are still making, is the hasty application of quantitative research methodology to the strategic accountability of Christian ministries.[3]

- Both conventional (quantitative) and unconventional (qualitative) factors need to be integrated seamlessly into planning and evaluation, lest missionary endeavors result in mere proselytism rather than true conversion. Result-based management (RBM) has pitfalls; in particular, the "result" that it produces may be not real but rather just a bubble. In many cases, solid results are contingent upon healthy processes. Perhaps process-based management (PGM) should be adopted for strategic accountability in mission, for we do not own the result but are called to be faithful in the process (see 1 Cor. 3:6). Any strategy should aim at long-term effectiveness rather than short-term efficiency.

3. This statement was made by a Gallup Korea speaker during a seminar in 2010 on research methodology hosted by the Korea Research Institute of Mission (KRIM).

## MISSIOLOGICAL CONSULTATIVE PROCESS

A tool that has been significantly helpful to me in sharpening my insight into strategic accountability has been the missiological consultative process of the Wycliffe Global Alliance. Lest we as Wycliffe personnel should become trapped without a kingdom perspective in our own myopic spheres of endeavor—Bible translation, for example, and its related tasks—the international leadership team of Wycliffe Global Alliance decided to invite Bill Taylor, former director and current ambassador-at-large of the World Evangelical Alliance's Mission Commission (WEA MC) to walk us through a missiological consultation in 2006. As a revered leader whose work is in accordance with the WEA MC slogan ("reflective practitioner") and who is well versed in both theory (theology/missiology) and practice, Taylor was an obvious choice. This event evolved into an annual consultative process with a variety of facilitators, with the result that the Wycliffe Global Alliance leadership team also aspired to become reflective practitioners and became increasingly better equipped for strategic planning and accountability. Wycliffe Global Alliance took a further step in this direction by appointing a director of missiological development who is also responsible for establishing and running a missiological institute.

One prominent benefit, among many, that I personally gained from this consultative process was a fresh look at our paramount goal, Vision 2025.[4] Instead of taking just the numbers—the year 2025, for example, and the remaining 2,200+ language communities still needing God's Word in their mother tongues—I began to dig deeper into the undergirding strategic themes of urgency, sustainability, capacity building, creative strategies, and partnerships (see accompanying table), matters that are qualitative in contrast to the numeric and temporal goals. As an aspiring reflective practitioner, I realized that Wycliffe Global Alliance as a missional community needed not only to adopt the slogan of seeing a Bible translation program in progress in every language still needing one by the year 2025 but also, and more importantly, to undertake an intense, ongoing process of reflection built on these five strategic themes.

---

4. *The Vision 2025 Resolution, adopted in 1999 by the Wycliffe International organizations and key partners, states,* "We embrace the vision that by the year 2025 a Bible translation project will be in progress for every people group that needs it" (www.wycliffe .net/AboutUs/Vision2025/tabid/98/language/en-US/Default.aspx).

## VISION 2025, *supported by:*

- Urgency
- Capacity Building
- Sustainability
- Creative Strategy
- Partnership

**Table 20.1.**

Strategic themes undergirding Vision 2025

Wycliffe Global Alliance should aim at organizational (internal) transformation before attempting to transform others. The current leadership team, called the Global Leadership Team (GLT), is committed to this process, and many partners are following suit.

## MULTILATERAL ACCOUNTABILITY—A KEY TO STRATEGIC ACCOUNTABILITY WITHIN THE CHURCH

Robert Linthicum correctly notes that significant systemic change "cannot occur . . . unless the articulated values . . . are truly embraced, and that cannot occur unless structures function to implement those values and unless individuals who run those structures work for the interests of the people [involved]. *Only when individuals and structures and values change do you have systemic change.*"[5] Four areas of multilateral strategic accountability are key to systemic transformation of Korean (or other Majority World) church and mission: institution and structure, a corporate culture of shared values, a wider community of learners and reflective practitioners, and partnership.

### Institutional and Structural Issues

On the home front, it is crucial for any institution to have a functioning system of checks and balances governing the relationship between board and administration. Although such structures exist in most Korean Christian institutions and not-for-profit organizations, I have rarely observed a truly well-functioning board. For years, various executive directors of Korean Christian and mission organizations have approached

5. Robert Linthicum, *Transforming Power: Biblical Strategies for Making a Difference in Your Community* (Downers Grove, Ill.: InterVarsity Press, 2003), pp. 25–26 (italics in the original).

me asking for formal or informal consultations. Almost always their frustration has been caused by malfunctioning boards, either inactive or hyperactive. Most boards I observed were simply nominal and thus inactive, assuming that the executive director and/or the administrative team would do what was needed for the organization without being held accountable.

Occasionally, hyperactive boards try to micromanage the executive director and his team, constantly stepping on the CEO's toes. Such boards simply do not understand board-administration dynamics and ignore or lack governance policies. My experience suggests that one of the most urgent issues to be addressed if there is to be healthy strategic accountability in any Korean Christian/mission organization is the establishment of a functioning board with integrated knowledge of the organization's history, mission, vision and core values, strategies, and structure.

On the field, it is crucial to have a solid receiving structure or system. If there is a sending system, there should be a receiving system as well. Surprisingly, though, among the more than 180 Korean mission agencies, not many have a field structure. In that sense, Korean mission practices are often compared to a baseball game without a catcher. Many Korean missionaries are on their own; they do not belong to any agency or structure and therefore are not accountable to anyone. And many mission agencies do not have a field system that is adequate to hold their members accountable.

In 2004 several Korean mission leaders started the annual Bangkok Mission Forum to address the focal issues of Korean mission. The first forum identified various issues and reached a consensus that accountability was the most crucial and most urgent. The theme of the second forum, held the following year, was "Korean Mission and Accountability."[6] The second forum saw a heated debate on the cause of and remedy for the lack of accountability among many Korean missionaries and agencies. This forum eventually concluded that a healthy receiving structure on the field was the key to strategic accountability. I chaired the discussion and compiled the summary that appears as the appendix to this chapter.

6. The papers presented at the Bangkok forum were compiled and published as *Hanguk Seongyo-wa Chaengmu* (Korean mission and accountability: The second Bangkok mission forum), ed. Bangkok Mission Forum Committee (Seoul: Hyebon Publishing, 2006).

## A Corporate Culture of Shared Values

In a healthy community, core values are formed, co-owned, and transferred naturally to the next generation. The well-being of a community is therefore more fundamental than structural change, for the existence of a healthy corporate culture is a key to sharing and transferring values. Promoting healthy accountability in the context of community is both biblical and practical. The late Linsu Kim, a distinguished scholar of business administration and a former board chair of Global Missionary Fellowship, the incorporated umbrella organization of Wycliffe Korea (Global Bible Translators), emphasized the importance of cultivating a corporate culture of shared values; in the Korean context, the function of senior members as role models is crucial to this process. In keeping with the Korean proverb "If upstream is clean, so is downstream," when senior members demonstrate integrity and accountability, junior members will feel obliged to follow their example. This is healthy social pressure embedded within a corporate culture. Within a healthy community, wrong can be corrected by "speaking the truth in love" (Eph. 4:15). It is important for Korean mission not to copy any Western system blindly, especially when individualism is embedded within the latter. It will take mutual (Western and non-Western) efforts to come up with a *global* accountability system.

## A Wider Community of Learners and Reflective Practitioners

Strategic accountability presupposes healthy strategies that are biblically sound and clinically proven. But how can we determine whether a given strategy is healthy? Again, it takes a community—more precisely, the hermeneutic community, both synchronic and diachronic. We are standing on the foundation laid by the diachronic covenant community, on wisdom accumulated through the ages that provides continuity and safeguards. The truth is not found for the first time after two millennia of church history; to claim otherwise is heretical. Studying and learning from the Christian classics is very important in this regard. Korean mission has much yet to learn from the history and legacy of the church. Without that recognition, there is no hope of achieving strategic accountability.

We also need a synchronic community that not only will add value to the corporate wisdom but also will interpret together the new things

God is doing here and now. How the early Christian community discerned the will of the Holy Spirit together is noteworthy: "*It seemed good to the Holy Spirit and to us* not to burden you with anything beyond the following requirements" (Acts 15:28 NIV). The tragic Afghanistan incident in 2007—in which two young men out of twenty-three short-termers were killed by members of the Taliban and which resulted in the untimely closure of most ministries in Afghanistan in which Korean missionaries were involved—was a negative example of one Korean mission agency blindly following its own strategy without proper consultation with the wider Korean mission community. Although a member of both Mission Korea and Korean World Mission Association, the agency ignored repeated warnings from both organizations about its actions.[7] A similar unfortunate event, hosted by another organization, occurred in 2011 in a sensitive Muslim country. Again, the advice of the wider mission community went unheeded.

Intentional effort is required to broaden the contemporary (synchronic) community for maximum synergy in understanding the times in order to know what to do (see 1 Chron. 12:32). The formation of a wider community of learners and reflective practitioners will enable us, through cross-fertilization, to establish the best practices for many difficult situations and to confirm and reconfirm healthy strategies. Korean mission has not generally been active in sharing and collaborating with the wider mission community, and it is crucial now for it to come out of its hermit-like seclusion and to mix and mingle with the global hermeneutic community. This engagement is an important prerequisite for healthy strategic accountability.

Listening to and interacting with Thai church leader Anusun Bunnit during the Second Bangkok Mission Forum, for example, turned out to be a rare chance to evaluate Korean mission from a recipient's point of view. According to Bunnit, the majority of Korean missionaries in Thailand focus mainly on constructing material objects, such as church buildings, without training indigenous leaders. He implored the forum participants to select and send only those who had a solid track record of discipleship; the rest should be recalled. The church of Thailand also had money, he said, but was in desperate need of outsiders' help in training leaders.

7. For details, see "2007 South Korean Hostage Crisis in Afghanistan," http://en .wikipedia.org/wiki/2007_South_Korean_hostage_crisis_in_Afghanistan.

An ethnically Korean Chinese woman I met at the Amsterdam 2000 conference on evangelism revealed a similar case. Delighted to be meeting a Korean-Chinese delegate, I approached her, but she not only seemed somehow unexcited but in fact flatly rejected me. I was embarrassed but had no option other than to keep my distance. The problem was that we were in the same hotel and daily commuted to and from the convention center on the same bus. I therefore mustered enough courage to approach her again, asking if she had previously had any negative experiences with Koreans. Yes, she said, rather apologetically this time. What she revealed flabbergasted and shamed me. Her tone in considering Korean missions was similar to that of Anusun Bunnit, but her evaluation was much worse. In a nutshell, some Korean missionaries and their sending churches had in effect committed sheep stealing with the aid of a huge amount of money. Most heartbreaking was the loss of her long-standing disciple, which the delegate regretted not because of his move to another leader but because of his betrayal of the Gospel for money.

These two cases are just the tip of a huge iceberg. Korean missions cannot afford to let such inordinate and irresponsible events happen again and again. We must heed such wake-up calls, which should lead to healthy strategic accountability. To be accountable to God and the global mission community, we need to establish various strategic Korean mission forums, while also being actively involved in global and regional forums. I am glad to see the recent proliferation of Korean mission forums such as the Bangkok Mission Forum, Sorak Mission Forum, Korean Diaspora Forum, and Korean Diaspora Missions Network. Korean missions, however, should also participate in strategic global and regional forums more actively, thereby learning from and contributing to the wider mission community.

## Partnership Issues

A final issue to be addressed in terms of multilateral accountability is partnership. Although partnership has already been considered in this chapter to some degree, in light of its significance for strategic accountability, it is worth digging deeper. The recent appearance of partnership as a buzzword is a mixed blessing. On the one hand, the Christian world, especially the evangelical camp, is finally recognizing the significance of partnership, but on the other hand, one wonders whether this language will prove to be merely another pep talk. I sincerely hope and pray that the global mission and the church worldwide will take partnership seriously enough to make a substantial commitment to it.

Many people already know the practical benefits of partnership. Those attending the Korean Global Mission Leadership Forum in February 2011 did not have to be sold on the practical benefits of partnership; numerous books and articles both within and outside Christian circles provide powerful proof of its effectiveness. Two cases related to Korean mission are cited here to provide further verification. In the early 1990s I was asked by Global Missionary Fellowship (GMF) to visit several Latin American countries to consult with national church leaders about the possibility of sending GMF missionaries. My first experience of interaction with Latin American leaders provided a steep learning curve. During the visit one leader said rather bluntly that he would not welcome one more Korean because of divisions and conflicts among Korean missionaries in his country. He was a convert from Catholicism, which maintains an ostensible unity, but having observed ugly feuds among Korean missionaries who had come all the way to Latin America to preach a supposedly better truth, he was wondering whether he had been right in deciding to convert to Protestantism.

During the same trip one Peruvian church leader virtually burst into tears upon meeting me. I was, he said, the very first Korean mission leader to visit with the national church first in order to consult on whom to send and for what purposes. He had been praying eagerly that one day Korean missions would learn to respect and work in partnership with the national church, and finally I was there, in front of his desk, the answer to his prayer! Bishop David Zac Niringiye made a similar comment during the Mission Korea 2010 conference. Requested to provide an honest critique of Korean missionaries in Africa, the bishop said that most of them had never made any contact with African churches; they had neither consulted nor formed partnerships with them. Many Korean missionaries came of their own volition, doing whatever they wanted to do and ignoring the African churches. Such missionaries, he added, are not needed on the mission field today.

Such experiences are not solely the responsibility of individual Korean missionaries. In many cases sending churches play their part, especially megachurches. Global Bible Translators (GBT) recently had to pay a painful price for a megachurch's "good will" that lacked the spirit of partnership. A GBT member was working as a Bible translator in a rather sensitive area. His sending church, one of the largest in Korea, decided to shoot video footage of his family at work. According to the original agreement, the film would be viewed only within the church, and only to encourage prayer support within the congregation. The producer felt, however, that, since the material had turned out so well, it could be developed into a documentary film for public viewing. Without consulting GBT or even the missionary featured in the recording, the film was put into production and given a public showing. By the time GBT and the field organization realized what had transpired, it was too late. Since public knowledge of their work could result in serious legal action by the government of the country involved, this family was asked to leave the field immediately, and the film was removed from public theaters.[8]

## KINGDOM PARTNERSHIP AS GOD'S WAY OF DOING HIS MISSION

When I joined Wycliffe some thirty years ago, my challenge, I thought, was to adjust to the predominant Western culture. Despite myself, I often tried to think and behave like a Westerner, or at least to pretend to do so. I even endeavored to make Wycliffe Korea (GBT) as Western as possible. As the number and size of non-Western constituencies grew, however, Wycliffe eventually had to face the challenge of making itself truly international, instead of maintaining the status quo as a West-centered multinational club. In the process, both Westerner and non-Westerner had to adjust and meet each other midway. It has been an exciting journey of discovery as we have sought to move toward a healthy multicultural community, which, I believe, is a crucial prerequisite for kingdom partnership and for the realization of ultimate strategic accountability.

---

8. In a similar vein, the following comment by Jonathan Bonk is worth considering: "Megachurch congregations, eager to do good and to do it quickly and efficiently, bypass traditional mission agencies, oblivious of the painful lessons learned from decades of missionary work and deep familiarity with indigenous peoples. They cannot waste years or even months learning another language, becoming comfortable in another culture, and identifying more than superficially with another people. The tedious, time-consuming business of incarnation—Jesus was a three-mile-an-hour Palestinian Jew—is not an option. They have no time to be truly converted themselves" (Jonathan J. Bonk, "Mission as Invasion?" *International Bulletin of Missionary Research* 34, no. 2 [April 2010]: 66).

One of the best models for conceptualizing kingdom partnership is the so-called sailboat paradigm.[9] Space does not allow me to pursue this metaphor here, other than to say that, if we are concerned about the form strategic accountability should take in the future, the image of a sailboat, versus a motorboat, is worth close collaborative consideration; I believe it well pictures God's strategy of *missio Dei*. The sailboat approach will involve strategic collaboration between the emerging Majority World, whose strength is in general principles and a global/holistic approach, and the conventional West, whose strength is in its approach to details and analysis. These complementary members of the one body must be interconnected organically and synergistically for the sake of the ultimate cause. It takes the global church to accomplish the global mission. It takes the nations, after all, to reach the nations!

## APPENDIX

The Second Bangkok Mission Forum: Wrap-up Session of Day 2, May 11, 2005 (compiled by Min-Young Jung)

I.  For a healthy accountability system, it is crucial to establish and implement an on-field receiving system/structure.

    A. Decisions should be made on-site; remote control is unrealistic and ineffective.

    B. On-site ministry support, supervision, and member care are essential.

    C. Through formation of an on-site missional community, we can effectively prevent individualistic deviation. Communal discernment and plans are better than those of individuals.

II.  The role of on-field administration should include the following:

    A. Total care—spiritual, physical, emotional—of missionaries and families.

    B. Strategic, work-related, administrative, technical support.

9. See Alex Araujo, "To Catch the Wind: A New Metaphor for Cross-Cultural Partnership" (paper presented at the Coalition on the Support of Indigenous Ministries, Lombard, Ill., 2008), and Min-Young Jung, "Sailboat Paradigm: A Biblical Partnership of the Global Mission Era" (paper presented at Sorak Mission Forum, Seoul, Korea, 2009); see also "Sailing Friends," http://sailingfriends.wordpress.com.

       C. A system of accountability involving strategic plan and implementation, management, supervision, evaluation, and discipline.

III. Two conditions for the establishment and implementation of on-site administration are (A) a change of perspective and (B) structure.

       A. It takes a kingdom-first mind-set.

          1. Volunteerism is both a strength and a weakness of not-for-profit organizations. Volunteerism becomes a great strength when a healthy community culture is cultivated. Otherwise it can become extremely individualistic.

          2. Recovery of community is urgently needed. We have to guard against the tendency to take advantage of community for achieving personal ambitions; rather, we should cultivate a culture of commitment for the community goals and accountability.

          3. We should train leaders who can foster teamwork on the mission fields. This skill should be developed in seminary education and missionary training.

       B. The establishment of effective and implementable structure is necessary.

          1. We need to study, evaluate, and contextualize the established structures and systems developed by Western missions.

          2. Internationalization of home-grown mission agencies (in Korea and in the Diaspora) is necessary. We need to analyze, evaluate, and upgrade Korean models with field structure (e.g., Paul Mission).

          3. We need to learn from the example of the ecumenical movements, especially models in which Korean missionaries are working under the authority of indigenous churches.

4. We can set up desirable on-field structures through interdenominational and interagency networks.

   a. We need a "holy rectangular relationship," i.e., dialogue and collaboration between missionaries, agencies, sending churches, and indigenous churches.

   b. We also need to actively utilize established networks of missionaries, indigenous churches, mission agencies, etc.

   c. Once a broader network is established, every on-field ministry should be in line with agreed-upon principles and guidelines. The network should screen projects and ministries that are against the agreed-upon principles and strategies.

   d. The missionaries and agencies participating in the broader network should abide within the agreed-upon ethical code of conduct. For example, a mission agency should not accept a missionary who is being disciplined by another agency.

IV. The establishment and implementation of a multilateral accountability system are crucial.

   A. For an on-site accountability system, it is important to listen to the indigenous church. (In that regard, the Bangkok Mission Forum invited Elder Anusun Bunnit for a Thai church leader's evaluation of Korean mission.)

   B. A bilateral accountability relationship between mission agency and local (sending) church is important.

      1. They should share the responsibilities of missionary selection, management, care, etc. It is important to put special weight on the sending church's evaluation/reference in the missionary selection process.

      2. The sending church should be given the chance to participate in such crucial decisions as missionary allocation, redeployment, and change of ministry.

# 21

## Response to Min Young Jung, "Strategic Accountability"

*John McNeill*

MIN YOUNG JUNG'S CONTRIBUTION to this volume will resonate with many readers. How indeed can missionary activities be guided so that they are done in God's way?

In his chapter Jung outlines the topic of strategic accountability and points out that as missionary organizations work on the specifics of missionary tasks, one set of values needs to run throughout their structure, from top to bottom. His emphasis on the top-down nature of example-setting in Korean culture is worthy of careful note by Westerners.

Jung's experience with and careful thought about organizational structures are clear from his chapter. Also worthy of attention are cultural issues relating specifically to Koreans. As I raise the questions mentioned below, however, I want to emphasize that I have great respect for Koreans and their contribution to the work of the kingdom. I pose these questions in the hope that the enthusiasm, discipline, and energy that Korean missionaries show can be even more effectively channeled.

When discussing Korean top-down authority (his use of the Korean proverb "If upstream is clean, so is downstream" is telling), Jung warns against copying Western corporate culture, which is deeply influenced by individualism, a point that is very clear and helpful. Yet Korean culture is not without individualism too, but individualism of a different kind from that in the West. What I am calling Korean individualism is based on Korea's sense of its national uniqueness, a self-understanding that encourages Koreans as a group to follow an individualistic path separate from the community of nations. Such national-level individualism could seriously hinder the kind of cooperation that dialogue at events such as the Korean Global Mission Leadership Forum seeks to foster.

Toward the end of his contribution Jung mentions the example of a Korean megachurch that "lacked the spirit of partnership" (p. 275). This problem seems to be widespread among megachurches in North America as well but is perhaps particularly acute in Korea because of the tendency for more churches there to be "larger than life." Perhaps the kind of national-level Korean individualism suggested above can also become characteristic of a megachurch and the subculture that it develops. An understanding of megachurch phenomena might help us to prepare guidelines that could prevent the problems in mission activity that can be caused by the power and subculture of such churches.

Power issues are also raised in Jung's chapter. He mentions examples from China and Thailand, where Korean money has represented a serious missionary problem. Because of their great financial resources, Korean missionaries in both places have been able to avoid the real work of mission and have been empowered instead to engage in building projects and, to use Jung's term, sheep stealing. A clear definition of mission is required, and flexing of economic muscle in order to manipulate local people or fulfill a personal agenda does not qualify as part of that definition.

In addressing diachronic community, Jung writes that Koreans have not learned enough from the Christian classics. If this is so, to paraphrase Shakespeare's *Julius Caesar*, "It is a grievous fault, and grievously do we also suffer therefrom in the West." But our shared weakness is no excuse for not doing better. It has been apparent to me for years that some Korean missionaries are repeating the very mistakes that, citing instances from past Western-mission experience, I warn my students against. History teaches serious and valuable lessons; Korean missionaries and Western missionaries should each encourage the other to give serious study to and learn from the examples of the past.

A personal story sheds light on some of the issues mentioned in this response. Some years ago I met representatives of a Korean mission in Russia. At the time we met, the Korean missionaries saw me as an answer to their needs, a theologically trained and Russian-informed person who could help them design their program for pastoral training in Russia. For several years I worked with them both as a teacher and as one who strategized with them about curriculum. At one point in our cooperation, as I taught a course on pastoral care, I mentioned the biblical limits of any human authority, including that of a pastor. The teaching was so well received by both the students and the seminary staff that someone decided to have it transcribed and distributed in the national magazine for their churches in Russia. When some of the local Korean missionary pastors, however, read that a teacher at their seminary was saying that their authority was limited by God and should be resisted if it spoke against the clear will of God, they were very upset. As a result I was shunned by the seminary, never told what the problem was, and never invited back. Fortunately, a friend who was an insider told me what had happened, and at least I could understand where I stood. What I experienced, it seems, was a pulling together of Korean ranks in order to fend off dealing with a conflict, one that, according to my insider friend, still has *not* been dealt with internally more than a decade later. This example leads me to wonder how cooperation within what Jung calls our synchronic community can be improved so that non-Koreans can be full partners in the process of dealing with hard issues that arise among their Korean sisters and brothers, and vice versa.

Jung ends his paper with a sailing image that has particular resonance for me, a lifelong sailor. Sailing is a complex activity, one that, unlike motorboating, is not directly helped by the application of horsepower (read "money"). A good sailor knows and depends on wind and water as well as the boat. Boats of course differ, but so too do wind and water. The surface of water tells the trained eye a lot about wind, but it also hides invisible currents that are vital to the progress of the boat. And wind: what a mystery is hidden in the simple movement of air! Each body of water affects wind differently because of its environment. Varying shorelines and the differential heating effect of the sun greatly affect wind, its intensity, and its direction and duration. The most expert sailor is greatly hindered in new waters until he or she learns the subtleties of the local environment, wind, and currents, usually partly from experience, but largely from locals. Sailing provides many obvious lessons for missions.

# 22

## Accountability in Mission Partnerships: Case Studies from Wycliffe Global Alliance

### *Kirk Franklin*

M ISSION AGENCIES IN THE twenty-first century are assisting people of all nations to serve in all nations. This worldwide mission service is made possible by a complex set of ministry partnerships involving the sending church, the sending mission structure, and the receiving church or receiving agency. Into this mix come the missionary and the relationship with his or her supervisor. In fact, the missionary may have a whole set of supervisors—home church pastor(s), mission agency administrators and leaders, and in-country team leaders or receiving partner-agency leaders.

What follows are recent case studies provided by administrators affiliated with Wycliffe Global Alliance.[1] These case studies demonstrate unique cross-cultural experiences. The insight gained as we reflect on these studies and the lessons learned from them will enable us to better prepare the next generation of missionaries and ministry partners.

### CASE STUDIES INVOLVING CROSS-CULTURAL MISUNDERSTANDING

In the following case studies some of the missionaries come from high-context cultures, and some from low-context cultures. In high-context

1. Wycliffe Global Alliance is the new name for Wycliffe International, formerly known as Wycliffe Bible Translators International. Wycliffe Global Alliance, with more than 100 affiliated organizations, is linked together by a common vision to see Bible translation and related services provided for minority people groups.

cultures the "communication or message is one in which most of the information is either in the physical context or internalized in the person, while very little is in the coded, explicit, transmitted part of the message." In contrast, "in low-context cultures, people pay special attention to explicit communication and to ideas."[2]

*Study 1: Expectations in a Reporting Relationship*

An experienced Australian missionary couple began working in a Pacific Island country. The couple did not submit the required monthly reports outlining their current activities and goals for the next month to their supervisor. They also did not take the time to meet face-to-face with their supervisor to develop their annual plan. The supervisor, an experienced missionary from Finland, became concerned about this absence of information and personal interaction because he felt it was his responsibility to plan with the couple. In consequence, he set up a two-way radio meeting with them to discuss when they could meet face-to-face.

During the radio conversation the Australian couple indicated that they were fine and were making good progress. They said they did not see any need to be accountable to their supervisor. They were adamant that their accountability was solely to their church and sending organization. The couple said that coming to the mission's administrative center just to meet with their supervisor would take too much time and cost too much money. Therefore they politely declined the request. The supervisor, however, insisted they must meet. His insistence shocked the couple, who still refused to change their plans. The result was that the supervisor viewed the couple as individualistic, stubborn, and unwilling to submit to his authority, while the couple saw their supervisor as power hungry and not at all understanding of their situation. Eventually the couple agreed to meet the supervisor but felt forced into the situation, and they made travel arrangements reluctantly.

During preparations for the meeting the supervisor agreed that the couple could have an advocate, a colleague from Australia, attend the meeting with them. After both the couple and their supervisor had had the opportunity to explain their perspectives more clearly, each party began to see that the other had valid points, and a compromise was reached.

2. James E. Plueddemann, *Leading Across Cultures: Effective Ministry and Mission in the Global Church* (Downers Grove, Ill.: IVP Academic, 2009), p. 78.

LESSONS LEARNED

Meeting face-to-face using an appointed advocate greatly helped to put matters on neutral ground and resulted in an acceptable way forward. It became clear, for both the Australian couple and their Finnish supervisor, that better orientation at the very beginning of the relationship regarding expectations and mutual responsibilities might have prevented the situation from arising in the first place.

### Study 2: Expectations in a Consultative Relationship

A partner organization in East Asia received an Australian couple who were highly qualified to work as advisers with the local government. The wife had a postgraduate degree in education. An Asian colleague who had developed good government relations and spoke the national language fluently took the wife to visit schools in the area where she would work on education issues. She did not yet speak the national language and so relied on her Asian colleague to interpret for her. As she worked through the curriculum of the local schools with the provincial and local government officials, the Australian expert told her Asian colleague to explain to the officials the deficiencies she found in the curriculum. Her colleague explained that it would be inappropriate to tell the officials of these problems directly. The Australian insisted, however, that the officials be told directly and clearly. The colleague did as he was told, and as expected, the officials were unhappy because they had been made to look ineffective, causing them to lose face.

This incident had an impact on the Australian's relationships with the officials. Each time she submitted recommendations for approval, they were rejected. Even if her observations were accurate, the damage had been done.

Eventually another Asian joined the Australian couple. This time when revisions were needed, the Asian invited local officials and teachers to meet together and to provide input on changes that needed to be made. The Asian was so successful in eliciting contributions that all future recommendations were approved.

LESSONS LEARNED

New personnel, regardless of where they come from, need to acquire an understanding of the values and practices of the people they are to serve before they begin their assignment. Being right is not the most critical factor for a successful partnership and ministry effectiveness. Partnerships in which all participants can give their input in an accepting environment will have the greatest impact.

## Study 3: Saving Face

Leaders from Asian sending countries required their new candidates to go to Australia to gain proficiency in English before beginning formal missionary training. The regional director for Asia, who was from the United States, thought it would be beneficial to expand the training facility in Australia to accommodate more Asian students. Many experienced people were available to train the new candidates at the facility.

The regional director for Asia raised the idea at a regional meeting with directors from the Asian sending countries. Since no negative responses to the idea were made, he decided to take a vote. The leaders looked at one another, and they all agreed. The regional director then asked who would financially support the project. Again, the leaders unanimously raised their hands, indicating agreement.

Upon returning home, the Australian leader of the training facility initiated the expansion. The Asian country leaders, however, did not send in their expected financial support. Frustrated, the regional director asked the finance manager to visit the leaders in each country and to encourage them to be accountable for the support they had promised.

As the finance manager met informally with the leaders, what had happened became clear. Even though they all greatly admired and respected the regional director, none of the leaders really liked the proposed project. They felt it was an expense that most pastors in their countries would not support.

Their "lack of accountability" was clarified. They voted "yes" with their raised hands but "no" with their inaction. As one leader observed, "We could not bear to see our regional director lose face in front of all of us. We had to publicly affirm him, or else we would be publicly disgracing him."

### LESSONS LEARNED

In a "shame" culture, issues related to saving face apply not only to those from that culture but also to expatriates working in that culture. "Accountability" needs to be understood in context to ensure that the expectations of those in leadership are realistic.

## Study 4: Expectations of a New Worker

The Latin American was well educated and very successful. After receiving her missionary calling, she enrolled in training to become a missionary. During training, her gifts in key ministry areas were noted, as well as her high degree of motivation. Her mission supervisor was a senior administrator from the United States with more than twenty years of service, which included work in South America.

Approximately two years into her field term, the Latin American missionary experienced severe exhaustion and was sent to a nearby counseling center for help. An analysis of the previous two years showed that since her U.S. supervisor resided out of the country, the missionary had tried to make too many decisions on her own. As a consequence, she had readily overcommitted herself and had focused on projects other than her primary task of language learning. Her actions had quickly led to burnout and a personal crisis. The U.S. supervisor's method of relating to the missionary had been friendship oriented. This approach had not communicated clearly the seriousness of the situation to the Latin American missionary. From the missionary's cultural perspective, the friendship style of oversight adopted by the supervisor did not match the gravity of the situation. Consequently, the missionary had not made changes in her work habits that might have prevented the burnout she experienced.

The Latin American missionary eventually returned to her home country after being stabilized at the counseling center, but it took approximately eighteen months for her to recover fully from the experience, even with continual counseling during her time at home.

### LESSONS LEARNED

This incident could have been prevented had the supervisor more clearly outlined expectations for the early years of the Latin American missionary's service. The supervisor should have more fully explored the expectations for supervision during the missionary's pre-field orientation, including discussion of cultural perspectives from both the supervisor's culture and the missionary's culture.

*Study 5: "Borrowing a Knife"*

A New Zealander who had extensive experience in a Southeast Asian country was given the new role of building relationships with a local Christian ministry. He went to a meeting with the ministry's leader. Afterward, as was his practice, the New Zealander wrote a summary of the meeting, highlighting the main points. One of the issues he mentioned was the lack of engagement by the ministry's board in the development of strategy and direction by the ministry's leader. In response, the ministry's leader wrote the New Zealander a nice note of appreciation, which he copied with the New Zealander's report to his board. The leader's action greatly upset the New Zealander because protocol in his culture dictated that he be asked for permission before his written communication was more widely distributed.

LESSONS LEARNED

After this event, the New Zealander shared the incident with a Singaporean colleague. This friend immediately understood what had happened. (There is even an appropriate Chinese phrase that in English means "to borrow a knife to kill someone.") The ministry's leader was frustrated with his board, but for cultural reasons he could not confront it directly. He therefore "borrowed a knife" from his New Zealand staff member in order to emphasize a point of contention with his board in a face-saving manner. Once this action was understood by both the New Zealand staff member and the Asian ministry leader, the relationship between the two men worked more smoothly. When time is taken to understand how culturally mandated actions might affect those coming from other cultures, trust is built, and good will is established.

## CASE STUDIES EMPHASIZING THE IMPORTANCE OF RELATIONSHIPS

Cross-cultural ministry contexts can place strains upon interpersonal relationships. At the heart of the challenge is the ability to work through disagreements. Legitimate forms of behavior and action need to be identified so that people will listen very carefully to each other. Sherwood Lingenfelter points out that "when we allow disagreements to reach a point where we judge and condemn one another's spirituality, we destroy any possibility of working effectively together. The commands of

Scripture make it clear that the first and most important criterion in our relationships is that we love one another."[3]

What follows are case studies about cross-cultural relationships between missionaries in teams or between ministry partners.

## Study 6: Becoming Part of the Conversation

Representing my mission agency, I showed up for a meeting with a long-time partner in West Africa. Upon my arrival I learned that the agenda was already set and contained a list of five demands for me to deliver to my international board. I was to give the response from my board at the next meeting with the West African partner. When I delivered the demands to my board, which is very culturally diverse, a colleague from the Pacific Islands questioned whether or not what had been written by the West African partner was truly the crux of the matter. It seemed to him that the purpose of the demands was primarily to gain attention. The West African partner felt our organization was not really listening, because we had previously come with our own agenda all set. We had to admit that we had not focused on building a relationship with this partner.

### LESSONS LEARNED

What is said of Asia seems to be true in Africa as well: one needs to meet with someone three or four times before one can become part of the conversation. Sometime later, when I returned for a visit to the West African partner, I attended a prayer meeting at the organization's office and then took a couple of its leaders out to lunch. Later when it came time for me to give my response from our board, I hesitated because my statement would likely not meet the demands the partner apparently wanted. But after I had made a feeble attempt at responding, one of the board members whom I had taken to lunch said, "I think we can set the demands aside for now." Continuing to build trust has been crucial to making progress in this relationship. Where trust has been built, good accountability on both sides will likely result.

3. Sherwood G. Lingenfelter, *Leading Cross-Culturally: Covenant Relationships for Effective Christian Leadership* (Grand Rapids: Baker Academic, 2009), pp. 64–65.

*Study 7: A Clash of Expectations*

Two single women from Eastern Europe were on their first assignment with a West African partner ministry. As the women settled into their assignment, they were able to develop a very good working relationship with the project director, a local citizen. However, the perspectives of the two women and the project director on the nature of the partnership differed, which eventually led to a problem.

The project director's strategy required that the entire team work together on a particular item. One of the Eastern European women was more compliant than the other, so she went along with this requirement without making any comment. However, the other woman felt this arrangement did not make the best use of her time, since the team was usually working on something outside her ministry specialty. She had already made plans for what she was going to contribute to the project with her expertise; but as a result, since her skills differed from those of the rest of the team, including her Eastern European colleague, she usually found herself sitting through meetings, day after day, with nothing to do. Having an outgoing personality, she followed her understanding of Scripture and went directly to her West African project supervisor and asked to be excused from these meetings. He agreed, without appearing to be offended by the request. Only much later did it become apparent that their relationship was deteriorating.

Later an African friend of the Eastern European women explained to them what he thought had happened. Since the two women were financially supported by sources outside Africa and therefore were not dependent on the local ministry, the supervisor felt powerless to stop the strong-willed woman from doing what she wanted. He did, however, view her straightforwardness as an affront to his authority as project leader. But all this was revealed only after she had left West Africa.

## LESSONS LEARNED

This breakdown in communication and friendship could possibly have been avoided if the Eastern European woman and her West African supervisor had been able to discuss their expectations of each other from the very beginning. If the supervisor could have clarified each team member's role, including differences in expectations likely to arise from their differing cultural contexts, then all team members' roles would have been understood from the outset.

## Study 8: Understanding Each Other's Culture First

Two missionaries from Eastern Europe arrived in West Africa to serve under a ministry partner. They purchased two motorbikes, using funds provided by a U.S. funder. When the assignment of one of the women was coming to an end, the missionary needed to dispose of her motorbike. She felt that if she gave the bike to her local supervisor, it would be used for his personal needs. Instead, she wanted to give it to another local person, who was directly involved in ministry with the local rural communities. She did so. She later discovered, however, that she should have officially presented the keys to the partner organization leader and asked him to transfer the use of the motorbike to the local ministry colleague she wanted to help. The details are sketchy, but the resulting disagreement ended in the ministry supervisor's giving the Eastern European woman a very poor final evaluation for her work on the project. Before the evaluation, however, she had been given no indication that she had done anything inappropriate.

She had worked on the project wholeheartedly, and the local people loved her and were grateful for all she had done. They sent her on her way with a celebration and several awards, and she left with a clear conscience. It was only after she had returned home that she received her supervisor's review, and though she held nothing against him personally, she was devastated to receive such a negative report.

Eighteen months later the supervisor wrote the Eastern European woman a heartfelt apology for the broken relationship and the pain he had caused her. He took full responsibility for what he had done. The woman responded by giving forgiveness to her former supervisor and was able to let go of any anger she felt. She came out of the conflict stronger and more mature.

### Lessons Learned

It became apparent that much of the difficulty could have been avoided with a better understanding, on both sides, of the differences between the Eastern European woman's culture and that of her West African supervisor—and of how those differences influence attitudes and behaviors. The experience was painful and disillusioning for the Eastern European sending organization and staff. Through it they learned some of the new realities missionaries face in various parts of the world. This case study is now used in this Eastern European country for orienting new missionaries to cultural differences and differing attitudes toward possessions.

*Study 9: Get the Terminology Right*

In the past, Singapore sending-office administrators felt quite frustrated whenever they were informed by one of their missionaries, after the fact, that the missionary had made changes to his or her assignment. When alterations were made by the missionary without consulting either the sending office or the missionary's home church (which often provided the major portion of the missionary's financial support), complications usually ensued. The sending office would find itself in the awkward position of having to speak with the church leadership to explain and apologize for the lack of consultation. It became apparent that these missionaries did not understand the need for accountability to their home church, the sending office, and the field administration. Analysis of the problem made it clear that using the terminology of "prayer and financial supporters or partners" was too weak. The wording was not sufficient to lead missionaries to understand the necessity of communicating with these stakeholders and of being accountable to them.

Other problematic factors included the fact that mission policies were based on Western thinking, with its emphasis on individual rights and on individuals making their own decisions. The Singaporean (and, generally, Asian) world is, in contrast, based on community rights, in which decision making is shared. Within the mission organization's system of financial support, there was no employer in the traditional sense, so missionaries got the false impression that they could do whatever they wanted.

### Lessons Learned

It was determined that the sending organization needed to change the terminology it used and then reorient all parties. The term "stakeholder" replaced words such as "partner" and "supporter." The missionary, home church, sending office, and field organization were all identified as equal stakeholders. No change of program or other major decision should take place without the agreement of all stakeholders. This modification has resulted in much clearer and better working relationships over the years.

*Study 10: Work and Recreation Combine*
*to Build Healthy Relationships*

An impasse had been reached in the ministry relationship. The two mission organizations, one a Latin American multinational and the other a North American multinational, wanted to partner; but after multiple e-mails and written and signed agreements, the leaders of both organizations were frustrated. A formal partnership had been formed, but it was far from being operational. Anti–North American feelings and hurts of the past from real or supposed slights had fueled the fire. Prejudice and concern for individual rights had added to the mistrust and misunderstanding. A North American organization with egalitarian, individualistic attitudes was running up against a Latin American hierarchical, communal/relational organization. Each needed the other, but neither could determine how to move forward.

The problem stemmed from the two organizations' lack of relationship outside of the work environment. This obstacle was put into words by one of the Latin American colleagues: "You schedule a meeting, then once it is over, you take off or run to another meeting. We, in contrast, will meet, work together, and then go somewhere and relax and play together."

LESSONS LEARNED

Within this particular cultural mix, a relationship needed to extend beyond the discussion table. Only when work and recreation were combined could issues of trust be resolved. Then progress was made, along with solid accountability in the working relationship. Once the two organizations were able to develop a work/play relationship, other cultural differences receded in significance and were more easily understood and accepted. This example underscores the awareness that "people have relationships, organizations don't."

## CONCLUSION

Missionaries, like all human beings, are naturally influenced by their own culture. Mission administrators also are influenced by their cultures of upbringing and by the unique organizational cultures of their mission agencies. International mission bodies are caught up in a sometimes intricate dance in which they attempt to please a multitude of cultural "players" and work with diverse ministry partners. Deft footwork is required for a strong performance both in the area of accountability and in extending member care.

# 23

## Response to Kirk Franklin, "Accountability in Mission Partnerships"

### Hyun Mo (Tim) Lee

A S WE SEEK TO understand the practical problems posed by strategic accountability, the field-based case studies discussed by Kirk Franklin provide useful points of reference and illuminating examples. Franklin's case studies demonstrate that cultural issues can be a crucial contributing cause of failure in strategic accountability for internationalized mission agencies. To lack understanding of a different culture creates unnecessary conflict. Two practical steps that can help in overcoming such conflict are, first, to enhance both pre-field and in-field orientation programs (to a certain extent, failure of orientation programs can be attributed to a lack of cultural understanding) and, second, to place increased emphasis on relationship-building skills within ministries, bringing to the fore the importance of relationships. Building relationships has long been a problem in ministry, but it should become a core value in light of our newfound awareness of cultural difference. Let me elaborate these two steps within the context of issues raised by Franklin.

### LACK OF CULTURAL UNDERSTANDING AND FAILURE IN STRATEGIC ACCOUNTABILITY

Mission agencies often fail to recognize the differences between high-context cultures and low-context cultures.[1] Korean missionaries, for

1. "High-context culture" and the contrasting "low-context culture" are terms pre-

example, typically reflect their high-context culture, and as a result, in a ministry setting they are more likely to rely on their own feelings and subjective judgments than on policies or rules set down by their sending agencies. This approach has benefits—for example, flexibility and the ability to respond rapidly to needs in the field—but its practitioners might be viewed by Western supervisors as individualistic and dogmatic. By contrast, missionaries from North America typically demonstrate features of their low-context cultural background. Instead of recognizing the crucial contributions made by feelings and intuition gained in the field, they tend to stick strictly to the rules and policies of their sending agencies. These missionaries can seem impervious to the needs of their fields, and their ministry may bear little fruit. Supervisors are more ready to give weight to low-context culture, while field workers often prefer the responses prompted by high-context culture. Non-Western missionaries tend to put more emphasis on the values of high-context culture, but Western missionaries take low-context culture for granted and as a result criticize non-Western workers for dismissing rules and working on their own. Similarly judgmental, the non-Western missionaries condemn Western workers for their bureaucratic attitude and blind obedience to rules and policies. Such cultural differences create significant barriers to partnership and make the determination of strategic accountability difficult.

Also of relevance are the differences between a relationship-centered culture and a responsibility-centered culture. Relationship is typically regarded as a core value in the non-Western world, where proper relationships are believed to sustain society, and where to break a relationship in order to fulfill a responsibility is recognized as an evil. Maintaining proper relationships and adhering strictly to the law are often incompatible. Non-Western society usually employs a double standard: if an individual upholds public order and social justice at the expense of doing harm to a relationship, he or she is considered legally correct but might be denounced by community members as a traitor or

---

sented by the anthropologist Edward T. Hall in his book *Beyond Culture* (Garden City, N.Y.: Anchor Press, 1976). In a high-context culture, much is left unsaid, left to the culture to fill in. Words and word choice become very important in higher-context communication, since a few words can communicate a complex message very effectively to an in-group (but less effectively outside that group), while in a lower-context culture, the communicator needs to be much more explicit, and the value of a single word is less important. The culture of most Western societies is low-context.

untrustworthy. Face-saving is evident in personal relationships. To disgrace someone is extremely foolish behavior, and doing so could break a relationship. The wounds of a broken relationship are most painful, and therefore the value placed on maintaining a relationship is higher than that placed on respecting and carrying out a responsibility. By contrast, in Western societies individual responsibility is clearly a social norm. Persons who tell lies or break rules in order to retain a relationship become morally suspect. Furthermore, since in Western societies morality is connected to religious belief, a person's faith may also be questioned. Relationships that get in the way of fulfilling one's responsibility must be broken. Such cultural differences create many problems for collaboration between Westerners and non-Westerners. Seen from a legalistic perspective, Western missionaries are strong, but when they are viewed from an emotional standpoint, criticism is inevitable.

## OVERCOMING THE LACK OF CULTURAL UNDERSTANDING

Multicultures and multinationalities are realities that most mission agencies today cannot avoid. Previously, mission agencies mostly included Western missionaries, and therefore the minority non-Western missionaries simply had to adjust to Western cultural norms. Now the tables have been turned. The norms of Western culture cannot remain the norms of mission culture. The case studies and lessons provided by Kirk Franklin return us to the two measures outlined in the introduction to this response, which will help in this transition.

### Reinforce Orientation Programs

The content of both pre-field and in-field orientation programs must become more detailed; the case studies such programs consider must become more comprehensive. When the mission fields were dominated by missionaries who held Western values, it was possible to proclaim a single standard that could be understood and obeyed by all. This method of accountability is no longer valid. Standards and values among missionaries who work together are highly diverse. Rules that are comprehensible to all parties must be put in place, and strategies that are acceptable to both Western and non-Western missionaries must be developed. If a policy does not ring true for either group, it should be changed. Mission agencies that refuse to engage in such endeavors face inevitable internal conflicts.

### Teach Relationship-Building Skills

Formerly, supervisors laid stress on the value of communication as a means to avoid conflict. We now need, however, to move beyond communication skills and to look instead at what I would like to call relationship-building skills. From the Western perspective, time and energy spent on building relationships may seem wasted. In light of the facts, however, that the number of non-Western missionaries is growing at a fast pace and that most mission fields are located in non-Western areas, we should recognize the crucial nature of relationships. Most non-Western missionaries are aware, without any additional training, of the importance of relationships, but the topic needs to become an acknowledged component in training programs for Western missionaries. Moreover, Western mission agencies should revise their regulations to include the concept of relationship. They absolutely must learn about and understand high-context culture. Administrators may feel that high-context culture is to a certain extent problematic, but they should be aware that it exists in the mission field and that the efficiency of their ministries would be enhanced if high-context cultures were understood. It is fully appreciated that missionaries from a low-context culture find it quite difficult to act according to the norms of a high-context culture. Nevertheless, it is absolutely essential for missionaries from different contexts to understand each other.

## DEFINING AND DEMANDING STRATEGIC ACCOUNTABILITY IN A MULTICULTURAL SETTING

Mission leaders must discard the preconception that the evaluation norms of Western society must be correct. Even biblical norms often leave room for relative views when they are approached from a different cultural perspective. Today Western mission agencies should have evaluation standards that are broader than those used when Western churches were working alone. In some instances our evaluation system must be changed to increase the weight given to the efficiency of a ministry and decrease the weight given to strict policy observance. If missionaries serve in a relationship-centered culture, questions about their relationships with native partners and with fellow missionaries from other cultures should be considered. Ask the hard question: Which is likely to have greater effect—observance of strategy statements that originate in Western concepts, or efforts to understand and accept local values and to adjust to the cultural norms of a specific mission field?

## FURTHER QUESTIONS

An issue not covered by Kirk Franklin's case studies but also worthy of consideration concerns differences in spiritual gifts or methodologies in cross-cultural settings. For example, Korean missionaries are strong in direct evangelism and church planting. Many years ago a certain international mission agency in Asia prohibited missionaries from church planting in their first term, regardless of their background. Korean missionaries who seemed to be capable of planting churches because they had been brought up in a similar cultural background and had had good church-planting experiences were prohibited from planting churches because of policy decisions made by senior Western missionaries. When the mission agency attempted to initiate disciplinary action against a Korean missionary who had successfully planted a church in his first term, member missionaries from non-Western countries felt a stirring of anger. The methodology of ministry should be able to be flexible in terms of culture and nationality; mission strategies could then be adjusted in light of realities in the mission field.

# 24

# Bringing the Insights of Semantic Analysis to Bear on Missionary Accountability

## *A. Scott Moreau*

IT IS A SIGNIFICANT challenge to summarize deliberations focused on a particular topic without simply offering a summary of what has already been stated in the preceding chapters. Rather than offer a synopsis, I will use a concordance approach in which I examine the vocabulary used in the chapters by each group (Korean and North American) to uncover the hidden curriculums expressed in the terms used by each.

The expression "hidden curriculum" was popularized by Benson Snyder in his 1970 examination of formal educational settings.[1] I adapt the term here to refer to values or orientations that underlie the trajectories of the discussion and the positions taken by participants. A parallel though more provocative term would be "hidden agendas." The methodological assumption driving my approach is linguistic in nature: someone writing about a topic (in this case, accountability) draws explicitly and implicitly from his or her value system. Authors consciously use specific terminology to make their case, but they also unconsciously use language that reflects values that undergird their thought processes. The semantic analysis that follows stems from this assumption.

## METHODS

From the corpus of documents as they were originally presented at the Korean Global Mission Leadership Forum, edited versions of which ap-

---

1. Benson R. Snyder, *The Hidden Curriculum* (New York: Alfred A. Knopf, 1970).

pear as these chapters, it is possible to examine the hidden curriculum by exploring the vocabulary used by the two groups. Although several of the papers and responses were written in Korean and translated into English, in every case the Korean author knows English and delivered the paper in English, ensuring a high level of correspondence between what was intended by the author and the English translation used in this analysis.

The process I used was to merge all the Korean case studies and responses into one file, and all the North American case studies and responses into a second file. Chris Wright's Bible studies, which were developed with a purpose different from that of the other presentations, are not included in the analysis. I then ran a concordance macro on each file, which gave these results: the original Korean papers had a total word count of 28,968, using a 4,713-word English vocabulary, and the original North American papers had a total word count of 21,540, using a 4,062-word vocabulary.

Since the assumption guiding my methodology is that *relative* vocabulary use exposes underlying values, I needed to compare the *frequency* with which terms occur, rather than the raw count. Thus, if the North American papers use a word 100 times, how many times would the Korean authors need to use that word for it to appear with the same frequency in the Korean papers? The Korean *total* word count was 34 percent larger than the North American total word count.[2] Thus, the same word would need to appear 134 times in the collated Korean papers to match the frequency of its appearance in the North American papers.

A specific example illuminates this comparison. All the papers focused on issues related to "accountability." This word and its variants such as "accountable" are found 186 times in the North American papers and 218 times in the Korean papers. To compare these two numbers, I multiplied the North American count (186) by 1.34 for a "frequency equivalent" of 250 (rounded). In other words, "accountability" was used more frequently by the North Americans than by the Koreans. Since the papers wrestle with issues of accountability in mission, we should expect to see both groups use that word and its variants frequently in relation to other terms. Indeed, it was the eighth most commonly used word in the North American papers and the ninth most commonly used word in the Korean papers, clearly reflecting the primary theme of the gathering.

2. More precisely, the Korean total word count was 34.485 percent greater than the North American total word count. Exact numbers have been used for all calculations in this chapter; the results and figures shown in the text have been rounded.

In itself as an overt term, however, "accountability" does not expose the hidden curriculum of either group. To get at the hidden curriculum, we need to identify terms emphasized by one group in contrast to the other. Having established a frequency count for every word, I next followed a five-step process to uncover such terms:

1. All variations on each word (plurals for nouns, tenses for verbs, etc.) were clustered or grouped together in a single count.

2. All the North American counts were multiplied by 1.34485 to obtain a prorated, or relative, total count for each word.

3. All words were listed alphabetically, and then the frequency counts for each word (or word group) were compared.

4. The word counts were then filtered. For words (and variants) used fewer than 100 times, as prorated, only those for which the count of one group was at least double the other group were retained. For words (and variants) used more than 100 times, those that were used by one group at least 50 percent more frequently than by the other were kept. Finally, proper nouns (e.g., Americans, Bible, Christians, Koreans, Asia, Europe), proper names of authors or Christian figures (e.g., Christ, Paul), and common words (e.g., what, where, with) were deleted. This filtering process yielded 142 words for the Korean papers and 139 words for the North American papers.

5. As the last step, the remaining words from the two lists were grouped into clusters.

The assumption underlying this process is that, as authors write, many aspects of word choice lie outside their conscious awareness, and therefore their vocabulary can be revealing of the hidden curriculum I hoped to uncover.

At the same time, my clustering of these terms into groups did not take place in a vacuum. This step was taken *after* all the papers had been presented. During the forum, time was allotted after every pair of papers for questions and answers, as well as additional comments from the presenters. Furthermore, during the time the participants spent together there was a constant stream of table talk over meals and discussions as those attending the forum traveled together in vans each day from hotel to meeting venue, to churches, to meals, and back to the hotel at night. My clustering of terms, while drawing solely on the final version of the papers as presented, was carried out in light of the larger setting of the consultation.

I would argue, then, that the picture given by the terminology does demonstrate, in aggregate, ideals that undergird ways the participants think about and envision accountability from within their cultural frames of reference.

## SEMANTIC-DOMAIN ANALYSIS OF TERMS USED MORE FREQUENTLY BY THE KOREAN PARTICIPANTS

The filtering process mentioned above yielded 142 words that the Korean presenters used with markedly greater frequency than did the North Americans. Using the applet available at www.wordle.net, I generated a "word cloud" to depict visually which terms were most strongly emphasized in the Korean papers (fig. 24.1). In this image the size of the word indicates the frequency with which it occurs in the Korean papers.

A quick glance at the resulting map shows that terms such as *support, organization/organize, field, work/worker, culture/cultural,* and *finance* were more significant in the Korean discourse about accountability than in the North American discourse. While this image offers an overall sense of the hidden curriculum, we need a more differentiated approach to see clearly which themes emerge.

**Figure 24.1.**

Words and variants used by Koreans far more frequently than by North Americans

### Semantic Analysis of Word Clusters

Taking the Korean list, I grouped 99 words and variants (out of 143 words) into thirteen clusters. Another person might have clustered the terms differently. Having read the papers, listened to the presentations, and participated in the informal discussions during the consultation, I took into consideration the themes and variations I had encountered, as well as the overall fit of ideas expressed in the cluster as a whole. It would have been instructive, if time had allowed, to have compared my clustering with a clustering undertaken independently by one of the Korean participants. Eight of the thirteen clusters, in my judgment, have reasonably direct bearing on ways the Korean participants framed the issue of accountability.[3] Using the multiplier indicated above, in each cluster table that follows I indicate how many times a term appears in the Korean papers and the number of times it appears in the North American papers. The totals for each table indicate how often words within that cluster appear in each set of papers and enable us to gain a sense of the comparative significance of the vocabulary in the cluster across the papers as a whole.

I arranged the clusters into three sets, consisting of three, three, and two, plus one "floating" cluster. The first three clusters (K1–K3) comprise technical terms that, taken together, indicate areas to which the Koreans paid more attention in their delineation of accountability than did the North Americans. Cluster K1 comprises terms that are oriented toward specific structural or organizational components. Are they also constraints? Do we see care and precision evident in the nomenclature for structural elements in an organization, experienced as constraints on how the Koreans discussed accountability? While this cluster may not round out a general picture of what organizational structures should be, it does suggest that knowing the correct terms and using them regularly were more significant to the Korean participants than to the North American participants.

Given the relative emphasis cluster K1 places on organizational nomenclature, the terms grouped into cluster K2 indicate an expectation of procedures or order within the organizational structures. Picking up on the theme of explicit terminology, cluster K3 contains concrete terms related to monetary or fiscal concerns. There is more than one possible explanation for the usage that this cluster illustrates. Perhaps Korean participants desired to address issues that they anticipated would be of concern to the North American participants; the frequent

---

3. Over forty words and variants did not readily fit into any cluster, which is not surprising, given their apparent randomness. For example, Koreans used "tentmaker" seven times more often than North Americans. While this statistic indicates that the Korean participants consider tentmaking in relation to accountability more frequently than do the North American participants, "tentmaker" does not fit into any of the clusters.

use of these terms may be connected to Korean expectation that, for North Americans, accountability revolves around finances. Alternately, Koreans may, in fact, be most concerned about the monetary component of accountability and so may have consistently (though perhaps not consciously) used financial nomenclature that denotes this concern. A more in-depth analysis of these three clusters might include an exploration of elements in the papers that are identified as "typical" or "regular" in regard to agencies' "operations" and "practices," perhaps shedding light on why the terminology is significant.

| Cluster K1: Organization | | | Cluster K2: Methods | | | Cluster K3: Finances | | |
|---|---|---|---|---|---|---|---|---|
| Term | Kor | NA | Term | Kor | NA | Term | Kor | NA |
| dispatch | 30 | 0 | method | 12 | 1 | income | 6 | 0 |
| headquarters, HQ | 56 | 2 | type, typical | 13 | 3 | disburse | 9 | 0 |
| institute, institution | 12 | 1 | procedure | 13 | 4 | dollar | 24 | 1 |
| department | 55 | 13 | operate, | 25 | 11 | profit | 38 | 4 |
| govern, governance | 9 | 3 | operation | | | cash | 12 | 1 |
| system, systematic | 57 | 17 | regular | 18 | 8 | exchange | 19 | 3 |
| legal | 17 | 5 | practical, | | | amount | 36 | 12 |
| organization, | | | practice | 55 | 27 | purchase | 14 | 5 |
| organize | 221 | 95 | TOTALS | 136 | 54 | donate, donor | 26 | 11 |
| committee | 28 | 13 | | | | fund | 66 | 30 |
| manage, manager, | | | | | | finance | 148 | 90 |
| management | 46 | 23 | | | | TOTALS | 398 | 157 |
| TOTALS | 531 | 172 | | | | | | |

The next set of clusters (K4–K6) focuses on nomenclature of hierarchy and social mores. Given the values traditionally assigned to Korean culture and worldview, it is not surprising to see that clusters K4 and K5 contain terms related to obedience and authority. Accountability was framed in hierarchical vocabulary far more frequently by the Korean participants than by the North Americans. Hierarchical constructions were especially important in relation to the role of the senior pastor; their frequency indicates why the phrase "relational economics" was repeated in formal and informal discussions during the consultation. The terms gathered in cluster K6 connect to the terms in K4 and K5 in that Koreans who do not obey those in authority would be deemed by other Koreans to be failing to act in a cooperative fashion, and as noted in several papers, they would face significant sanctions for unharmonious behavior. That the terms in clusters K4, K5, and K6 are used far more frequently by the Korean authors than by the North American writers indicates their relative importance in the Korean context and helps explain why Koreans express frustration that North Americans really do not understand the significance of these issues and how they play out in Korean discourse on accountability.

The usage pattern evinced by these three clusters highlights disparities between Koreans and North Americans and can be read to suggest that Korean discourse on accountability connects along hierarchical lines, with those above holding formal titles and those below being obliged to maintain harmony in the community by means of both their behavior and their attitude.

| Cluster K4: Obedience | | |
| --- | --- | --- |
| Term | Kor | NA |
| bound, boundary | 9 | 0 |
| ethics, ethical | 7 | 0 |
| rule | 16 | 0 |
| law | 27 | 1 |
| according | 26 | 4 |
| tradition | 11 | 3 |
| absolute | 11 | 3 |
| must | 54 | 13 |
| allow, allowance | 56 | 17 |
| loyalty | 7 | 3 |
| obey, obedience | 7 | 3 |
| maintain | 16 | 7 |
| order | 37 | 16 |
| **TOTALS** | **284** | **70** |

| Cluster K5: Authority | | |
| --- | --- | --- |
| Term | Kor | NA |
| below | 14 | 1 |
| selected | 15 | 3 |
| senior | 17 | 4 |
| status | 16 | 4 |
| designate | 30 | 8 |
| elder | 12 | 4 |
| refer, reference | 19 | 7 |
| own, owner | 67 | 42 |
| **TOTALS** | **190** | **73** |

| Cluster K6: Cooperation | | |
| --- | --- | --- |
| Term | Kor | NA |
| harmonize | 5 | 0 |
| intercede | 18 | 3 |
| network | 32 | 7 |
| cooperate, cooperation | 34 | 8 |
| support | 288 | 139 |
| **TOTALS** | **377** | **157** |

In the final three clusters, K7 and K8 are linked, and K9 stands on its own. The first two group around ideals and values that permeate the Korean papers. Cluster K7 shows that terms related to groups are used more frequently by the Korean participants, which is not surprising, given the more collective nature of Korean culture. Cluster K8 contains terms that can be understood as modes of cooperation and values linked to those modes. Again the explanation for the more frequent use of some terms (e.g., transparency) by Korean authors may be found either in the desirability of the values these terms portray or in perceptions of North American understandings of accountability. Certainly, the use of these terms undergirds the cooperation nomenclature seen in K6.

Cluster K9 was a surprising discovery. Vocabulary of negation can be read in a variety of ways. Its use by Korean participants may express a sharper focus on the value of prohibitions, or it might indicate that boundary lines are more clearly drawn for the Korean participants than for North Americans. A deeper exploration of these terms in their original linguistic settings would be required to discern their focus and significance, but the fact that the Koreans used negations in their papers far more frequently than did North Americans is likely connected to the orientation toward obedience and authority seen in clusters K4 and K5.

| Cluster K7: Community | | | Cluster K8: Values | | | Cluster K9: No | | |
| --- | --- | --- | --- | --- | --- | --- | --- | --- |
| Term | Kor | NA | Term | Kor | NA | Term | Kor | NA |
| associate, | | | honest | 9 | 0 | cannot | 21 | 8 |
| association | 22 | 7 | efficient | 13 | 0 | without | 41 | 20 |
| society | 17 | 5 | adopt, adoptable | 11 | 1 | not | 214 | 131 |
| join | 21 | 7 | Confucian | 9 | 1 | **TOTALS** | **276** | **159** |
| body | 52 | 19 | proper | 12 | 3 | | | |
| member | 104 | 46 | balance | 13 | 4 | | | |
| team | 65 | 36 | health, healthy | 34 | 13 | | | |
| community | 83 | 55 | transparency | 36 | 13 | | | |
| **TOTALS** | **364** | **175** | **TOTALS** | **137** | **35** | | | |

## Conclusion for Korean Nomenclature

What does this examination of the vocabulary used by Korean participants as they reflected on accountability enable us to say about a possible hidden curriculum? As we reflect on this question, we must keep in mind that these clusters focus only on the terms used far more frequently in the Korean papers than in the North American papers and therefore illuminate only the *differences* evidenced by the vocabulary of the two groups, not the similarities. This semantic-domain analysis can therefore usefully be integrated with the review of the papers themselves that is contributed to this volume by Steve Moon. Figure 24.2 highlights eight of the cluster sets emerging from the variances in vocabulary of the Korean participants. It offers a snapshot of vocabulary clusters, highlighting key areas that they mentioned more frequently than their North American counterparts did.

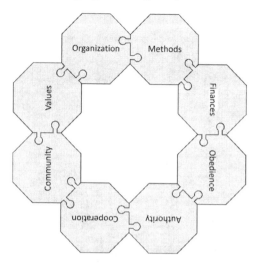

**Figure 24.2.**
Korean vocabulary clusters

In contrast to the North American participants, the Korean participants discussed organizational structures that are specific, concrete, collective, and hierarchical. Authority was presented through a nomenclature of status that flows from top to bottom. Together these clusters give us a picture of obedience to rules that follow "relational economics" based in authority or status rather than "policy economics." This picture is enhanced by the greater Korean use of terms focusing on community and harmony. The semantic domain for accountability for the Korean participants incorporates words for authority, specificity of methods, hierarchy, obligation, and community.

## SEMANTIC-DOMAIN ANALYSIS OF TERMS USED MORE FREQUENTLY BY THE NORTH AMERICAN PARTICIPANTS

The filtering process outlined above (points 1–5) identified 139 words (and variants) used by the North American presenters far more frequently than they were used by the Koreans. Following the pattern of the previous section, I generated a word cloud to depict visually the terms emphasized more frequently in the North American papers (fig. 24.3). As with the Korean word cloud in figure 24.1, the size of the word in the map indicates the number of times it occurs in the papers scrutinized.

A quick glance at the map demonstrates that words such as *agency, partner/partnerships, serve/service/servant, relationship, report/reporting,* and *supervise/supervision* played a far greater role in the North American discourse. While this offers an overall sense of the hidden curriculum, an additional approach is needed in order to see how these individual terms might blend together.

**Figure 24.3.**

Words and variants used by North Americans far more frequently than by Koreans

### Semantic Analysis of Word Clusters

I follow the same format in this section as I did in the section on the semantic domain of Korean terms. Taking the North American word list, I clustered 121 words and variants (out of 139 words) into fourteen groups, eight of which have the most direct relevance to accountability.[4] In each of the cluster tables that follow and using the prorating multiplier discussed above, I indicate how many times each term appears in the North American and Korean papers. The totals at the bottom of each table again allow a comparison of the frequency with which words related to each cluster's theme appear in each set of papers.

The first three clusters show the North American tendency for active initiation and engagement, together with an expectation of success. Cluster NA1 as a whole shows that, in discussing accountability, the North American participants were far more likely than the Korean participants to use terms related to active engagement. Further buttressing this orientation toward active engagement, the terms grouped in cluster

---

4. As with the Korean vocabulary, several words did not fit any cluster. For example, North Americans used "heart" almost three times more often than Koreans, but "heart" does not fit in any of the clusters.

NA2 show that the North Americans used words expressing initiation and initiative more frequently than did the Koreans. Given the extensive use by the Koreans of terms related to hierarchy and authority, the contrasting levels of usage evident within these two clusters of vocabulary are not surprising. Cluster NA3 comprises terms that express expectations of success or movement toward success. The more frequent use of terminology expressing optimism fits the "can do" orientation that characterizes North Americans.

| Cluster NA1: Active Engagement | | | Cluster NA2: Initiative | | | Cluster NA3: Optimistic Expectations | | |
|---|---|---|---|---|---|---|---|---|
| Term | Kor | NA | Term | Kor | NA | Term | Kor | NA |
| note, noted | 26 | 3 | initiate, initiative | 23 | 1 | impact | 20 | 1 |
| intervene, intervention | 12 | 3 | seek | 19 | 2 | forward | 17 | 2 |
| describe | 19 | 7 | expand | 9 | 1 | positive | 11 | 2 |
| comment, commenting | 13 | 5 | engage | 30 | 4 | confidence | 9 | 2 |
| expose, exposure | 11 | 4 | proactive | 11 | 2 | succeed, success | 32 | 9 |
| review | 26 | 10 | sponsor | 12 | 3 | expect, expectation | 46 | 21 |
| respond respondent | 51 | 24 | extend | 16 | 6 | possibility | 27 | 14 |
| challenge, challenged | 30 | 14 | approach, approached | 19 | 9 | potential | 13 | 7 |
| question, questionable | 30 | 14 | go | 38 | 20 | **TOTALS** | **176** | **58** |
| continual, continue | 31 | 15 | provide | 85 | 52 | | | |
| serve, service, servant | 100 | 65 | **TOTALS** | **261** | **100** | | | |
| **TOTALS** | **347** | **164** | | | | | | |

The next set of three clusters relates to understanding, methods, and outcomes. Cluster NA4 groups terms used by North Americans in expressing an emphasis on clarity (explain, clear, apparent), attending to the larger picture (frame, pattern, environment), and identifying important components (axiom, character, focus, key). Concern to identify key underlying components and their contribution to the broader picture was more deeply embedded in North American discourse on accountability than for the Koreans. Cluster NA5 contains terms of connection and progression—North Americans were more likely to identify or discuss sequential movement in accountability. Cluster NA6 shows the North American penchant for keeping the end in sight in their papers.

If the first three clusters indicate a "can do" rhetoric, the second set indicates a "how to" approach that has outcome or completion in mind.

| Cluster NA4: Seeing What Is Important | | | Cluster NA5: Linear Progression | | | Cluster NA6: A Purposeful End | | |
|---|---|---|---|---|---|---|---|---|
| Term | Kor | NA | Term | Kor | NA | Term | Kor | NA |
| apparent | 16 | 0 | link | 12 | 0 | reconcile, | | |
| axiom | 7 | 0 | subsequent | 7 | 0 | reconciliation | 9 | 1 |
| explain | 9 | 1 | lesson | 17 | 1 | outcomes | 9 | 2 |
| clear, clearly | 43 | 6 | list | 30 | 3 | complete, | | |
| frame | 11 | 2 | mechanism | 8 | 1 | completing | 30 | 8 |
| character, | | | next | 16 | 3 | purpose | 20 | 10 |
| characteristic | 17 | 4 | movement | 12 | 5 | goal | 23 | 12 |
| pattern | 12 | 3 | program | 42 | 19 | conclude, | | |
| information | 32 | 12 | **TOTALS** | **144** | **32** | conclusion | 20 | 11 |
| part, partial | 34 | 13 | | | | **TOTALS** | **112** | **44** |
| significant | 20 | 8 | | | | | | |
| environment | 15 | 6 | | | | | | |
| focus | 31 | 15 | | | | | | |
| key | 13 | 7 | | | | | | |
| **TOTALS** | **261** | **77** | | | | | | |

In the final set of three clusters, NA7 and NA8 are linked, while NA9 stands apart. The terms in cluster NA7 show a use of vocabulary relating to performance assessment. It is tempting to pair the outcome-oriented vocabulary in cluster NA6 with the assessment vocabulary in cluster NA7 as indicators that being able to see how well goals are met is more typical of the North American than the Korean presentations. Only through examination of the assessment terms in their rhetorical contexts—that is, what they are paired with—would we be able to establish the role of assessment within North American accountability discourse.

| Cluster NA7: Assessment | | | Cluster NA8: Supervision | | | Cluster NA9: Females Noted | | |
|---|---|---|---|---|---|---|---|---|
| Term | Kor | NA | Term | Kor | NA | Term | Kor | NA |
| assess, assessment | 16 | 2 | assign, | | | woman | 31 | 1 |
| adequate, | | | assignment | 23 | 3 | she | 54 | 8 |
| adequacy | 22 | 3 | supervise, | | | her | 134 | 75 |
| criteria | 19 | 3 | supervision | 91 | 18 | **TOTALS** | **219** | **84** |
| perform, | | | compliance | 12 | 3 | | | |
| performance | 12 | 6 | official | 12 | 4 | | | |
| effect, effective | 56 | 28 | oversee, | | | | | |
| appropriate | 23 | 12 | oversight | 12 | 5 | | | |
| **TOTALS** | **148** | **54** | report, | | | | | |
| | | | reporting | 93 | 58 | | | |
| | | | **TOTALS** | **243** | **91** | | | |

Cluster NA9 does not necessarily link to any of the other clustered ideas, but it does show that, in their exploration of accountability, the North American participants specifically identified women 2.6 times more frequently than did the Korean participants. This imbalance may simply result from differences in language usage. Contemporary North American discourse is gender explicit, with the third person nonneuter pronouns (she, her, he, him) typically referring only in gender-specific ways. In contrast, the Korean use of English in the papers was more gender nonspecific, using "he" and "him" both when an individual male was meant and to refer to a person in general, whether male or female. Given the continuation of male-dominated leadership in Korean society as a whole—including in ministry settings—and the changes that have taken place in North American gender roles over the past several decades, this differential is not surprising.

### Conclusion for North American Nomenclature

How might we summarize the hidden curriculum of the North American participants as they wrote on accountability? Again the reader must remember that the North American clusters discussed here focus only on terms used far more frequently in the North American papers than in the Korean presentations. Thus, what follows illustrates only the *differences* evidenced by the vocabulary of the two groups, not the similarities. Figure 24.4 highlights eight of the cluster sets emerging from the variances in vocabulary of the Korean participants.

In contrast to the Koreans, terminology employed by the North American participants pointed toward action, expectation, progression, purpose, and assessment. Here we encounter in a new context the message of American slogans such as Nike's "Just do it" and U.S. president Barak Obama's "Yes we can!" 2008 campaign slogan. This vocabulary is all the more significant in light of the negative terms used more frequently by Koreans than North Americans (cluster K9). This "can do" approach that characterizes many North American ideals also demarcates North American discourse on accountability.

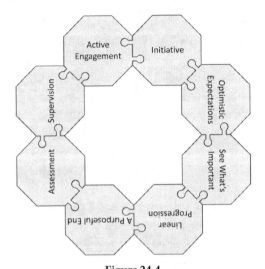

**Figure 24.4.**

North American vocabulary clusters

## CONCLUSION: DIFFERENT FRAMINGS
## OF ACCOUNTABILITY

The hidden curriculums uncovered by the analysis in this chapter suggest that Koreans and North Americans who choose to partner together will face significant challenges in developing a mutually acceptable approach to accountability. For example, Korean expectations that are related to hierarchical authority, obedience, and specific organizational titles will mix poorly with North American expectations of initiation, engagement, and optimism about linear progression toward a purposeful end. It could potentially be very helpful for both groups to know in advance how each frames its discussion of accountability, although that knowledge in itself will not alleviate stress arising from differing perspectives.

A telling example of this point is provided by the expression "relational economics." The term was used in one of the case studies and reiterated during several question-and-answer sessions. For Koreans, relational economics drives accountability, but the exposure of the Korean hidden curriculum enables a better understanding of this concept. The clusters in our analysis help uncover Korean "relational economics" as not egalitarian but hierarchical, the proper form of interpersonal relationship as tacitly understood by Koreans. This hierarchical framing has well-defined constraints that can be seen in the clusters, including obligation, harmony, and precise organizational roles—all defined and applied from a Korean perspective.

Thus, Korean missionaries on the field believe that correct behavior incorporates a flexibility that means shame is not brought to the organization or its leaders. For example, they might value contravention of written policy when that policy clashes with the maintenance of harmony and obedience to authority. Generally speaking, Koreans who note such a breach of policy would likely choose not to mention it, knowing that to do so could bring disarray to the ministry both on-site and back home. North Americans, in contrast, would be more likely not only to mention any disregard of policy but even to force an investigation of the matter. This response fits with the ideals identified in the North American hidden curriculum, such as initiative, the identification and assessment of what is important, and progressive steps to deal with significant issues. The American approach, however, would be deemed so offensive by the Koreans that major conflict would be all but inevitable.

The consultation did not resolve these differences. Exploring the two hidden curriculums gives ground, however, for both groups to find ways to move toward mutual understanding and formation of a common approach to accountability, one that recognizes the desires and framework of each group and finds ways to deal with the conflicts that will inevitably arise.

# 25

## Highlights of the Korean Global Mission Leadership Forum

### Sang-Cheol (Steve) Moon

THE KOREAN GLOBAL MISSION Leadership Forum held at the
Overseas Ministries Study Center, New Haven, Connecticut, in
February 2011 consisted of ten plenary presentations and responses,
two Bible studies, three gatherings for small-group discussion, and
four prayer sessions. This summary chapter seeks to highlight some of
the main points made in the position and response papers that were
presented at the forum and subsequently edited for publication in this
volume.

Timothy Kiho Park's chapter addresses several questions relevant
to the volume as a whole: What is accountability? Why is missionary accountability important? What are the problems of the Korean church in
relation to accountability? Who has accountability in mission? For what
are mission leaders accountable? After acknowledging these significant
issues, Park lists twelve suggestions for increased accountability in mission. His answers to the first two questions, on the nature and value of
accountability, are based on his personal exegesis of biblical passages
and on his interpretation of the relevant literature. To identify current
problems of accountability facing the Korean mission movement, he
draws together responses made during group discussions in which experienced Korean missionaries who are studying at Fuller Theological
Seminary's School of Intercultural Studies participated. Park's suggestions for higher accountability in mission—for example, closer coopera-

tion between missionaries, mission agencies, supporting churches, and on-field organizations; development of detailed policies; and creation of missionary care systems—are both practical and concrete.

Geoffrey Hahn's response to Timothy Kiho Park's chapter centers on a discussion of the compatibility of—and tension between—two mission values: contextualization and ecclesiology. The former is emphasized by mission agencies, the latter by sending churches. Despite this tension, Hahn holds that regard for neither ecclesiology nor contextualization should diminish. Rather, he argues, both approaches can continue to be valued highly if their apparent contradictions are addressed through "a partnership of equals characterized by grace" (p. 70). Hahn concludes that grace is necessary in every sphere of partnership.

Stanley Green first addresses accountability in light of the Bible and then turns to current research to consider a range of definitions of accountability. In doing so, he points not just to accountability as restrictive control but also to accountability's positive dimensions, namely, that it can "strengthen trust and confidence by increasing transparency [and] improving performance" (p. 76). To counter "accountability myopias," Green proposes a kingdom-oriented approach that promotes healthy interdependent relationships between sending and receiving partners. His model of an inclusive, participatory accountability in the Spirit is the Jerusalem council in Acts 15. This council voluntarily surrendered power to the Spirit's leading among the whole people of God, who were equal partners in the mission of God yet represented different groups within the early church. Green posits: "Partnership in the Gospel thus came to mean sharing power, becoming open to new traditions, and allowing the Spirit to direct the decision-making process" (p. 79). His concluding remarks emphasize the building of internal capacity within nonprofits for adaptive learning.

N. Yong Sung's consideration, in his response to Stanley Green, of the notions of upward and downward accountability leads to an emphasis on "*coram Deo* consciousness" (p. 83). Sung points out that two kinds of policies, namely, sound financial and ministry policies, are essential to good accountability. He emphasizes the importance of independent church growth, although he does not exclude the need for partnering churches to help each other. This position differs slightly from Green's emphasis on an interdependent relationship, but the opinions of these two leaders are not far apart. Furthermore, Sung's incarnational model of accountability sounds very similar to Green's kingdom approach to accountability.

David Yoo uses the first half of his chapter to introduce the overall ministry of SaRang Community Church, in Seoul, and the vision of its World Mission Department. The second half is devoted to introducing the church's accountability in mission and, more specifically, in administration, finance, and recruitment. One impressive effort in the cause of administrative accountability in SaRang Community Church is that prayer items are gathered from missionaries for sharing with church members, who can therefore intercede for the missionaries during both large-scale and small-group prayer meetings. Such effort not only reinforces administrative accountability but also reflects the church's commitment to engage in spiritual support for the missionaries through spiritual warfare.

Sherwood Lingenfelter's response to Yoo's chapter focuses on five areas: accountability structures, recruitment and training, finance and property, policies, and assessment of ministry effectiveness. In dealing with each of these issues, Lingenfelter both affirms current practice and, through his questions, suggests additional processes and actions for improvement. Analysis of his questions or observations reveals that they center on the need for evaluation: of missionary candidates, the effectiveness of the training curriculum, mission organizations, the financial accountability structure, ministry effectiveness, and the intercessory prayer meetings. In his concluding comments Lingenfelter raises the need for solid study by missionaries of the culture and nation to which they are sent and for development by mission agencies of policies for missionary care that will help prevent missionary attrition.

Larry Fullerton's statement that mission is part of the very DNA of Black Rock Congregational Church, in Fairfield, Connecticut, well expresses that church's commitment to missions. Numerical data support his contention: 25 percent of the church's total operating budget is given to the cause of missions. Fullerton explains the application process for missionaries in detail, focusing on ways the church seeks to strengthen accountability between missionaries and the church by means of the procedures it follows. The church's Mission Covenant clearly communicates the expectations and responsibilities of the local church. Black Rock's policy for its annual missions conference is also inspiring. Fullerton shares the church's success story briefly; the not-so-successful stories he considers in more detail. The negative experiences draw our attention to the local congregation's role in keeping the missionaries and supporting churches accountable to each other. The whole point of accountability is well summarized in Fullerton's final paragraph, as he notes that missionaries who live within the church's "requirements of accountability" find that they "can count on the members of Black Rock Church to pray for them and to be on their side in the midst of the rigors and spiritual battles of ministry" (p. 156).

Won Sang Lee's response to Larry Fullerton holds up Black Rock Congregational Church as a model for other congregations to emulate. He makes special mention of the church's Board of Missions handbook and its Mission Covenant (the latter is found in appendix A of Fullerton's chapter). Lee recommends the handbook—which spells out the process missionary applicants are to follow and makes clear the church's guidelines for missionaries it supports—to "any local church serious about deepening accountability in its mission program" (p. 178). He observes that the church's Mission Covenant with missionaries it supports helps to "ensure that the church's mission goals are well carried out" (p. 178) and asks whether a similar covenant between the church and mission agencies might be useful. He concludes by emphasizing the matter of spiritual accountability, noting that "spiritual maturity will be the answer to many problems"; we therefore have a need for "continual evaluation of each missionary's spiritual progress" (p. 180).

Bahn Seok Lee begins his chapter by mentioning several financial scandals within Korean and Korean American mission agencies and organizations. He then considers cultural aspects of these issues and their systemic causes before adopting a historical perspective. Lee's diagnosis is that "the concept of accountability, separate from relationships, is still foreign to many Korean organizations and their leaders" (p. 186). A clue to the failure of accountability to take root can be discerned, he suggests, in the concepts of absolute loyalty and hierarchical relationship, but systemic weaknesses must also be recognized, such as the lack of financial management and financial statements, of accounting principles, and of Korean governing law. Finally, Lee suggests that solutions might be found in education that leads to greater awareness of the issues involved, the enactment of more specific laws, and the creation of an organizational supervisory body.

In his response to Bahn Seok Lee's chapter, Marvin Newell quotes a psychological study in order to assert the importance of normative parameters or standards. From Acts 5 he draws four overriding transcultural and transtemporal principles related to property's value, vulnerability, and visibility and to property owners' stewardship responsibilities. In light of the realities of the Korean situation as presented by Lee, Newell raises the question whether long-term partnerships between Korean mission entities and Western ones are "realistic and sustainable" (p. 204). Perhaps here we need more discussion for clarification of the presenter's intention and the issues at stake. For ease of review and clarity, Newell clusters together the consequences of financial misappropriation suggested by Lee. They present a significant cautionary list. In his concluding question, regarding "prepackaged or culturally unimplementable" accountability, I understand Newell to be calling for a deeper understanding of one another across cultures.

Hunter Farrell's chapter deals with cases of sexual abuse in the missions community. This kind of sharing takes courage and Christian maturity. Farrell explains how the Independent Abuse Review Panel (IARP) was chartered by the General Assembly Council (GAC) Executive Committee of the Presbyterian Church (U.S.A.) in 2003 to investigate allegations of abuse in PC(USA) mission fields. In October 2010 the panel issued a 546-page report that considered a total of thirty incidents of abuse that had occurred in eight countries. The IARP report noted the correlation between boarding school settings and instances of abuse. One of the unfortunate factors involved was the organizational and administrative changes that the PC(USA) was undergoing during the period in question, which introduced significant uncertainty into the life and work of missionaries. After sharing some of the points raised by the report, Farrell introduces steps that the Executive Committee of the General Assembly Mission Council (GAMC) took in response to the report. One of the decisions made by the committee was that a letter of apology should be issued to the victims of the abuse; a public apology was also communicated through a press conference. Farrell points out in his conclusion that the self-understanding of the Reformed church as always being reformed is reinforced through the course of confession and healing.

Yong Cho's response to Farrell's chapter approaches the issues involved from three angles—biblical, administrative, and cultural. His concern about public humiliation and the dangers of slander seems to be an effort for pursuing Christian maturity in ecclesiastical review and judicial proceedings. Administratively, Cho points to an area of potential vulnerability, stating that he knows of no Korean mission agency with a policy in place for dealing with allegations of child sexual abuse. Finally, he warns mission agencies to be alert to self-destructive cultural trends and to resist being caught up in them.

Missiologist Shin Chul Lee presents a case study of the Korea Presbyterian Mission (KPM), established by the Korea Presbyterian Church (Kosin). After introducing the Kosin denomination, he clarifies the aims and terminology of his case study and the organizational system of KPM. He suggests measures that would improve financial transparency and accountability within KPM in its relationship with supporting churches, with the KPM Committee, and with its missionaries. For Lee the connections between KPM and the Korea Presbyterian Church (Kosin) congregations need to be strengthened. A pattern of designated giving that bypasses both administrative fees and the normal budgetary processes points to deficiencies in collaboration and partnership between the two related entities. Lee also suggests the establishment and promotion of a general fund that would provide more equitable distribution of support among the missionaries.

Dick McClain summarizes Lee's chapter in a positive light before making five recommendations on the basis of his expertise and personal experience. He suggests, first, that the authority of KPM missionaries to receive designated funds directly from their supporters should be limited. Second, he recommends that KPM enhance the services it provides to local churches and to its missionaries. Third, with reference to the general fund, McClain suggests retaining the personal touch of individualized support for missionaries, while using the organizational structure for administration and to set the direction of mission endeavors. His fourth recommendation is that the agency's finances should undergo an independent audit annually. Fifth, he recommends that missionary budgets be segmented into "launch," "missionary support," and "ministry/project support" in order to provide a more adequate way of projecting actual costs and administering donor support.

Jerry Rankin's case study of administrative accountability centers on his experience as president of the International Mission Board (IMB) of the Southern Baptist Convention. His basic standpoint is that the IMB has a strong accountability structure, although it faces new challenges with the growing influx of missionary members from the Majority World. His discussion outlines the core competency that the IMB emphasizes in pre-field orientation and training programs, and he stresses the importance of accountability to peers and team ministry leaders. Many observers would agree with his diagnosis of weaknesses present in Korean missions' handling of accountability, and the advice he offers is detailed. At the deeper level of worldview exegesis, Rankin points out the challenges that a face-saving culture, which discourages confrontation, poses in the area of accountability.

The response of Young Choon Lee and Elaine Lee to Rankin's assessment answers many questions raised by his presentation. Having outlined WEC International's organizational structure and practices, the authors turn their discussion to WEC's experience with Korean workers. In their eyes, communication presents a major area of challenge, as also do vision and strategy because of the implications those hold for administrative accountability. Their conclusion includes the important observation that cultural differences in understanding of such concepts as team, leadership, and decision making have been at the root of much misunderstanding and frustration. Often, the authors suggest, the point at issue is not a matter of right or wrong, or of biblical versus unbiblical, but of different values and preferences.

Min Young Jung's chapter raises a significant question: how strategic should a strategy be? He goes on to outline the missiological consultative process that Wycliffe International has gone through. His main thesis is that the Korean church (and/or the Majority World) needs multilateral strategic accountability. Under this heading, Jung raises four sets of issues relating to institution and structure, a corporate culture of shared values, the wider community of learners and reflective practitioners, and partnership. One conclusion he reaches is that we need to move toward becoming a healthy multicultural community, something that is crucial as a prerequisite for kingdom partnership.

In his response to Min Young Jung, John McNeill immediately embarks on a major discussion of corporate culture. He suggests, importantly, that Koreans are not free from individualism but that they show a different type of individualism than is common in the West, warning that "national-level individualism" (p. 281) could hinder desirable international cooperation. McNeill also observes that some Korean missionaries are repeating the very mistakes against which he warns his students. His comments show the need for the kind of forum from which this book arises.

Kirk Franklin shares ten case studies involving cross-cultural misunderstanding. He has selected examples that illustrate situations involving missionaries from high-context cultures as well as ones from low-context cultures, as defined by the anthropologist Edward Hall. After each case study Franklin clarifies the lessons it offers. The conclusion he draws from this material is that both missionaries and mission administrators are naturally influenced by their home culture, as well as by the organizational culture of their mission agencies. These facts offer complex challenges to mission communities in the areas of accountability and providing member care.

In his response to Kirk Franklin, Tim Hyun Mo Lee raises further questions related to strategic accountability. First, is lack of cultural understanding a significant cause of failure in the area of strategic accountability? It is certain, Lee suggests, that cultural differences create many conflicts in the context of collaboration between Westerners and non-Westerners. Second, how can the lack of cultural understanding be overcome? He offers two possible solutions: reinforcing orientation programs, and strengthening skills for relationship building. Third, how can strategic accountability be defined and demanded in multicultural settings? Lee argues that the presence of multicultural teams means that Western mission agencies should develop broader standards of evaluation than before. Under the heading "Further Questions," he concludes that mission strategies should remain flexible, able to adjust to changes in the mission field.

The focus on accountability at the Korean Global Mission Leadership Forum enabled one of the most significant areas of weakness in the Korean missionary movement to be addressed. For this we can be thankful. A significant lesson is being learned, although much homework is still required if progress is to be made. I personally appreciate the collective sensitivity, wisdom, and maturity exhibited in this international missiological (and hermeneutical) community.

# Appendixes

## *Participants*

Rev. Shin Jong (Daniel) Baeq
SEED International
Merrifield, Virginia

Dr. Gary Bekker
Executive Director
Christian Reformed World Missions
Grand Rapids, Michigan

Dr. Jonathan J. Bonk
Executive Director
Overseas Ministries Study Center
New Haven, Connecticut

Rev. Dr. Yong Joong Cho
Director
Global Partners Research and Development Center
Seoul, Korea

Rev. Dr. B. Hunter Farrell
Director of World Mission
Presbyterian Church (USA) Worldwide Ministries
Louisville, Kentucky

Mr. Kirk Franklin
Executive Director
Wycliffe Global Alliance
Melbourne, Australia

Rev. Jon Fuller
International Director for Mobilization
OMF International
Singapore

Rev. Larry Fullerton
Missions Pastor
Black Rock Congregational Church
Fairfield, Connecticut

Rev. Dr. Patrick Fung
General Director
OMF International
Singapore

Rev. Stanley W. Green
Executive Director
Mennonite Mission Network
Elkhart, Indiana

Dr. Paul R. "Bobby" Gupta
Hindustan Bible Institute and College
Chennai, India

Rev. Dr. Geoffrey W. Hahn
Deputy International Director for the Americas
SIM International
Fort Mill, South Carolina

Rev. Min Young Jung
Associate Director
Wycliffe Global Alliance
Singapore

Mr. Hangjun Kim
Cornerstone
Asia

Rev. Jin Bong Kim
International Church Relations Assistant to the Executive Director
Overseas Ministries Study Center
New Haven, Connecticut

Rev. Seung-Ho (Stephen) Kim
Korea National Director
OMF
Seoul, Korea

Rev. Sun Man Kim
Senior Pastor
First Korean Presbyterian Church of Hartford
Manchester, Connecticut

Dr. Bahn Seok (Peter) Lee
Cornerstone
Asia

Mrs. Elaine Lee
Deputy International Director
WEC International
Singapore

Rev. Henry Lee
Korean Field Director
Frontiers
Seoul, Korea

Dr. Hyun Mo (Tim) Lee
Professor of Missiology
Korea Baptist Theological University/Seminary
Daejeon, Korea

Prof. See Young Lee
Graduate School of International Studies
Seoul National University
Seoul, Korea
Former U.N. Ambassador
Former International Director of Come Mission

Dr. Shin Chul Lee
Korea Presbyterian Mission (KPM–Kosin)
    and Professor of Missiology
Korea Theological Seminary
Chunan, South Korea

Dr. Won Sang Lee
President
SEED International
Merrifield, Virginia
Senior Pastor Emeritus
Korean Central Presbyterian Church
Centreville, Virginia

Rev. Dr. Wonjae Lee
General Secretary
General Board of Mission
Korean Methodist Church
Seoul, Korea

Rev. Young Choon Lee
Deputy International Director
WEC International
Singapore

Dr. Sherwood G. Lingenfelter
Professor of Anthropology and Former Provost
Fuller Theological Seminary
Pasadena, California

Rev. Dick McClain
President and CEO
The Mission Society
Norcross, Georgia

Dr. John McNeill
Professor of Missions and Anthropology
Providence University College and Seminary
Otterburne, Manitoba, Canada

Dr. Sang-Cheol (Steve) Moon
Executive Director
Korea Research Institute for Mission (KRIM)
Seoul, Korea

Dr. A. Scott Moreau
Professor of Missions and Intercultural Studies
Wheaton College Graduate School
Wheaton, Illinois

Dr. Marvin J. Newell
Executive Director
CrossGlobal Link
Wheaton, Illinois

Rev. Daniel J. Nicholas
Director of Communications and Publications
Overseas Ministries Study Center
New Haven, Connecticut

Dr. Kiho (Timothy) Park
Director of Korean Studies and Associate Professor of Asian Mission
School of Intercultural Studies
Fuller Theological Seminary
Pasadena, California

Dr. Yong Kyu Park
Professor of Church History
Presbyterian General Assembly Theological Seminary
Seoul, Korea

Rev. Greg Parsons
General Director
U.S. Center for World Mission
Pasadena, California

Rev. Jerry A. Rankin
President Emeritus
International Mission Board of the Southern Baptist Convention
Richmond, Virginia

Mrs. Jewel Showalter
Area Representative to the Middle East/North Africa
Eastern Mennonite Missions
Salunga, Pennsylvania

Dr. Richard Showalter
President
Eastern Mennonite Missions
Salunga, Pennsylvania

Rev. Dr. Nam Yong Sung
Senior Pastor
SamKwang Presbyterian Church
Seoul, Korea

Rev. Dr. Christopher J. H. Wright
International Director
Langham Partnership International
London, England

Rev. Dr. Seung Kwan (David) Yoo
Mission Pastor
SaRang Community Church
Seoul, Korea

# Sponsors

First Korean Presbyterian Church of Hartford
Manchester, Connecticut

SaRang Community Church
Seoul, Korea

Rexahn Pharmaceuticals, Inc.
Rockville, Maryland

New Haven Korean Church
Hamden, Connecticut

Institute for the Study of American Evangelicals (ISAE)
Wheaton College
Wheaton, Illinois

Korean Central Presbyterian Church
Centreville, Virginia

SamKwang Presbyterian Church
Seoul, Korea

Council of Korean Churches of Connecticut
Glastonbury, Connecticut

United Church of Westville
New Haven, Connecticut

Word of Life Press
Seoul, Korea

# Contributors

Jonathan J. Bonk is Executive Director of the Overseas Ministries Study Center, New Haven, Connecticut; Editor of the *International Bulletin of Missionary Research*; and Director of the online *Dictionary of African Christian Biography*. Before moving to New Haven in 1997, he served for twenty years as professor of Global Christian Studies at Providence College and Theological Seminary in Canada. He was raised in Ethiopia by missionary parents, serving there with his wife in famine relief, 1974–76. He is best known for his book, *Missions and Money: Affluence as a Western Missionary Problem* (Orbis, 1st edition 1991; 2nd edition 2007), recently translated into Korean (Christian Literature Society of Korea, 2010), and is editor of the *Encyclopedia of Mission and Missionaries* (Routledge, 2007).

Yong Joong Cho is currently Director of Research and Development at Global Partners, International Director of Global Network Mission Structures, and Copresident of the East-West Center for Missions Research and Development. He served as chairman of the Preparation Committee of Tokyo 2010, an international centenary celebration of the Edinburgh 1910 World Missionary Conference. Earlier he served as international director of Global Partners, working in over 30 nations, and as general secretary of World Korean Missionary Fellowship. He has worked in the Philippines, Myanmar, India, and the United States, and has established two theological schools, in Myanmar and India. After studying civil engineering at Korea University, he studied theological subjects in the United States: Trinity College (B.A.), Trinity Evangelical Divinity School (M.Div., Th.M.), and Trinity International University (Ph.D.).

B. Hunter Farrell serves as the Director of World Mission for the Presbyterian Church (U.S.A.). He is a graduate of Fuller Theological Seminary, Pasadena, California; earned the Ph.D. in cultural anthropology from the Pontificia Universidad Católica del Perú; and served as a Presbyterian mission coworker in theological education and community development in Congo (1981–82, 1986–90) and Peru (1998–2007).

Kirk Franklin grew up in Papua New Guinea (PNG), the son of American linguists/Bible translators. Returning to PNG as an adult, he met his Australian wife, Christine, there. Kirk has held leadership positions with Wycliffe in PNG and Australia and now is the President/ CEO of Wycliffe Global Alliance. The operational headquarters is in Singapore, but Kirk remains in Melbourne to be with his family as Christine continues to serve with Wycliffe Australia.

Larry Fullerton is Executive and Missions Pastor of Black Rock Congregational Church in Fairfield, Connecticut, having been called to the church in 1997. Previously he served six years as a captain in the United States Air Force and later as excutive and missions pastor of College Church, Wheaton, Illinois (1975–96). He is a graduate of Gordon Conwell Theological Seminary, South Hamilton, Massachusetts. Fullerton is a member of the Board of Trustees of the Overseas Ministries Study Center, New Haven, Connecticut.

Stanley W. Green serves as Executive Director of Mennonite Mission Network, a position he assumed in 1993. He previously served as president of the Council of Anabaptists in Los Angeles, conference minister with the Southwest Mennonite Conference (Arizona and California), and an urban missiologist in Los Angeles, California, with the Mennonite Board of Mission's Evangelism and Church Development Department. Originally from South Africa, Green served in pastorates at Congregational churches in his home country. He and his family also served a five-year term as missionaries in Jamaica. Green completed a master's degree in missiology at Fuller Theological Seminary in Pasadena, California, and is currently a Ph.D. candidate there.

Geoffrey W. Hahn is SIM International's Director for the Americas. Previously, as a missionary in Ecuador for ten years, he was involved in church planting, health, radio, and leadership ministries before moving to an international role as director of ministry development for SIM. Hahn holds a B.A. in philosophy from Wheaton College, Wheaton,

Illinois; an M.Div. from Trinity Evangelical Divinity School, Deerfield, Illinois; and a D.Min. from Denver Seminary, Littleton, Colorado.

Min Young Jung became Associate Director of Wycliffe Global Alliance in 2008. He joined Wycliffe Bible Translators in 1983 and served as a Bible translator in Indonesia from 1986 to 1996. He was then appointed a codirector of Global Bible Translators, which is Wycliffe Korea. Since 2002 he has, under Wycliffe Global Alliance, led the Asian Diaspora Initiative, which promotes Bible translation ministry among various diaspora communities.

Bahn Seok (Peter) Lee serves with Cornerstone in Asia.

Hyun Mo (Tim) Lee is Professor of Missiology at Korea Baptist Theological University and Seminary, Daejeon, South Korea. He joined the faculty in 1993 and chaired the world missions department for a decade before serving as dean for a year beginning in 2002. Since 2010 he has been chairman of the missions and evangelism committee of the Asian Pacific Baptist Federation, an affiliation of fifty-five Baptist conventions with 25,000 churches in twenty countries. Previously, he worked with JOY Mission, Seoul (1983–87) and was co-pastor of a Korean Baptist congregation in Dallas, Texas (1987–92). He is a graduate of Seoul National University (B.S.), Korea Baptist Theological University and Seminary (M.Div.), and Southwestern Baptist Theological Seminary (Ph.D.). His publications include *Introduction to Missiology* (2000), *Understanding Modern Mission* (2003), and *Senior Missionary* (2007).

Shin Chul Lee, a member of the Korea Presbyterian Mission (KPM) Executive Committee and head of the KPM Policy Committee, teaches missions at the Korea Theological Seminary, in Chunan, South Korea. For ten years he served as a KPM/WEC missionary among the Dagomba people in Ghana, West Africa. He recently received the Ph.D. degree from the University of Wales, Lampeter; his dissertation was on Presbyterian church planting in Korea. He is the author of "A Suggestion to Foster KPM Field Missions" (First KPM Bangkok Forum, 2004) and "The Purpose of KPM: Establishing Reformed Churches" (Second KPM Bangkok Forum, 2008).

Won Sang Lee is President of SEED International, a mission af-filiated with The Mission Exchange, with headquarters in Merrifield, Virginia. He served as senior pastor of the Korean Central Presbyterian Church, Centreville, Virginia, for twenty-six years (1977–2003). In 2010 he completed a Ph.D. at the University of Wales, Lampeter.

Young Choon Lee and his wife, Elaine Lee, currently serve as Deputy International Directors of WEC International. From 1993 to 2004, they worked with WEC in Mongolia in church planting and leadership training. They served as the leaders of the WEC team in Mongolia from 1994 to 2004. While there Young Choon also served as the Director of the Union Bible Training Center in Mongolia from 1999 to 2002. Young Choon received his M.Div. from Presbyterian General Assembly Theological Seminary, Chongshin University in Korea. Elaine completed an M.A. at Westminster Theological Seminary, Philadelphia, Pennsylvania.

Sherwood G. Lingenfelter, who came to Fuller Theological Seminary, Pasadena, California, in 1999, retired as Provost on June 30, 2011. He continues to serve on Fuller's faculty as Professor of Anthropology. Previously he served as professor of intercultural studies, provost, and se-nior vice president at Biola University, La Mirada, California. He earned the Ph.D. in anthropology at the University of Pittsburgh. Lingenfelter has served as consultant to SIL (Summer Institute of Linguistics) over the last two decades in Papua New Guinea, Borneo, Philippines, Africa, and Latin America. His publications on missions include *Ministering Cross-Culturally* (1986), *Transforming Culture* (1992, 1998), *Agents of Transformation* (1996), *Teaching Cross-Culturally* (2003) with his wife, Judith Lingenfelter, and a publication co-authored with Paul R. Gupta, *Breaking Tradition to Accomplish Vision: Training Leaders for a Church Planting Movement* (2006). His most recent book is *Leading Cross-Culturally: An Incarnational Model for Power-Giving Leadership* (2008).

Dick McClain, President and CEO of The Mission Society, Norcross, Georgia, since September 2009, came to The Mission Society in 1986 as its first director of missionary personnel. He subsequently served as vice president for mission ministry, vice president for church ministry, vice president for mission operations, and finally executive vice president and chief operating officer. The son and grandson of missionaries, Dick was born in China and grew up in India and Hong Kong. Prior to joining the staff of The Mission Society, he served as the youth minister of Crossroads Bible Church, an interdenominational congregation in the Panama Canal Zone. An ordained United Methodist minister, he served pastorates in West Michigan for eleven years.

John McNeill is Professor of Anthropology and Intercultural Studies at Providence College, Otterburne, Manitoba. He and his wife, Christel, have been involved in mission teaching and humanitarian work in Central and Eastern Europe since the 1970s. They are both staff members of YWAM and have often been on loan to other mission organizations.

Sang-Cheol (Steve) Moon is Executive Director of the Korea Research Institute for Mission (KRIM), Seoul, which was founded in 1990 by mission administrators as the research arm of Global Missionary Fellowship. He was KRIM's chief researcher (1990–98) before being named director. Moon is also Assistant Professor of Missiology at Hapdong Theological Seminary, Suwon, and Associate Pastor for Missions at Nam-Seoul Grace Church. He was a Mission Commission associate for the World Evangelical Alliance (1996–2004). Moon is a graduate of Pusan National University (B.A.), Asian Center for Theological Studies and Mission (M.A.), Korea Reformed Theological Seminary (M.Div.), and Trinity Evangelical Divinity School (Ph.D.). He is author of "The Protestant Missionary Movement in Korea: Current Growth and Development" (*International Bulletin of Missionary Research*, April 2008).

A. Scott Moreau is Professor of Intercultural Studies at Wheaton College, Wheaton, Illinois, and Editor of the *Evangelical Missions Quarterly*. He is coauthor of *Introducing World Missions: A Biblical, Historical, and Practical Survey* (2004), editor of Baker Academic's ongoing Encountering Mission series, general editor of the *Evangelical Dictionary of World Missions* (2000), and managing editor of the Network for Strategic Missions Knowledge Base. A graduate of Wheaton College and Trinity Evangelical Divinity School, Moreau served for fourteen years with Campus Crusade for Christ, including as a physics and general science teacher at Ntonjeni Swazi National High School,

Swaziland (1978–80), and professor of theology and missions at Nairobi International School of Theology, Nairobi, Kenya (1984–91). He also was a deputy administrator of the Accrediting Council for Theological Education in Africa.

Marvin J. Newell is Executive Director of CrossGlobal Link, Wheaton, Illinois. He and his wife, Peggy, served as missionaries for fifteen years in Indonesia, where his main responsibility was teaching and administration at the national Bible college. Before assuming leadership of CrossGlobal Link, Newell served as Asia-Pacific regional director with TEAM for six years and then as professor of missions and intercultural studies at Moody Theological Seminary for eight years. Newell has a D.Miss. from Trinity Evangelical Divinity School, Deerfield, Illinois, and is the author of *A Martyr's Grace* (Moody Publishers, 2006) and *Commissioned: What Jesus Wants You to Know as You Go* (ChurchSmart Resources, 2010).

Kiho (Timothy) Park is Director of Korean Studies and Associate Professor of Asian Mission, in the School of Intercultural Studies, Fuller Theological Seminary, Pasadena, California. He served as a missionary in the Philippines for fifteen years with the Global Mission Society (GMS), the missionary arm of the General Assembly of the Reformed Presbyterian Church in Korea. He is a graduate of Chongshin University (B.A.), Presbyterian General Assembly Theological Seminary, Chongshin University (M.Div.), and Fuller Theological Seminary (Ph.D.).

Yong Kyu Park is Professor of Church History in Chongshin University's Presbyterian General Assembly Theological Seminary, Seoul, Korea, and also Director of the Korea Institute of Christian History (KICH). A specialist on the Pyengyang Great Revival, Park is a graduate of Sung Kyun Kwan University, in South Korea (B.A.); Presbyterian General Assembly Theological Seminary, Chongshin University (M.Div.); Western Evangelical Seminary, Portland, Oregon (M.A.); and Trinity Evangelical Divinity School, Deerfield, Illinois (Th.M., Ph.D.). He is author of the two-volume *History of the Korean Church* (2004). In 1994, his *History of the Early Church* earned Park the Best Theologian of the Year award from the Korea Evangelical Theological Society.

Jerry A. Rankin served with the International Mission Board (IMB) of the Southern Baptist Convention for forty years, the last seventeen years as president. President Emeritus since August 2010, he is an Adjunct Professor at Mississippi College, Clinton, Mississippi. Appointed to Indonesia in June 1970, he and his wife, Bobbye, served as missionaries in Asia with the IMB for twenty-three years. Rankin was associate to the IMB's area director for South and Southeast Asia (1982–86), administrator for the denomination's mission work in India (1986–87), and area director for Southern Asia and the Pacific (1987–93). A Mississippi native, Rankin is a graduate of Mississippi College, Clinton, and Southwestern Baptist Theological Seminary, Fort Worth, Texas. He is author of *A Journey of Faith and Sacrifice: Retracing The Steps of Lottie Moon* (1996) and coauthor of *Spiritual Warfare and Missions: The Battle for God's Glory Among the Nations* (2010).

Nam Yong Sung is Senior Pastor of SamKwang Presbyterian Church in Seoul, Korea, and Professor of Missions and Intercultural Studies at the Graduate School of Chongshin University. A former Global Mission Society/SIM missionary in Nigeria, he taught at Igbaja Theological Seminary and Jos ECWA Theological Seminary. Sung is also Executive Editor of the *Korean Mission Times*. He is a graduate of Dankook University (B.A.); Presbyterian General Assembly Theological Seminary, Chongshin University (M.Div.); and Trinity Evangelical Divinity School (Ph.D.).

Christopher J. H. Wright became International Director of the Langham Partnership International in 2001. He has also served as chair of the Lausanne Movement's Theology Working Group (2005–11) and as chair of the Theological Resource Panel of TEAR Fund since 2001. In 1983 he moved to India with his wife, Liz, and four children to teach at Union Biblical Seminary in Pune for five years. At this time he and Liz were mission partners with Crosslinks, an evangelical Anglican mission agency. In 1988 he returned to the U.K. as academic dean (1988–93) and then principal (1993–2001) of All Nations Christian College, Ware, Hertfordshire, England, an international training center for cross-cultural mission. Ordained in the Anglican Church of England in 1977, he served as an assistant pastor in the Parish Church of St. Peter and St. Paul, Tonbridge, Kent, England. He has written several books, including *The Mission of God* (InterVarsity, 2006) and *The Mission of God's People* (Zondervan, 2010).

Seung Kwan (David) Yoo currently serves as Mission Pastor at SaRang Community Church in Seoul, Korea, overseeing SaRang's domestic and international mission ministry. In this role he draws on his experience in the corporate world and as SaRang's first lay tentmaking missionary. He is secretary general of International Operation Charity in Korea, Inc., a board member of the Lausanne International Strategic Working Group, a board member of the Global Inter Missions Network (GIMNET), and an international consultant for SIM. He received his Ph.D. from Baikshuk University.

# Bibliography

"Accountability." http://en.wikipedia.org/wiki/accountability.

ActionAid International. *Alps: Accountability, Learning, and Planning System.* www .actionaid.org/sites/files/actionaid/actionaids_accountability_learning_and _planning_system.pdf.

Ahn, Hee. "Jikjangin Gibudanche Biriro Gibu-uihyang Eopseojyeo" (Forty percent stopped giving because of scandals in public nonprofit organizations). *Chosun Newspaper,* November 29, 2010.

Araujo, Alex. "'To Catch the Wind: A New Metaphor for Cross-Cultural Partnership." Paper presented at the Coalition on the Support of Indigenous Ministries, Lombard, Ill., 2008.

Baker, Dwight P., and Douglas Hayward, eds. *Serving Jesus with Integrity: Ethics and Accountability in Mission.* Pasadena, Calif.: William Carey Library, 2010.

Bangkok Mission Forum Committee, *Hanguk Seongyo-wa Chaengmu* (Korean mission and accountability: The second Bangkok mission forum). Seoul: Hyebon Publishing, 2006.

Barrett, David B. "The Status of the Christian World Mission in the 1990s." In *Mission in the Nineteen Nineties,* ed. Gerald H. Anderson, James M. Philips, and Robert T. Coote, pp. 72–73. Grand Rapids: Eerdmans, 1991.

Beals, Paul E. *A People for His Name.* Rev. ed. Pasadena, Calif.: William Carey Library, 1995.

Bebbington, D. W. *Evangelicalism in Modern Britain: A History from the 1730s to the 1980s.* London: Unwin Hyman, 1989.

Black Rock Church Missions. www.brcc.org/missions/missions.html.

Bonk, Jonathan J. *Missions and Money: Affluence as a Missionary Problem—Revisited.* Rev. and expanded ed. Maryknoll, N.Y.: Orbis Books, 2007.

———."Mission as Invasion?" *International Bulletin of Missionary Research* 34, no. 2 (April 2010): 65–66.

Bosch, David J. *Transforming Mission.* Maryknoll, N.Y.: Orbis Books, 1999.

"A Brief Statement of Faith." In *The Constitution of the Presbyterian Church (U.S.A.),* part 1: *The Book of Confessions,* pp. 263–75. Louisville: Office of the General Assembly, 2004.

Brown, Arthur J. *Mastery of the Far East: The Story of Korea's Transformation and Japan's Rise to Supremacy in the Orient.* New York: Charles Scribners, 1919.

Christensen, Rachel Atkin. "Accountability Mechanisms and Mission-Based Activity: A Nonprofit Agency Serving Immigrants and Refugees." Master's paper, Virginia Polytechnic Institute and State Univ., 2002. http://scholar.lib.vt.edu/theses /available/etd-04262002-105015/unrestricted/MajorPaperChristensen.pdf.

Clark, Charles Allen. *The Nevius Plan for Mission Work, Illustrated in Korea.* Seoul: Christian Literature Society, 1937.

Cohen, Richard. *Coming Out Straight: Understanding and Healing Homosexuality.* Cleveland, Ohio: Oakhill Press, 2000.

Cornwall, Andrea, Henry Lucas, and Kath Pasteur. "Introduction: Accountability Through Participation; Developing Workable Partnership Models in the Health Sector." *IDS Bulletin* 31, no. 1 (2000): 1–13.

Ebrahim, Alnoor. "Towards a Reflective Accountability in NGOs." In *Global Accountabilities: Participation, Pluralism, and Public Ethics*, ed. Alnoor Ebrahim and Edward Weisband, pp. 193–224. Cambridge: Cambridge Univ. Press, 2007.

"Emil Brunner." *Columbia Encyclopedia*, 6th ed. 2008. www.encyclopedia.com/doc/1E1 -Brunner.html.

Evangelical Council for Financial Accountability. "ECFA Standard 3—Financial Oversight." www.ecfa.org/Content/Comment3.

Evangelical Joint Accounting Committee. *Accounting and Financial Reporting Guide for Christian Ministries.* Rev. ed. Norwalk, Conn.: EJAC, 2001.

Evinger, James, Carolyn Whitfield, and Judith Wiley. *Final Report of the Independent Abuse Review Panel, Presbyterian Church (U.S.A.).* Louisville, Ky.: PC(USA), 2010.

"Final Report of the Independent Abuse Review Panel—Presbyterian Church (U.S.A.)." www.pcusa.org/resource/final-report-independent-abuse-review-panel-presby.

*Final Report of the Independent Commission of Inquiry.* Louisville, Ky.: Presbyterian Church (U.S.A.), 2002.

Financial Accounting Standards Board. "Statement of Financial Accounting Standards No. 117: Financial Statements of Not-for-Profit Organizations." June 1993. www .ecfa.org/Content/Comment3.

"5 wol 17 il Gidoggyo Yeongjeog Olympic Yeollinda" (On May 17th, Open the Spiritual Olympics of Christianity). *Bit-gwa Sogeum* (Light and salt), April 1995, pp. 18–25.

Hall, Edward T. *Beyond Culture.* Garden City, N.Y.: Anchor Press, 1976.

Hayward, Douglas, and Paul E. Langenwalter. "Holding Missionaries Accountable: A Proposed Code of Ethics for Missionaries Based upon the Code of Ethics of the American Anthropological Association." In *Serving Jesus with Integrity*, ed. Baker and Hayward, pp. 343–73.

Herman, Judith. *Trauma and Recovery: The Aftermath of Violence—from Domestic Abuse to Political Terror.* New York: Basic Books, 1997.

Hood, Jason. "Theology in Action: Paul and Christian Social Care." In *Transforming the World? The Gospel and Social Responsibility*, ed. Jamie A. Grant and Dewi A. Hughes, pp. 129–46. Nottingham: Apollos, 2009.

Hucker, Charles O. *China's Imperial Past: An Introduction to Chinese History and Culture.* Stanford, Calif.: Stanford Univ. Press, 1975.

Hwang, Yong-hyun. "Segye Bogeumhwa-leul wihan Umjigimdeul" (The movements for world evangelization). *Bit-gwa Sogeum* (Light and salt), September 1992, pp. 52–57.

Jang, Dong Min. *Daehwaro Puleoboneun Hangukgyohoesa* 1 (Korean church history opened through dialogue 1). Seoul: Revival and Reformation, 2009.

*Je 53hoe Chonghoerok* (The fifty-third General Assembly records, the Korean Presbyterian Church). Seoul: Presbyterian Church of Korea, 1968.

Jeon, Ho-jin. "Hanguk Gyohoe Hyeon Hwang-gwa Banghyang" (The status and direction of the missions of Korean churches). *Seonggyeong-gwa Sinhak* (Bible and theology) 16 (1994):16–43.

Jeong, Insook. "2009 Seonkyosa Pasong Hyeonhwang" (Statistics of missionaries in various nations as of 2009). *KWMA Newsletter*, March 19, 2010, pp. 4–5; www.kwma.org.

Johnson, Todd M., and Kenneth R. Ross, eds. *Atlas of Global Christianity*. Edinburgh: Univ. of Edinburgh Press, 2009.

Johnstone, Patrick. *The Church Is Bigger Than You Think*. Pasadena, Calif.: William Carey Library, 1998.

Johnstone, Patrick, and Jason Mandryk. *Operation World*. 6th ed. Waynesboro, Ga.: Authentic Lifestyle, 2001.

Jung, Min-Young. "Sailboat Paradigm: A Biblical Partnership of the Global Mission Era." Paper presented at Sorak Mission Forum, Seoul, Korea, 2009.

———. "Seongyo-wa Chaegmu" (Mission and accountability). In *Hanguk Seongyosa-wa Chaegmu*, ed. Bangkok Mission Forum Committee, pp. 19–42.

Kang, Seung-sam. "The Foreign Mission of the Korean Presbyterian Church, 1965–1990." In *Chonghoe Baegnyeonsa*, ed. Yong Kyu Park, 2:327–53.

———. "The Korean Presbyterian Church and Overseas Mission." In *Chonghoe Baegnyeonsa*, ed. Yong Kyu Park, 1:403–52.

Kerns, Kevin P. *Managing for Accountability: Preserving the Public Trust in Public and Nonprofit Organizations*. San Francisco: Jossey-Bass Publishers, 1996.

Kim, Gi-Yul, and Byun Youngseon. *Biyeongli-beobin Hoegye-wa Seomu Silmu* (Accounting for nonprofit organizations and practical tax accounting). Rev. ed. Seoul: Samil Infomine, 2010.

Kim, Hwal-Young. "Seongyo Hyeonji Haengjeong System" (Field administrative system). In *Hanguk Seongyo-wa Chaengmu*, ed. Bangkok Mission Forum Committee, pp. 215–28.

Kim, In-ho. "Hanguggyohoe Haeoe Seongyo-ui Yeogsa-wa Jeonmang" (The history and prospect for foreign missions of the Korean church). Paper presented at Mission Korea Conference, Seoul, 2001.

Kim, Jung-nam. *Jonggyo Beobin-ui Seomu-wa Gyohoe Jaejeong Gwanli* (Tax accounting for religious organizations and for church financial management). Seoul: Doseo Choolpan Youngmoon, 2004.

Korean World Missions Association. www.kwma.org.

Korea Presbyterian Mission. *KPM General Regulations*.

Korea Presbyterian Mission. *KPM Internal Regulations*.

Kouzes, James M., and Barry Z. Posner. *The Leadership Challenge*. San Francisco: Jossey-Bass, 2002.

Kwolek, Susan, and Karyn Popovich. "Strategic Accountability Agreements." www .healthcareleadershipconference.ca/assets/Popovich_-_Strategic_Accountability _Agreements%5B1%5D.pdf.

Lederleitner, Mary T. *Cross-Cultural Partnerships: Navigating the Complexities of Money and Mission*. Downers Grove, Ill.: IVP Books, 2010.

Lee, Byunghan. "Jisang Gonggaehae Uihok Jegi" (Opened the facts to eliminate suspicion). *Korea Times*, April 20, 2010. www.koreatimes.com/articles/589231.

Lee, Seok. "After Yonggi-Cho, Door Has Opened, but. . . ." *Sisa Journal*, September 30, 2010. www.sisapress.com/news/articleView.html?idxno=53278.

Lee, Seungkyu. "Yerang Seongyohoe Daepyo Hoengnyeong mit Chakbok Hyeomuiro Gusok" (Arrest of representative of Yerang Mission for accusation of embezzlement). *NewsNJoy*, December 20, 2007. www.newsnjoy.co.kr/news/quickViewArticleView .html?idxno=20979.

Lee, Timothy S. *Born Again: Evangelicalism in Korea*. Honolulu: Univ. of Hawaii Press, 2010.

Lingenfelter, Sherwood G. *Leading Cross-Culturally: Covenant Relationships for Effective Christian Leadership*. Grand Rapids: Baker Academic, 2009.

Linthicum, Robert. *Transforming Power: Biblical Strategies for Making a Difference in Your Community*. Downers Grove, Ill.: InterVarsity Press, 2003.

Mandryk, Jason. *Operation World*. 7th ed. Colorado Springs, Colo.: Biblica Publishing, 2010.

McCubbins, Michael D. "Missionary Accountability." www.biblebaptistarleta.org/b _missionary_accountability.pdf.

Missionary Kids Safety Net. www.mksafetynet.net.

Moon, Steve Sang-Cheol. "Gwangbok 60nyeon-gwa Seongyo Hanguk" (Sixty years of liberation and mission Korea). *Mokhoe-wa Sinhak* (Ministry and theology), August 2005, pp. 68–73.

———. "The Protestant Missionary Movement in Korea: Current Growth and Development." *International Bulletin of Missionary Research* 32 (April 2008): 59–64.

Neely, Alan. "The Teaching of Missions." In *Toward the Twenty-first Century in Christian Mission*, ed. James M. Phillips and Robert T. Coote, pp. 269–83. Grand Rapids: Eerdmans, 1993.

Nelson, Martin L. *Directory of Korean Missionaries and Mission Societies*. Seoul: ACTS, 1979.

Newbigin, Lesslie. *The Gospel in a Pluralist Society*. Grand Rapids: Eerdmans, 1989.

Nisbett, Richard E. *The Geography of Thought: How Asians and Westerners Think Differently . . . and Why*. New York: Free Press, 2003.

Oak, John H. *Called to Awaken the Laity*. Glasgow: Bell & Bain, 2009.

Paik, George Lak. *The History of Protestant Missions in Korea, 1832–1910*. Seoul: Yonsei Univ. Press, 1970.

Park, Myung Soo. *Hanguk Gyohoesa-ui Gamdongjeogin iyagi* (Moving story of Korean church history). Seoul: KookMinIlBo, 2006.

Park, Timothy Kiho. "The Influence of Korean Mission on the World Missionary Movement in the Modern Era." *Global Mission Advance* 46 (2009): 56–58.

Park, Yong Kyu. *Hanguk Gidokgyohoesa* (History of the Korean church). Vol. 1, *1784–1910*. Seoul: Word of Life Press, 2005.

———, ed. *Chonghoe Baegnyeonsa* (One hundred years of the General Assembly of the Korean Presbyterian Church). 2 vols. Seoul: General Assembly of the Presbyterian Church, 2006.

Peters, George W. *A Biblical Theology of Missions*. Chicago: Moody Press, 1984.

Plueddemann, James E. *Leading Across Cultures: Effective Ministry and Mission in the Global Church*. Downers Grove, Ill.: IVP Academic, 2009.

Pollock, David C., and Ruth E. Van Reken, *Third Culture Kids: The Experience of Growing Up Among Worlds*. 2nd ed. Boston: Nicholas Brealey Publishing, 2001.

Presbyterian Church of Korea. *Presbytery Records*. Seoul: Christian Literature Society, 1907.

Presbyterian World Mission. "Presbyterian World Mission Strategic Direction." http://missional.info/archives/125.

"Sailing Friends." http://sailingfriends.wordpress.com.

Scanlon, Leslie. "Six Persons Named by Abuse Review Panel in Physical, Sexual Abuse Investigation." www.pres-outlook.com/news-and-analysis/1-news-a-analysis/10520

-six-persons-named-by-abuse-review-panel-in-physical-sexual-abuse -investigation-.html.

Shidlo, Ariel, Michael Schroeder, and Jack Drescher, eds. *Sexual Conversion Therapy: Ethical, Clinical, and Research Perspectives*. New York: Haworth Medical Press, 2001.

SIL International. www.sil.org.

Silva, Raul. *Post-traumatic Stress Disorders in Children and Adolescents*. New York: Norton, 2004.

Smith, Megan, ed. *Child Sexual Abuse: Issues and Challenges*. Hauppauge, N.Y.: Nova Publishers, 2008.

Snyder, Benson R. *The Hidden Curriculum*. New York: Alfred A. Knopf, 1970.

Sohn, Chang-nam. "Seongyeo Danche-eui Jaemoo Jepyo-e Gwanhan Yeongoo" (Study of financial statements for mission organizations). Paper prepared for Korean World Missions Association, Seoul, Korea, 2004.

Taylor, William D. *Kingdom Partnerships for Synergy in Missions*. Pasadena, Calif.: William Carey Library, 1994.

———, ed. *Too Valuable to Lose: Exploring the Causes and Cures of Missionary Attrition*. Singapore: WEF Missions Commission, 1997.

"2007 South Korean Hostage Crisis in Afghanistan." http://en.wikipedia.org/wiki/2007 _South_Korean_hostage_crisis_in_Afghanistan.

Underwood, Horace G. "Principles of Self-Support in Korea." *Korea Mission Field* 4, no. 6 (June 1908): 91–94.

Vergara, Robert. "What's the Difference? A Comparison of Cultural Traits: Korean and American." Paper prepared for Cornerstone Ministries International, Seoul, Korea, 2008.

"Vision 2025 Resolution." www.wycliffe.net/AboutUs/Vision2025/tabid/98/language/en -US/Default.aspx.

Welsch, Glenn A., Charles T. Zlatkovich, and John Arch White. *Intermediate Accounting*. 3rd ed. Homewood, Ill.: Richard Irwin, 1972.

Wolf, Thomas. *Managing a Nonprofit Organization in the Twenty-first Century*. New York: Simon & Schuster, 1999.

World Christian Database. *www.worldchristiandatabase.org*.

Wycliffe Global Alliance. www.wycliffe.net.

Yoo, Seung-Kwan (David). "Jeonsinja Seongyosajuui Gwanjeomeseo bon Jiyeok-gyohoe Pyeongsindo Jeonmunin-seongyo Lideosip-gwa Seongyo-jeonryak" (Lay professional mission leadership and the mission strategy of the local church in the viewpoint of every believer missionaryhood). Doctoral thesis, Baekseok Theological Seminary, 2008.